CAMPAIGN
HAWAI'I

An Inside Look at Politics in Paradise

CAMPAIGN
HAWAI'I
An Inside Look at Politics in Paradise

Rick Tsujimura

WATERMARK
PUBLISHING

ISBN 978-1-935690-82-5

Library of Congress Control Number: 2016953448

Media excerpts used with permission. All photography and campaign memorabilia from the author's collection except:
Front cover (sign holders): *The Honolulu Advertiser*
p. 54 top and p. 57 top: Courtesy Ruth and Marcus Oshiro
p. 60 bottom: Ed Greevy

Design and production
Ingrid Lynch

Watermark Publishing
1000 Bishop St., Ste. 806
Honolulu, HI 96813
Toll-free 1-866-900-BOOK
sales@bookshawaii.net
www.bookshawaii.net

Printed in the United States

"Yet even sparrows dream, have hopes, aspire. They raise their eyes and see the eagles soaring the skies and the falcons flying with wings outspread, cleaving the wild winds and bracing the storms. Has never a sparrow dreamed of being an eagle? Or of flying with the wings of a falcon? Yet how many sparrows would dare essay the impossible to fly beside an eagle or to dive where the falcon dives? He quails instead with fear lest the eagle look upon him and see him only as prey, lest the falcon fall upon him and slay him on the wing. But the dream continues; the hope never dies, and even a sparrow can aspire."

—Samuel Crowningburg-Amalu, *Jack Burns: A Portrait in Transition*

Contents

❧

Foreword

~&~

Modern Hawaiʻi's political history began with the Democrats' take-over of the territorial legislature in 1954. That election ended more than a half-century of Republican Party rule. Five years later, Hawaiʻi became the nation's fiftieth state.

Most of the men and women who shaped that revolution are now gone: World War II veterans like Dan Inouye and Spark Matsunaga, Governor John A. Burns, the indomitable Patsy Takemoto Mink and thousands of labor union members across the Islands.

But another generation of young people took it further. They made Hawaiʻi into the nation's most Democratic state. Today Democrats hold the governorship, its four-person congressional delegation, all but one seat in its twenty-five-member state senate, and all but seven seats in its fifty-one-member house of representatives.

Many of those who effected that transformation never held public office themselves. They were, in the words of the late Robert Oshiro, "sparrows," who, campaign after campaign, handled the essential tending of the grassroots.

In 1970, Oshiro ran Governor Burns' last campaign. Among the young men hanging around Burns headquarters was Rick Tsujimura, a nineteen-year-old, third-generation American of Japanese ancestry. He took his political instruction from Sensei Oshiro, then and for a decade or more to come. Among the *sensei's* lessons:

"Relationships are what count in politics—the touches."

"Once a person contributes time to a campaign, he or she becomes loyal, while money represents only a betting marker rather than loyalty."

"Campaigns are like wars. The guy in the foxhole with you becomes your brother—once a comrade in arms, always a comrade in arms. Loyalty is all-important in politics."

"Strategy is the single most important element in a political campaign."

"Media is like an air force in politics; you can soften the ground, but it can't take the territory. It takes grassroots. Politics is all about relationships—that's how you take and hold the ground."

In 1978 incumbent Governor George Ariyoshi faced a tough re-election challenge from Honolulu mayor Frank Fasi. Fasi enjoyed a seventeen-point lead in early polling. Oshiro ordered a monster rally in Aloha Stadium and tapped twenty-seven-year-old Tsujimura to organize it. Fifty thousand was the goal—50,000 bodies, 50,000 *bentos* and balloons, the best entertainers in the Islands and plenty of fireworks.

Tsujimura and an army of his comrades pulled it off—50,000 gathered in Aloha Stadium in the name of a politician. It's never been done before, and it's never been done since.

I first met Tsujimura two years later. At twenty-nine he was running Eileen Anderson's campaign to unseat Fasi as Honolulu's mayor. Whatever the burdens of his position, he bore them lightly. He smiled easily and gave this scribe all the access I requested.

He also won, vanquishing the longtime nemesis of the Burns-Ariyoshi wing of the Democratic Party.

Or so it seemed. Four years later, Fasi defeated Anderson in her bid for re-election.

But Tsujimura's place in Hawai'i politics was now well established— always on the inside, always beside a score of comrades in arms whose contributions and skills he's always generously acknowledged.

They would win elections and they'd lose a few. Very few.

With equal measures of intelligence and humility, Tsujimura explicates both victories and defeats in *Campaign Hawai'i: An Inside Look at Politics in Paradise*. Students of politics, take out your notebooks and sharpen your pencils.

Dan Boylan
Emeritus Professor of History
University of Hawai'i – West O'ahu

Introduction

❦

Sparrows appear throughout this book. In the beginning, "sparrow" was the code word for stalwarts of the John A. Burns and George R. Ariyoshi campaigns. But the allusion is more than just literary metaphor. It is also a metaphor for the hundreds, if not thousands, of little folk who usually go unnoticed in local politics. While eagles and hawks are solitary, sparrows are communal—though they aren't all alike, nor do they all do the same things at the same time. Sparrows are everyday people, not flashy in their various gray-brown hues, and except for their insistent chirp, you'd probably just walk right by them. One of the purposes of this book is to recognize them, to share the stories of those whose actions helped shape Hawai'i—not from the halls and offices of power, but from their work in fields and factories and homes. These are the true heroes and heroines of Hawai'i politics.

Much has been written about the Island political scene by a plethora of people, many much more knowledgeable about these events than I. But this book tells the story from a sparrow's-eye view—not so much a historical account of events, but as a record of the lessons learned in my nearly fifty years of exposure to the political process in Hawai'i. The accounts related here are recounted as I saw them, and I apologize at the outset if my recollections are disputed by others.

This recounting is not to convince the reader that my choice of candidates was correct. Rather, it is to detail the experiences of just one of the little sparrows who worked on these campaigns—events as my colleagues and I saw them. Some of my co-workers' experiences are attributed here and some are not, mostly at their request. While I haven't spoken with all of the candidates covered in the writing of this book, those with whom I have conferred have been kind enough to indulge me with their own recollections. In large measure my personal interactions with them are included, but I have also relied upon news accounts to capture the essence of what a campaign is like for the campaign volunteer—that unsung hero or heroine—whom we all have met but seldom recognize. This book is really a tribute to them, the sparrows.

Finally, I owe much to the generation that preceded me. As a very young person in the 1970s, my access to local Democratic Party movers and shakers was decidedly limited, and I was fortunate to be allowed entrée at an early age into the campaigns of Governors Burns and Ariyoshi, and later with the campaigns of Governors Cayetano and Abercrombie; to be recruited to run the successful campaign of the first female mayor of Honolulu, Eileen Anderson; to be involved in the campaigns of Arnold Morgado, Jeremy Harris and Kirk Caldwell for mayor of the City and County of Honolulu; to understand the lessons of defeat that followed the congressional campaign of John Craven; and to witness the noble attempt by my friend Randy Iwase to run for governor against an incumbent juggernaut with little support from those he had campaigned for and served in the past. Each campaign brought lessons on loyalty and how fleeting it can be, as well as the opportunity to test theories and ideas passed on and learned from my political mentors and teachers, and to synthesize new ideas and theories of politics and strategy. I owe a debt of gratitude to these individuals for being able to be a part of their individual campaigns, and from whom I learned the lessons and principles articulated herein.

Events in this book are drawn from a variety of sources, many from the public record, others from presentations and recollections by friends and colleagues. I do owe a great debt of gratitude to Robert C. Oshiro, my political mentor and friend of many years. RCO, as many of us referred to him when speaking in the third person, or Bob, when we spoke to him directly, provided much of the underpinnings of my political thinking, analysis and theory. From 1970 when I first met him until his passing, RCO had a great influence in my life, and what is captured here is in many ways a tribute to him. I also owe much to the friends I have met over the years in the political process. I will acknowledge them all in the text of this book, as this is the only way for me to remain faithful to the context of their influence.

I hope that for those who experienced these times in the same environment, you will recall and recollect your own experiences and share them with friends and family. Pass your stories down to your progeny. To the students of politics, I hope the stories bring some life to events that they may have heard about, but whose details have faded with time. To the student of ethics and management, I hope this book will reinforce the belief that values and relationships count more than people usually acknowledge. To my colleagues and to future political types, I hope this book provides some guidance to the management of campaigns, the expectations of candidates and the different roles of both campaigns and candidates. It is my hope and belief that the lessons I learned will be transmitted and shared with another generation—that memories may have faded but will not be forgotten.

Special thanks to Andy Chang, Ann Yotsuji, Randy and Jan Iwase, Gary Nakata, Harry Mattson, Norma Wong, Charlie Toguchi and Gary Caulfield for reading my drafts. As I began to write this collection of thoughts, I found my memory failing me like a flickering light bulb. Fortunately, these close friends were able to screw the bulb tighter, tap it a few times or just replace the dead elements. Thanks to Ruth and Marcus Oshiro for their generosity in sharing family photos and approving their use in this book. Thanks also to Ben Kudo, who inspired me to start the book, and to whom its completion is due.

Finally, I owe much to the sacrifice of my wife, Ruth, and my three sons, who have endured much as I dabbled in this activity. To them, all my apologies for a short temper, the absence from home during their growing years and the silence brought by a desire to shield them all from what I knew—and sometimes from what I didn't. ❧

CHAPTER ONE

Beginnings

❧

**"You gain the goodwill of friends through kindness, favors,
old connections, availability and natural charm."**
—Quintus Tullius Cicero, *How to Win An Election*

Nineteen seventy was a seminal year in Hawai'i politics. Jack Burns was seeking re-election as governor, when a young lawyer from Wahiawā, a former state house representative from the same district, decided to surrender his own political ambitions and run Old Stone Face's campaign. Robert C. Oshiro was an uncommon man, who in many ways shaped Hawai'i's politics for decades to come. He was diminutive, unassuming, almost invisible if you were unobservant, with hazel eyes and wavy hair, and a look that pierced your inner soul. I met him after an event at the garden veranda at Washington Place, where the governor and his family lived.

My politics as a young university student was decidedly strange. I was a conservative, having been brought up under the umbrella of Baptist teachings at my alma mater, Hawaii Baptist Academy (HBA). My Sundays for as long as I can recall involved duty as a choirboy and altar boy at my Episcopal church, the Church of the Epiphany, at 10th and Harding Avenues in Ka'imuki. This was the home church of the Richardson family, including William S. Richardson, who would become Jack Burns' first lieutenant governor and his first selection for chief justice of the Hawai'i Supreme Court. As I recall, my parents campaigned for "Bill" in Ka'imuki, including around church.

I was a "good boy," meaning I didn't overtly disobey, but like all boys wasn't necessarily always "good" either. I had my share of fibs from not having homework assignments to offering excuses about my failing grades in elementary school. Neither of those fibs worked with my dad. And while I sometimes did wrong, I was always forgiven, probably to my parents' exasperation. It was at HBA that I hit my stride. Why and how is open to conjecture, but I suddenly turned my life and focus around. So my first advice to parents reading this is, yes, your child can turn things around, I did. I suspect it had much to do with my teachers—one of whom, Maureen King, endured me from my arrival at HBA until I left. Maureen and I are still friends after all this time, and she can take or absolve herself from any credit for the events in my later life. I can attest to her caring nature and abiding love for her students, many of whom she continues to counsel and advise decades later. I specifically recall that Maureen indulged my quirkiness and stubbornness as the editor of our high school yearbook. Whatever had been the norm was broken during my tenure and later restored when I was no longer editor. It was a portent of my future endeavors.

It was also during this time that I found myself joining the speech and debate team. For as many Saturdays as I can remember, I attended debate and speech tournaments from Kamehameha Schools Kapālama to Waiʻanae High School under the mentorship of Willis Moore, my high school speech teacher. Facing Oʻahu's best student speakers was humbling. It became clear that regurgitating facts was insufficient. You really needed to think and arrange arguments. More importantly, you needed to convince the judges of the soundness of your position. This, however, paled when compared with the experience of delivering an oration. To this day I am in awe of the talent of Waiʻanae students' ability to engage in the millennia-old human activity of storytelling. More than mesmerizing, this skill represented the proposition that anyone could succeed; and that there was much talent in those we thought had less. I learned a lot about people and more importantly about myself.

Politics is, after all, all about people. Its Greek origin in the word *politikos* refers to citizens—members of society governed by rules. Rules are established to define and express relationships between and among people. It is through relationships that people interact with other people. Politics, thus, in all its forms is about these relationships or the lack thereof. Politics is only seen through the eyes of people. If you don't know what to look for, you won't see what is there, no matter how obvious it is. If political actions do not make sense, seem strange or appear contrary to the public will, you must look at the relationships. Sherlock Holmes, written by Sir Arthur Conan Doyle, is often quoted as saying, "Eliminate all other factors, and the one which remains must be the truth."[1] But I think the better Doyle/Holmes quote is: "In solving a problem of this sort, the grand thing is to be able to reason backward. That is a very useful accomplishment, and a very easy one, but people do not practice it much. In the everyday affairs of life it is more useful to reason forward, and so the other comes to be neglected."[2] If you understand the motives of an individual you understand the decision. If you work backwards, the motives will be true even if you didn't find them first evident. Once you appreciate this, the politics of the individual are clear to see.

I may not have thought much about all this in high school, but as one grows older and matures, the idea grows stronger. We are different only because we think we are. As my friend Neil Abercrombie likes to point out, our diversity should define us, not divide us. Too often as a child I engaged in division rather than multiplication. But of course, I was a child.

Much of my intellectual difficulty growing up was resolving the conflicts between science and faith; in many ways politics offers a similar conflict. How can one harmonize disparate thoughts? The best example I can give is music. Music provides a language that brings disparate concepts into some kind of harmony. At its best, politics is like music; in order to be successful, in order to touch people and convince them of the cause you are campaigning for, one needs to resolve the conflicts between ideas, to harmonize them, using the points and counterpoints to full and rich complexity.

I felt that I was out of place in politics. I wasn't a group person. And that stems from my being an only child, as well one of the youngest grandchildren in my mother's large family. I grew up with a Burger King philosophy; I wanted to "have it my way." Being the youngest only led to indulgence. Politics at an early age was me, not they. However selfish

---

[1] Sir Arthur Conan Doyle, *The Sign of the Four*. Similar expressions occur in *The Adventures of Sherlock Holmes*, "The Adventure of the Beryl Coronet"; *The Memoirs of Sherlock Holmes*, "Silver Blaze"; *The Return of Sherlock Holmes*, "The Adventure of the Priory School"; *His Last Bow*, "The Adventure of the Bruce-Partington Plans"; *The Case-Book of Sherlock Holmes*, "The Adventure of the Blanched Soldier."

[2] Sir Arthur Conan Doyle, *A Study in Scarlet*.

that may sound, it allowed me the luxury of freedom from group-think or the confines of consensus, I was free to advocate quite different ideas in a harmonious pact.

I also found myself caught between the contradictions of patriotism and common sense. I was a pro-American hawk, but I didn't necessarily see that slogging through the mud in Vietnam was going to protect democracy. That said, many of my friends and other members of my generation did. For many reading this, that memory is a distant one. But for the members of my generation it is still as clear as day. I was distrustful of politicians, with their grandiose statements and promises, and their focus on what may have sounded great but had no relevance to the daily lives of ordinary people. In many respects it was like the television programming of the day. Like the popular Japanese program shown for decades in Hawai'i, *Abarenbō Shōgun*, right always triumphed over evil, but only after evil acknowledged right's righteousness and then turned on righteousness and argued that he was an imposter—because right wasn't the "right" thing for evil. I felt that like the *shogun* I wasn't being told the truth by our political leaders, and when confronted the "truth" showed itself to be no longer true.

With all of this in my head, I sat that evening like a "good boy" at Washington Place, surrounded by a multimedia program with two Kodak carousel projectors, a stereo tape recorder with a soundtrack on one channel and an electronic pulse on the other, fading the slides in and out on a screen about nine feet high. It was, to say the least, impressive. Remember this wasn't the age of large screen color television or Bluetooth-driven sound equipment, but the 1970s. It was eye-opening. As the presentation concluded I turned to my parents and said, "What a piece of propaganda!" All my parents could do is give me the eye, which meant, "Shut up! I know you don't want to be here, but we'll leave shortly." My parents were there because one of my dad's biggest customers was Minoru Hata of Y. Hata & Co., the big food distributor. Minoru and his brother Frank were influential political types, so when asked to attend, my parents could find no acceptable excuse not to.

So I sat there quietly, and then Governor Burns walked up to the microphone wearing his suit and said, "I hope you enjoyed that piece of propaganda!"

I was hooked. Here was a man, a politician no less, calling it like it is.

How can that be? All politicians were by definition liars. Look at what was happening on the national level in Vietnam. How could this guy be any different?

But he was. After listening to him answer questions from the audience of mostly Americans of Japanese Ancestry (AJA), I buttonholed him and we chatted for thirty minutes or so—me, an unknown, full-of-himself nineteen-year-old, and the governor of the state of Hawai'i. I can't recall what we discussed, but I think it had to do with Mainland milk imports and local dairy farmers' opposition. In any event, this smart-ass university student was trying to play "gotcha" with the governor. But I couldn't. In fact, the outcome was that I volunteered to help him in his campaign. It was an auspicious night, one that would alter the course of my life. From these incredibly naïve beginnings, I was allowed entrée to the core of the Burns political machine: Robert C. Oshiro, Don Horio and Dan Aoki. My life would never be the same. ❧

CHAPTER TWO

An Education

~❧~

"Ethics really involves much more than the mere problem of what
is right and what is wrong. It is in itself a science and is primarily
concerned with the definition of a man's character, with his
moral values and his duties as a human being."
—Samuel Crowningburg-Amalu, *Jack Burns: A Portrait in Transition*

"Politics is the most hazardous of all professions. There is no other in which
a man can hope to do so much good to his fellow creatures…and neither is
there any in which, by mere loss of nerve, he may do as widespread harm.
There is not another in which he may so easily lose his own soul, nor is
there another in which a positive and strict veracity is so difficult."
—Andrew Oliver, *Politics* [3]

"What a manager does can be analyzed systematically. What a manager has
to be able to do can be learned (though perhaps not always taught). But one
quality cannot be learned, one qualification that the manager cannot acquire
but must bring with him. It is not genius; *it is character*." (Emphasis added.)
—Peter Drucker, *Management*

It would be easy to fall prey to the seduction of politics, many have.
Maybe I was too naïve to consider the opportunity I had been afforded,
or maybe it was the rose-colored glasses I was wearing.

The next morning, following my conversation with the governor, I
met RCO at the Burns campaign headquarters on King Street. It was

---

[3] From a gift from Robert C. Oshiro printed by Continental Airlines, courtesy of John A. (Jack) Smith, undated.

the old Wong's Drapery building, which had a first floor, a mezzanine and second warehouse floor. RCO's office was on the mezzanine, and he was guarded—and I do mean guarded—by a stern woman named Shirley Kimoto. No one saw Bob except through Shirley. I was fortunate and was allowed in. We had a short conversation and Bob gave me the keys to the storeroom, which contained all the brochures and campaign paraphernalia for the campaign. My charge: Make sure that by the general election there would be enough stuff for the campaign. Wow! I had never had such responsibility before, and would you entrust some nineteen-year-old with all of the campaign paraphernalia, from brochures to pencils to bumper stickers to buttons? Bob did.

But I wasn't alone. I soon met a cadre of young people: Jim Kirchofer, Bob Fishman, Paul Aoki, Ed Correa, Jerry Kimoto, Ruby Kimoto (Shirley and Jerry's sister) and others. We were Bob's boys and girls.

I recall Bob showing us home movies of his own campaign in Wahiawā, in which he organized young people as "futurenauts." In those days "-naut" was a popular suffix—astronauts, aquanauts and so forth. In Bob's mind the 1970 election was about Hawai'i's future, and what role locally born youth would play in it. He was committed to the idea that we would play a big part. Tom Coffman recounts in his book, *Catch A Wave: Case Study of Hawai'i's New Politics,* that Bob was concerned about the tidal wave of newcomers to the Islands changing Hawai'i and its culture. He intended to instruct these young people in local politics— to be his disciples, if you will—and the ideas, thoughts and concepts that he had come to learn and appreciate. Newspaperman and political pundit Dan Boylan calls RCO "the wizard of Wahiawā." Bob was no wizard; but he knew politics, knew the players and had an innate ability to quickly assess and evaluate the strengths and weaknesses in people. And he wasn't afraid to test those strengths and weaknesses.

That election taught me that one must have faith in young people, and faith in others you do not know, or hardly know. How else do you explain a campaign chairman trusting a nineteen-year-old with the keys to the vault of campaign materials? It wouldn't happen today. And don't believe for a minute that Bob was xenophobic. My brothers in arms, Jim Kirchofer—"Patch," as we called him, for the eye patch he wore—and Bob Fishman, were not locally brewed individuals. Patch and Bob were from the Mainland, but their values were local. That's what RCO was focused on. Being local wasn't an incident of birth, he knew; it was a choice.

Later on, Bob Oshiro would recast his ideas on politics into his four principles of campaigning. And those four principles have stood the test of time.

This was 1970 and there were no campaign spending laws, no limitations on messages and content, no cable television. In fact, there were only three network stations—no Channel Five, no 'Olelo, no cable news, only the tried-and-true methods of one-on-one campaigning.

Bob believed in the grassroots base of campaigning and never lost sight of the importance of the relationships involved. But 1970 was the year Hawai'i was to be introduced to the thirty-minute campaign film, and Bob, ever the experimenter, went with it. The film "Catch A Wave" deeply touched many people who saw it. Its most famous line is delivered by Governor Burns, wearing shorts and speaking about leadership from the porch of his house in Kailua. "Any damn fool can take a stand!" he spouts angrily. "And I mean damn fool. Does that make sense, take stands?" This from Old Stone Face, as his supporters knew him. It made an impression. But most don't recall what he said after that, that a leader must bring people together and make things work for society and the community. Governor Burns got it right.

Leadership isn't about being a sycophant to the public or living by public opinion, but about leading public opinion. More important than doing the right thing politically is doing the right thing, period. In many ways that was one of the reasons he was faring poorly in the polls, as he faced his longtime opponent, Tom Gill. Governor Burns was thinking of the broader vision of and for Hawai'i, not what was politically expedient at the time. It was a fight between the moderates and the Democratic Party's liberal left, but more than that, it was a fight for the soul of the state.

This took courage. But Governor Burns had faced that test before when the legislature passed the abortion bill. As a devout Catholic, he was personally opposed to it. No doubt the bishop may have called him to remind him of his duties as a faithful member of the church. Yet Governor Burns allowed the bill to become law without his signature. Why? Was it a political act? Maybe, some might say.

But in "Catch A Wave," Governor Burns makes it clear that he is everybody's governor, and not just holding office to express his personal views.[4] Isn't that refreshing? A candidate who has the ethics to do the right thing—not what he wants, but what the public asks for and deserves. He certainly could have taken a stand and divided the community. Would that allow him to govern better? There is much to be learned from this man. While we can debate whether or not this was a political decision, we must admire the courage it took to do what he believed to be right.[5]

Governor Burns was also attacked that year for having "alarming friends" by his Republican opponent, Sam King, who would go on to become one of Hawai'i's most respected and beloved jurists. This comment was aimed at Jack Burns' character, insinuating that the governor was an honorable man, but one with unscrupulous friends. Even in those days, innuendo played deep in the public psyche. It did not work.

Candidate King was referring to the recent assassination of sitting state senator Larry Kuriyama in his carport in Pearl City. There was much speculation about the killing and it wasn't until 1989 that the hit man was identified.[6] But in 1970 the events were too recent, too real. King's allegation sounded as though he blamed Kuriyama's killing on Governor Burns.

Was it ethical to make such a claim? Was this negative campaigning? Was this a smear? Did King cross the line? We will never know what went through the minds of the voters, but Governor Burns survived the

---

[4] In fact, Governor Burns says that the bishop deals in black and white, while he himself has to deal with shades of gray. His balancing of his faith and his role as a public official should be a lesson for every politician.

[5] Further details about Governor Burns' life and career are available in the book *An Aura of Greatness* by his grandson Brendan Burns.

[6] In *The Honolulu Advertiser* dated September 18, 2005, Will Hoover writes, "Underworld hit man Ronald K. Ching—who in 1984 confessed to killing four men including a state senator and the son of the then-Honolulu prosecutor—died in his Halawa Correctional Facility cell yesterday morning, according to the Department of Public Safety... Ching was sentenced to life in prison on Aug. 24, 1985, for: shooting state Sen. Larry Kuriyama to death in his carport in 1970; murdering City Prosecutor Charles Marsland's son Charles Marsland III on a Waimanalo road in 1975... The murder of Kuriyama on Oct. 23, 1970 shocked the state. Kuriyama had been at a political rally attended by hundreds of people, including Gov. John Burns. He arrived home at around 11 p.m. and was gunned down by someone who shot him several times using a gun with a silencer. Kuriyama's family said they heard Kuriyama drive up and get out of the car. Then they heard several cracking sounds and the screams of the dying senator. Ching pleaded guilty to second-degree murder in the Kuriyama killing, saying that he 'agreed with others' to kill the senator. But he added that, 'Larry Kuriyama was shot by another in my presence with my aid and support.'" http://the.honoluluadvertiser.com/article/2005/Sep/18/ln/FP509180351.html.

onslaught of a bitter primary battle and an equally ambitious general election fight.

In the end 1970 was a victory for Governor Burns, Oshiro, Horio and Aoki.[7] And it was the setting of the stage for a relatively unknown state senator's rise to the office of governor. ❧

---

[7] Some have speculated about rivalries among Oshiro, Aoki and Horio, but I recall that Governor Burns' wife, Beatrice, told RCO that her husband "loved them all." Like a father with his children, he didn't pick favorites.

CHAPTER THREE

Work

❧

"'Working' the human being always means developing him.
The direction which this development takes decides whether the human
being—both as a man and as a resource—will become more productive
or cease, ultimately to be productive at all."

—Peter Drucker, *Management*

A campaign headquarters is always buzzing. Why? What's so important that so many volunteers are so busy?

Work and the presence of work is essential for a campaign. Having something for volunteers to do is critical to involving individuals in the process. But why? What is the magic?

The fact is, many campaign activities are really "make-work." So why waste people's time? In part, if a person wants to contribute time, the campaign needs to accommodate this contribution. If a campaign fails to do so, then the relationship between that individual and the campaign diminishes. Thus campaign "work" is a critical and necessary part of the process of building loyalty and allegiance.

For example, in 1970 Ed Correa and Paul Aoki were busy pinning supporters' locations on a huge senatorial map. It was a tedious job. Most local campaigns have done the same thing dating back to that election. While this provided a dramatic visual of where our supporters were located, it was never used as a practical campaign tool. It was always a make-work project for volunteers who had little skills in other activities.

Another activity in general use was the "*hui* book," a creation of Democratic campaign worker Kazu Sunada. Usually a pocket-sized booklet of several supporter cards, it has over the years morphed into various iterations, but the gist was to get someone to sign a card pledging support, obtain his or her address and phone number, enter this data into a hand-operated database by district and precinct and finally pin it to the maps.

These two activities were the *raison d'etre* for many campaign workers in Hawai'i. Mention a hui book to a person who was politically active in Hawai'i thirty years ago and you'll get an immediate reaction. But despite the wealth of data accumulated, without enough hands to sort, the data was for the most part inaccessible until the appearance of the personal computer. They were good ideas, but decades ahead of the technology. Now such data is accessed with the algorithms of computer experts crunching data.

In those good old days, having people look at these cards was primarily so that someone could say, "I know his/her family." And someone would make a call. The other was multiple touches by various people once some-one committed. And it was more to know who wasn't supporting the opposition as it was to know who was supporting your candidate. In this methodology it was a rudimentary poll—not scientific but effective—and also the basis for the "get out the vote" activities of more recent cam-paigns. It was effective because of this relationship building: the touches.

Work involved many other hands-on activities. Holding signs at vari-ous stretches of roadways, corners and junctions. Placing bumper stickers on supporters' cars. Walking the neighborhood in canvasses. Holding rallies in various districts. Hosting a coffee hour, which sometimes had no coffee, but beer and stew. This was all campaign work. And to vary-ing degrees all have stood the test of time. And some have become more involved than others. In 1970 these were basic, pure campaign events with narrow purposes. Canvassing brought neighbors in touch with neighbors. If a next-door neighbor asked you to vote for Jack Burns, you would more likely accept that friend's endorsement over some radio advertisement. If Uncle Masa said he was supporting Governor Burns, you'd likely support Burns yourself. If you went to a rally and saw your boss and colleagues there and they were supporting Governor Burns, so would you (nobody likes to be an outlier). And if you saw Auntie holding a "Burns for Governor" sign on Pali Highway, and you knew you'd be seeing her on Sunday, you'd better smile when she saw you driving by. Otherwise, "You goin' get it!"

There were armies of "bumper sticker-ers"—teams of folks who would ask you if they could slap a sticker on your car. That was better than just making stickers available, only to be taken but never used. Most supporters would take bumper stickers because they could be seen doing so. But despite the large quantity printed, few actually showed up on cars, thus the bumper sticker-er program.

All of these activities are "work." All involve sacrificing time, energy and, in some cases, money. But mostly it was time.[8] A lot of people helped, maybe not always enthusiastically or because they necessarily liked the candidate. In the old days, your day job might depend on who you supported politically.

Campaign work was a relationship between individuals who came together. These people worked together over the years, and relationships grew into friendships. Today this relationship is less in evidence, as much of this "work" has been handed over to computerized data analysis.

What's more, many people today are unwilling to announce their allegiances on their possessions. Consequently, the plethora of bumper stickers, which were so common during past campaigns, has been replaced by Facebook likes, supportive tweets and other affirmations of social media.

Yard signs, of course, are still very much in evidence today, as technology has rendered them even more accessible. In the '70s, yard signs were handmade, not printed *en masse* on corrugated plastic as they are now. Back then, you started with a paper sheet printed with your candidate's name, then spray-glued them to plywood panels, which were nailed or screwed to one-by-fours cut to four-foot lengths. The screwed variety was best as it allowed for disassembly for storage after the election. Many of these old paper signs had several layers of candidate posters glued to them as they were handed down from candidate to candidate. Banners were used, but they were also expensive and had to be silk-screened by hand; with technology this is now accomplished at a fraction of the cost and time.

Headquarters activities have also declined over the years. This is partly because the large numbers of workers once drawn from political appointees and public unions has shrunk, as alliances between unions and state

---

[8] Bob Oshiro once said that time is the most precious thing that people can contribute to a campaign. The corollary is, "Money is a cheap contribution"—i.e., it's a way not to contribute time, but to substitute for it. Once a person contributes time he or she becomes loyal, while money represents only a betting marker, rather than true loyalty.

and county administrations have evolved. Union membership in the past was aligned with the Democratic political establishment, a result of years of discrimination and oppression of the old Republican guard that once controlled local government and business. But today public unions and government administrations often find themselves much more at odds. This decline has also resulted in fractures between union retirees and current membership. While the interests of many retirees is to preserve the benefits they obtained from years of service, current members are more interested in salaries than benefits. This dichotomy creates a conundrum for union leaders forced to balance these countervailing issues. As a result, astute candidates now seek the support of the two groups separately, and cannot rely upon union backing without the extra effort. In the old days this dichotomy didn't exist. When union members were younger, raising young families, retirement benefits weren't an immediate concern, but wages were. Today, however, this divide between old and young union members has grown considerably.

To solicit union members, the "work" is done by union contacts, some of them close to leadership, but not necessarily to membership. Again, the relationships between union leaders and the political candidate is critical to pave the way for an endorsement, but not a sure way to secure the support of the rank and file. Candidates who don't receive endorsements must then contend that leadership's decision doesn't reflect the positions of the members. Union leadership and the rank and file are two separate groups; and it behooves the candidate to seek both. In fact, a union endorsement seldom means support from that union's rank and file; today's candidate understands that a union endorsement simply opens a forum and opportunity to reach its membership. It rarely means that union members are automatically voting for him or her.

Union support was not the sole venue of Democrats, by the way. US Senator Hiram Fong, a Republican, enjoyed strong union support during the many years he served. Why? Because of his deep relationships with union members and leadership during times when they needed him most.

In Bob Oshiro's day, "work" also meant seeking the best talent available. RCO always gave people a chance to prove themselves and gradually gave promising individuals more and more opportunities. He would coach and counsel them to draw out every grain of leadership they possessed, and promoted them to ever increasing positions of responsibility.

In that regard he was Confucius-like in his philosophy. Anyone who displayed a modicum of leadership was given more and more responsibility and authority, but if you didn't perform, no further assignments were given. Bob always had someone watching and waiting to step in as backup, in case someone failed to perform. Contingency plans were important. The campaign memoranda of the day always included planning documents with the roles of leaders and deputies outlined, and contingency plans placed in preparation.

It was Bob Oshiro who first referred me to the works of the late author and management consultant Peter Drucker, who wrote that "'Working' the human being always means developing...[the individual]."[9] And as Bob said, moving the vision of that individual from the ground under his feet to the horizon ahead became our clarion call. ⋙

---

[9] Peter Drucker, *Management*, (Harper & Row, 1974).

CHAPTER FOUR

Horizons

~&

"This spirit of a man and the ability of human beings 'to continue
dreaming the impossible dream, to pursue what is unattainable today
to make it tomorrow a reality'—this is the Jack Burns story...
To the young men and women of today, I would remind you that I, too,
was once as you are—filled with hopes, aspirations, ideals, and dreams.
With only these, I, too, became a sparrow."

—Robert C. Oshiro, *Jack Burns: A Portrait in Transition*

Most of us grew up being told to watch where we stepped. For those
growing up in rural Hawai'i, that was very practical advice. But
for politicians focusing on the ground under you or just in front of you,
makes you less of a visionary and more of a harbor pilot. Both are necessary. The harbor pilot knows the intricacies of navigating the near shore,
and that is particularly important for the achievement of specific goals.
But if you don't have an adventuresome spirit, a desire to discover new
things and places, life becomes very static.

In 1970 the shackles of the pre-statehood years were a thing of the
past. We were outward bound into new seas, new oceans, new waves
of discovery. Governor Burns brought an opportunity to rethink anew
what was, and to decide on what would be. It may have been a naïve
notion that Hawai'i could avoid the calamities of other societies, that
we could all live together, that we could have an ideal society, unbur-
dened by the strictures and norms of the Mainland. We could create a
multiethnic society based on a person's skills and intelligence and not
on power and intrigue. It was a time of hope and aspirations, ideals
and dreams.

After the 1970 election I returned to the University of Hawai'i, received my undergraduate degree in political science and headed off to law school.[10] In 1973 Governor Burns fell gravely ill with cancer and passed away. The baton was handed to his lieutenant governor, George R. Ariyoshi. Much has been much written by and about Ariyoshi,[11] and I needn't dwell on his years as LG and governor. But I will note that the Burns group, comprised of the late governor's old political allies, was not fully aligned with the group of supporters close to Ariyoshi. It took some time for the two groups to reach an equilibrium of sorts and finally become the Ariyoshi team. Some of this disparity would boil over into the 1980 election for mayor of Honolulu.

In 1974, a year after Ariyoshi had become acting governor upon Burn's death, he was running for election as governor. He faced several other candidates, including Tom Gill, state senate president Dave McClung and Honolulu's lesser-known upstart mayor Frank Fasi. I was in my second year of law school and although Don Horio[12] implored me to skip school in 1974, I decided that finishing law school was the better option. The Vietnam War was at its crescendo that year and I figured that finishing would give me an opportunity to sling law phrases rather than mud. Horio had me working on polling at the old Merchandise Mart building at the corner of Alakea and Hotel Streets. The labyrinthine structure was a peculiar place to stage a polling operation, but there we were. Since I had decided not to stay, my job was to bring in another person, Harry Mattson, to run the operation. As it turned out, Harry would continue in the business for decades to come, and we would be working together on political campaigns decades later.

---

[10] Bob Oshiro recommended that I go to law school. My intention upon graduation was to go to Japan to obtain a graduate degree in political science, focusing on political development around the turn of the twentieth century, and specifically why Japan and China developed differently. Why was the Meiji government successful, while the Qing dynasty in China fell after so many disastrous rebellions. Bob was persuasive, and with the help of Governor Burns, who wrote a letter of support to the only law school to which I applied, Loyola in Los Angeles, I was accepted. It was another turning point for me.

[11] See books written by Governor Ariyoshi: *With Obligation to All* and *Hawai'i: The Past Fifty Years, The Next Fifty Years*; and First Hawaiian Bank chairman Walter Dods' book, *Yes! A Memoir of Modern Hawai'i*.

[12] Later Don Horio's son would marry my cousin's daughter, making us relatives of sorts. His widow, Lila, and I remain friends today.

George Ariyoshi won the 1974 primary election and went on to beat Randolph Crossley in the general. Here's how the primary stacked up:

George Ariyoshi, lieutenant governor, 36.18%
Frank Fasi, mayor of Honolulu, 31.47%
Thomas Gill, former lieutenant governor, 30.08%
David C. McClung, state senate president, 1.79%
Henry deFries, 0.49%

Nineteen seventy-five was a big year for me. I graduated from law school midyear, took the Hawai'i State Bar Exam and began working at the AG's office under Ron Amemiya. I hadn't participated in the 1974 victory of Governor Ariyoshi and was reluctant to engage in the political scene due to my absence. But I was fortunate that Dan Aoki, Governor Burns' longtime aide, was still there on the fifth floor of the state capitol, working for the newly elected Governor Ariyoshi. Dan first told me that the only position available was a public defender job, working with Don Tsukiyama. Having married just after my graduation from law school, and with my wife still in law school herself, I needed a job, so I reluctantly set about contacting Don. He was a gracious man, especially knowing that I was a green attorney with no experience. Criminal law was not my cup of tea, but any port in a storm, I figured. A day later, Ron Amemiya called and offered me a position at the Attorney General's office and I jumped as fast as I could. I apologized to Don, but a civil job was much more appealing. Thus started my five-year tenure with the AG's office.

My assignment was the welfare division of the Department of Social Services and Housing (DSSH). That may be a mouthful, but it still doesn't give you a sense of the full breadth of the department, which included the prisons, welfare programs and vocational rehabilitation. Its director was Andrew I.T. Chang, who had been picked by Governor Ariyoshi as one of the "young" guys to lead state departments. Josh Agsalud would be another. Ron Amemiya, Wayne Minami and a host of thirty- to forty-somethings were tasked with leading this new administration into the future.

My first supervisor was a *kama'aina* named Jack Campbell, and my colleagues included Jim Dandar and Mike Lilly, who was the nephew of Amfac, Inc. executive Henry Walker.[13] Mike was also a seasoned veteran of the US Navy. So here I was, a no-experience, politically connected appointee in a sea of seasoned lawyers. I anticipated being in the background, but that was not to be.

I got my ticket to practice in October 1975, joined the AG shortly thereafter, and by November was in US district court all by my lonesome, on a motion for a temporary restraining order filed by the Legal Aid Society against the DSSH welfare division. It was a dark and stormy day, and as I walked from the AG's office on the fourth floor of the capitol to federal court, located in the downtown post office building, I felt I was heading to my doom. Federal judge Sam King sat on a podium high above the rest of us, with flowing red drapes in back of him. The court was empty except for the attorneys; but I could hear protestors outside chanting about the case. And there I was. Years of debating, oratory, law school melted away like an ice cube in the desert. My throat was dry and my mouth was parched. I stumbled at every turn, but I owe a great deal to Judge King, who recognized that this immature, inexperienced, first-time lawyer was probably appearing before him on his first case—and across from an opponent who was a seasoned Mainland attorney, Stan Levin. It looked like a rout, and leaving with dignity was all I could hope for. But Judge King in his wisdom allowed this young attorney to win a minor victory and denied Legal Aid's motion for a TRO. I could walk back bruised but with head held high. My boss, Jack, probably knew what I was in for, but he also needed to test me. Luckily I survived, and would thereafter spend days in the motions calendar at the federal and state courts on such cases.

Legal Aid was a tough opponent, not just because they were seasoned attorneys but because our department had difficulties writing regulations. Rules and regulations were a new thing. In the past the departments had pretty much done what it wanted, but Chapter 91, an infamous measure about rules creation, changed all that. Now agencies needed to articulate rules clearly and in compliance with federal law. These were new fields for the agencies, and there was a lot of stumbling. Invariably a lawsuit would be filed every Friday or Thursday for a TRO hearing to be held within a few days. Legal Aid was accustomed to flinging complaints under the

---

[13] I would later work for Henry Walker as one of Amfac's general counsels.

door to the AG's office after hours. By 1976 it was becoming a war.

So how do you win wars? Frontal attacks? *Banzai* charges? Strategic bombing? Sabotage? Attorney General Ron Amemiya, ever the strategist, decided to cut off funding to the Legal Aid Society at the state legislature, the largest source of their income. (You could do things like that forty years ago, but not today.) It worked, and Legal Aid agreed to talk before filing lawsuits. It did calm the waters. And I learned an important lesson, following on an old law school adage: If the law is on your side, argue the law. If the facts are on your side, argue the facts. If emotions are on your side, argue the emotions. If all else fails, make sure your client knows you're doing your best, make a scene and get yourself hauled out of court. The court may sanction you, but your clients will love you. Ron added a sidebar: If someone needs money from the legislature to attack you, cut the umbilical, or at least threaten to do so. That was a lesson in raw politics—not nice, but making sausage never is. ✒

CHAPTER FIVE

John Craven: The Mad Professor

❧

"Time is totally irreplaceable. Within limits we can substitute one resource for another... We can substitute capital for human labor. We can use more knowledge or more brawn. But there is no substitute for time."
—Peter Drucker, *The Effective Executive*

Maybe this chapter's title is unfair. Nineteen seventy-six was a year of change. Republican US Senator Hiram Fong had retired and Hawai'i's US Representatives Spark Matsunaga and Patsy Mink were vying to take over as his replacement. After defeating Mink for the Democratic nomination, Matsunaga beat former GOP governor William Quinn, Hawai'i's last territorial governor, for Fong's Senate seat by 40,000 votes, not a mandate but clearly decisive. Sparky would remain in the seat until his passing in 1990.

This led to a race for their two congressional seats. Department of Education and state government veteran Daniel Akaka sought the second congressional district, while Cec Heftel, the well-known owner of KGMB television and radio, was running for the first congressional district seat against an unlikely opponent, University of Hawai'i professor John Craven. Dan Akaka was a political protégé supported by the so-called Burns-Ariyoshi forces and was expected to win handily. Heftel was also expected to beat the political newcomer Craven. The fly in the ointment was that there appeared to be at least some enmity between Heftel and Ariyoshi. Craven was then recruited by the Ariyoshi group to run against Heftel. The man chosen to manage Craven's campaign was RCO. I got a call.

Honestly, in 1976, the last thing I needed to do was get involved politically again. My legal career was just starting and I believed that focusing on that was much more important. But Bob Oshiro had other ideas, and I signed on. Bob had set up campaign headquarters at the Chinese Cultural Center. Akaka's HQ was also there, but on the *mauka* side of the first floor courtyard. We were located towards the eastern end, under the parking structure by the elevators. This was a very small headquarters compared to our Wong's Drapery offices back in 1970. And the cadre of young people were somewhat different: Bob Nagao, Alan Tamayose, Ron Yokota, Jerry Kimoto, Shirley Kimoto, Mike Hee (son of Budget deputy director Jensen Hee) and the old man of the group, Tadashi Tojo. All would become close friends during this campaign.

It was a shoestring campaign. And because it was an election for national office, new federal campaign spending laws and restrictions applied. Bob was going to make this a grassroots campaign, not a TV/radio campaign, because we had no choice. So I'd do my day job then report to the headquarters on evenings and weekends. Every Saturday morning, Tadashi would bring hard boiled eggs from his farm. Remember Dr. Seuss' *Green Eggs and Ham*? Tadashi's eggs all had green yolks. They tasted fine; they just looked, well, green.

On this campaign, I recall that our passion for this new guy Craven was unwavering. John had a long résumé of making the most of our location in the middle of the Pacific. For young folks like us, the aspirational notions of more and better jobs for us and our kids resonated deeply, gutturally. Despite being a Mainland *haole*, we thought, John was a regular guy—weird at times (well, he was a professor), but a regular guy. More importantly, he was deeply committed to Hawai'i.

I remember our attempts to transform his "mad professor" look—his wardrobe, his wild hair flying in all directions, his socks that would invariably slip to his ankles and require constant attention to pull up. John was a great sport and a great candidate, never acting "habuts"[14] in front of us.

John Craven's defeat that year was hard to bear, and Bob knew that. He kept the HQ open for several months and we'd gather every Saturday like homing pigeons to talk about what we could have done.

This taught me the lesson of camaraderie. Campaigns are like wars. The guy in the foxhole with you becomes your brother. As in battle, you

---

[14] Local slang from the Japanese *habuteru*, meaning grumpy.

defend each other to the death. In many ways this explains the loyalty of fellow campaigners over the decades. Once a comrade in arms, always a comrade in arms. Loyalty is a rare trait but one that's essential in politics. It was a lesson that would stick with me.

Nineteen seventy-six also taught me that campaigns don't have to be big or well financed to be successful. Heftel won the primary with 47.18 percent of the votes cast, while Craven had 38.31 percent. My friend and later colleague Hal Jones,[15] who went on to become a GOP representative from east Honolulu, garnered 12.71 percent of the vote. Had Jones not been in the race, who knows what the outcome would have been. Bob was convinced we were just a few more weeks away victory. Time, however, is a ruthless midwife. A baby is born at a certain time regardless of the parents' desires. This was another good lesson.

The truth is that we were outspent. The other candidate had a much bigger persona and more gravitas among local business types, while John was, well, John. Craven was a nice guy, but an intellectual in a town that doesn't necessarily value intellectuals. A common statement then was that whichever way UH goes, the State goes the other way. This represented the notion that the university was out of touch with common people and couldn't connect with them. In many ways John wasn't the right candidate, and it also served to illustrate the same political axiom that Jack Burns had encountered with his nomination of Kenny Brown against Tom Gill in 1966.[16] Governor Burns was crushed by that election and never selected a running mate after that. For some time, Governor Ariyoshi also avoided making these choices himself, at least until 1980.

There is an appropriate postscript to this chapter, and one which many may not remember. The following is from John Craven's obituary in *The New York Times*:

John P. Craven, a former Navy scientist whose innovations in ocean technology and exploration led to some of the nation's most celebrated feats of espionage, died on Feb. 12 in Hawaii. He was 90...

---

[15] Hal and I would later become colleagues on the board of Global Hope Networks International, an NGO based in Geneva, Switzerland.

[16] One could take the contrary view, if one looked at the campaign of educator Dan Akaka, who did win. Maybe John was just a "bridge too far."

From 1959 to 1969, as chief scientist of the Special Projects Office, Dr. Craven led the Navy's drive to expand its presence into the crushing depths of the sea. Among other things, he turned submarines into spy machines that could reach down miles to inspect and retrieve lost enemy matériel, including nuclear arms... Dr. Craven was project manager for developing the Polaris, the world's first intercontinental ballistic missile that could be fired from a submerged submarine. It underwent test firing in 1960 and was in service for decades... In March 1968, a rich new target materialized when a Soviet missile submarine bearing code books, encryption gear and nuclear arms sank in the central Pacific. By all accounts, Dr. Craven and the spy sub located the wreckage more than three miles beneath the sea's surface...[17] The spy sub he devised made one of its greatest coups shortly after he left the Navy. In 1971, the Halibut stole into the Sea of Okhotsk north of Japan, found a telecommunications cable used by Soviet nuclear forces and succeeded in tapping its secrets. The mission, code-named Ivy Bells, was so secret that a vast majority of the submarine's sailors had no idea what they had accomplished. The success led to a concealed world of cable-tapping.[18]

John wrote a book published in 2001. When I ran into him at Honolulu International Airport baggage claim shortly after the book became available, I joked that if we knew then what we know now, I'm not sure we would have worked on his campaign. The nation and Hawai'i owes John Craven a heartfelt *aloha* for all he did. He is truly missed. ❦

---

[17] This was the famous *Glomar Explorer*, which was berthed at Honolulu Harbor. Little did we know that the ship wasn't looking for manganese nodules, reportedly a source of a potential economic boom for the Islands, but was in fact trying to salvage the sunken Russian submarine. See http://www.pri.org/stories/2015-09-07/ship-built-cias-most-audacious-cold-war-mission-now-headed-scrapyard.

[18] William J. Broad, "John P. Craven, 90, Pioneer of Spying at Sea, Dies," *New York Times*, Feb. 18, 2015, http://www.nytimes.com/2015/02/19/us/john-p-craven-90-scientist-who-shaped-cold-war-spying-at-sea-dies.html?_r=0.

CHAPTER SIX

George Ariyoshi: Quiet and Effective

๛

"Seven social sins: politics without principles, wealth without work, pleasure without conscience, knowledge without character, commerce without morality, science without humanity, and worship without sacrifice."
—Mahatma Gandhi

It had been four years since George Ariyoshi was first elected governor. He was now running for re-election. He wasn't flamboyant, nor was he loquacious. He was a typical AJA. We weren't brought up that way. But he had done a lot! And he had plans to do a lot more. He was forward thinking, concerned about our collective future. But in 1978 most knew nothing about what he had done or who he was. He was trailing in the polls.

Being the first non-haole governor had its drawbacks. Many had high expectations for change. But George Ariyoshi was a moderate, not a liberal. Secondly, while as governor he was the titular head of Hawai'i's Democratic Party, Ariyoshi's history with the party was spotty at best. Unlike his predecessor, who was a prominent architect of the party, Ariyoshi was mostly a bystander. This may have irked more than a few regulars, but he was after all the governor, and he deserved respect for his position. Ariyoshi had to earn the respect, however, of that base. And the way it was done at the party level was through the work of sparrows like Gary Caulfield, Dan Ishii, Brad Mossman, Clyde Sumida, Leighton Oshima, Everett Cuskaden, Sandy Ebesu, Benjamin and Franklin Kudo and many more "young

Democrats," who lined up the votes.[19]

Surrounded by a political team comprised of Walter Dods and Jack Seigle, who handled all media and communications; Ed Toma, Francis MacMillan, Jimmy Takushi and the old loyalists running the grassroots; Frank Hata, raising the money; and the Burns old guard led by Dan Aoki, the campaign seemed poised for success. But Ariyoshi was trailing, and there was a desire to bring in more guns. RCO answered that clarion call, although he wasn't especially happy about it. After 1970 and '74, he had returned to his Wahiawā roots and continued to practice law. But then, every four years like clockwork, the call would come. He was not a happy camper, closing up shop and referring his clients while he did his political duty. But Bob was like the legendary Cincinnatus who, when duty called, left his farm, defended the Republic and upon victory returned to the farm. Bob was Hawai'i's latter-day Cincinnatus.[20]

I believe 1978 was the year that Bob crystallized his political principles and ideas. His four requirements for a campaign volunteer were articulated. His concept of a flat campaign was one in which there were only Indians and no chiefs.[21] And most important of all was the requirement that we participate in a campaign because we are driven by a cause.

Bob had many great sayings. A campaign, he said, is based on multiplication and addition; not subtraction and division. That one has always remained with me.

On the true test of a volunteer: A person must be available, reliable, loyal and committed.[22] If you lack any of these traits, you won't be a productive volunteer. From a campaign perspective, a person who isn't available may never have existed. Someone who says he'll be there, but never shows up because they're always too busy, is unusable.

Similarly, a person who isn't reliable—e.g., says they'll be there and is perpetually late or misses appointments—might as well have said

---

[19] We were a somewhat "anal" bunch. I believe Clyde and Leighton, who ran one of the conventions, were the first to devise a "convention manual." I still have a copy. It described the rules and how everything has to work.

[20] Students of history might recall that George Washington also responded in Cincinnatus fashion after the Revolutionary War.

[21] My good friend Ed Hasegawa reminded me that the concept was that no matter who you were outside the campaign, in the campaign you were just one of the Indians.

[22] I have an original copy of that 1978 memo in my files.

they couldn't be there.

A person who flits from camp to camp, trying to get a better deal, isn't useful either. Trust in a campaign is paramount, and information shared indiscriminately or used to personal advantage to the detriment of the campaign is unacceptable. Likewise, a person who isn't committed, who is lukewarm and develops no fire in the belly for the candidate, is also unusable to the fullest extent.

These principles I believe are universal for all campaigns. And campaigns that adhere to these principles develop the strongest organizations. Those that don't adhere to them have weak structures and links, which in times of great stress will tear the organization apart. Campaigns are not won on paper; they are won in the heart.

The enemy isn't your political opponent; rather, it is the weakest links in your own organization. Bob knew this. His lectures—and yes, they were lectures, usually delivered in the late afternoon to the cabinet and appointees—were more admonishing than inspirational. After a decade of political superiority, there was a tendency to view winning as inevitable despite the closeness of prior victories. Bob may have seen that and thus the urgency with which he approached the political insiders.

My fortune lay in being involved in all of these meetings because, frankly, I was a political guy. But it was an opportunity to build relationships with cabinet and subcabinet throughout the administration. I got to know Andy Chang, not only as a client and a director, but personally. Similar political bonds were forged with Wayne Yamasaki, Don Botelho, George Freitas, Josh Agsalud, Ryokichi Higashionna, Jimmy Kumagai, John Farias and a host of others. For a young attorney these connections were invaluable and would certainly benefit me in my career.

The 1978 election was turning out to be a tough campaign. Governor Ariyoshi's main opponent would be Frank Fasi, mayor of the City and County of Honolulu. Fasi had the strength of the mayor's office; excellent fundraising capacity with his well-connected campaign treasurer, Harry C.C. Chung; control over building permits, water connections and sewer connections; and, perhaps most important, the prosecutor's office. He was and would continue to be the major threat to the State-level politicians. Fasi wasn't part of the old regime and, unlike Tom Gill, had no need of the old structure. He had built a new infrastructure. He was the exact opposite of Ariyoshi in many ways. Frank had his name on all the City construction signs, he had a color scheme on the bus, which matched his campaign colors; he appropriated the *shaka* sign as his symbol; and he wasn't, or at least we thought he wasn't, above paying volunteers to come from the outlying districts to wave Fasi campaign signs in town. What's more, he had his share of allies in the legislature.

Most who were involved remember the fights over the little traffic triangle where King Street splits into King and Kapi'olani Boulevard.[23] The battles to control this tiny piece of real estate are legend. Every day the sign-waving crews would get there earlier and earlier. I'm sure that both sides also did this, but I remember holding signs on Beretania Street by the capitol when Fasi supporters showed up and interspersed themselves between the Ariyoshi sign holders. There were no fisticuffs or brawls, but things got really tense, especially as the Fasi crew had one loud cowbell ringer.

Shows of force like this were common. How much effect did they have on the voters? No one really knows. But the polls weren't showing much movement in the early days.

A call from Bob one day led to the largest political rally in Hawai'i history. Bob asked me to grab a bunch of folks and come up with a rally at the newly built Aloha Stadium. As usual I said OK, not thinking very much about the details. I was just a good soldier, now twenty-seven years old. I called the ranking elements of the campaign together and started to describe what we were tasked to do. There was almost a visceral push-back. Ed Toma, the campaign chair, said that we needed to hold the rally at McKinley High School, Ariyoshi's alma mater. They'd done this before, and knew what to do and how to do it. Ed was absolutely correct. McKinley was a slam dunk. All twenty-five or thirty people in the room agreed. I marched back to Bob's office. He promptly said, "No! Stadium!" and I marched back as quickly as I marched over, and told the group, "No! Stadium!" That was the end of that.

Nine months out we were planning in earnest. We had a well-known local show promoter/producer, Dick Howard, along with entertainer Ray Tanaka. We met at the Musician's Union Hall on Kapi'olani and outlined a musical extravaganza depicting Hawai'i's history from primeval volcanoes to today. Bob had shared with me that he wanted this to be

---

[23] It is now occupied by an enormous fountain sculpture.

on a scale like the Nuremburg rallies of World War II. The scale of the endeavor was mind-boggling. It meant putting 50,000 people into Aloha Stadium. Before he'd had this idea, the best we'd been able to do was maybe 10,000, and that was pushing it. Logistically, 50,000 rally participants is simply a lot of people.[24] And we needed to feed and provide drinks for that crowd.

To the rescue came the governor's brother, Jimmy.[25] He was a miracle worker. He had standards, though. He wanted each bento to have a half *huli-huli* chicken, rice, a bun, *takuwan*, *kamaboko* and that green plastic thing that always gets put into it.

Close your eyes and think about 60,000 bento boxes filled with those ingredients.[26] We had fifty huli-huli chicken pits on the north side of the stadium started up the night before to cook the main course.[27] The surging orange glow was an incredible sight. Rice was being cooked at thirteen cafeterias[28] and trucked to the stadium for bento assembly.[29] Volunteers sliced the 60,000 pieces of kamaboko and takuwan. Could anyone actually do this? Today most would say "no can." But Jimmy did. With hundreds of volunteers.[30]

---

[24] Consider that an army division is 10–20,000 people. By comparison, we had to handle 50,000.

[25] Jimmy had a co-coordinator, Walter Yamashiro. Walter would become the head of the Office of Consumer Protection and would later perish in an American Airlines DC-10 crash at Chicago's O'Hare International Airport on May 25, 1979. Both my wife, Ruth, and I worked with Walter. She served as a deputy consumer protection specialist for him until his death, and I defended him on behalf of the AG in the case of Mitsuba Pub. Co. v. State.

[26] It was estimated that it would take 7.5 hours to cook the chicken. We figured we could cook 2,000 chickens at a rate of sixty minutes per bird, and we could pack 2,000 chickens every twenty-five minutes. This meant it would take the packing crew 6.5 hours to pack; thus the total time broken down per chicken was 45.5 minutes. That's how anal we were about the project.

[27] Ed Toma, Ariyoshi's campaign chair, headed the huli-huli chicken operation.

[28] Makalapa Elementary, Pearl City High, Moanalua High, Kapalama Elementary, Kalākaua Elementary, Kaʻewai Elementary, Kalihi Waena Elementary, Pearl City Elementary, Aiea High School, Moanalua Middle School, Aiea Intermediate School, Aliamanu Middle School and Radford High School. Just over 100 volunteers cooked and trucked 9,000 dry pounds of rice. By the way, we complied with all Department of Health food preparation regulations, including tuberculosis checks and x-rays. Our press release reported that 27,000 pounds of rice was cooked in all.

[29] Dexter Ego, a longtime volunteer at Democratic Party activities, managed the rice operations.

[30] Richard Sugita and Richard "Dickie" Okada prepared and poured the punch; Betty Nojima and Doris Ikeda were responsible for the packaging of the bentos; Charles "Charlie" Furuya was responsible for a group of volunteers who moved the bentos from the end of the line into

According to the fact sheet issued by the campaign to the press, we sold 65,000 tickets. Admission to the stadium was free, but you could buy a meal for $2.50. Other notable numbers:

- There were 60,000 bentos, 60,000 cold-cup drinks and somewhere between 12,000 and 18,000 cars.
- We cooked 15,000 whole chickens, 15,000 pounds of meat and 27,000 pounds of rice, and we prepared 60,000 cups of juice and 3,350 pounds of cabbage. We bought every single bag of kiawe charcoal in the state.
- 200 kegs of Primo beer were brought to the stadium and sold for thirty-five cents a cup.
- 10,000 bags of popcorn were brought to the stadium for distribution.
- 150 buses from around the island transferred people to the stadium, and we shuttled folks from Radford, Makalapa and Aliamanu to the stadium.
- There were some 4,000 volunteers to produce the event, and thousands of breakfasts and lunches were prepared to feed them.
- The committee paid the stadium $20,000 to rent the place.

Bob Nagao, who was tasked with handling communications that day, was busily setting up with his CB radio group. Communications would be critical as this was a multi-pronged event. He and his wife brought some tuna sandwiches to the baseball press box. I gobbled a few.

Here we were in the baseball press box, looking out at the orange glow in the north side of the stadium. As night came and the workers finished

---

the reefers; Everett Cuskaden, my colleague form the AG's office, had the food service duties; Bill Milks, another AG cohort, and Alan Ramos handled transportation; and another AG colleague handled communications. The food committee, besides those already mentioned, included Shota Sakai, Yuki Kitagawa, Tadashi Tojo, Charles Akama, Flo Anbe, Helen Inase, Jean Hara and Stanley Kumakura. Tiger Shinsato, along with Mike Amii, worked the manpower lists. John Tsutsumi of Fireworks, Inc. was our pyrotechnics guy. Interestingly, women outnumbered men on the volunteer list two to one. There are many others I will no doubt offend by omitting here, but my total counts show we had 103 volunteers to cook rice, 189 to cook the chicken, 972 to pack the bentos, 276 to serve, fifty people to prep the fruit punch, forty-one to cook breakfast and lunch for the volunteers and eight volunteers who went to Hawai'i Poi the day before to chop the cabbage placed under the chicken — 1,639 people in all.

rolling out tarps to cover the field (an Oʻahu Interscholastic League football game had been played that night), the stage was being constructed
from flatbed trailers. By my recollection, either six or nine of them. The
trailers and tractors had to have their tires deflated or they'd tear up the
field. As soon as they were done, a crew began decorating the stage.

We'd also ordered fireworks, which was to be the largest aerial
display ever in Hawaiʻi. Randy Iwase, my colleague from the AG's office,
volunteered to chair the balloon inflation crew on the north side of the
stadium. According to the fact sheet issued to the press, Randy's crew
blew up 17,000 balloons that night.[31]

We had a stellar cast of volunteers. Jensen Hee, deputy director of the
Department of Budget and Finance, handled the logistics. Mike Tokunaga,
deputy director of the Department of Accounting and General Services,
was responsible for ticket sales[32] along with Shirley and Ruby Kimoto's
brother Jerry. Bob Fishman, who was then the stadium authority's deputy
director, handled all the liaison work between the campaign and stadium
personnel. Hobe Duncan and Keith Haugen from the governor's office
handled media, Stan Suyat had poster duty and Chew Hoy Lee,[33] Kazu
Sunada and Mike Amii handled stage construction.

Crews were busily readying the tables on the north concourse to
assemble the bentos. As the sun rose, the volunteers began arriving.
Chicken was coming off the grills and being chopped in half to fit
into the bento box as rice began arriving from the multitude of schools
around Honolulu. Volunteers began to place the rice in the alumi-
num bottom with the cabbage, then the chicken, then the kamaboko,
then the takuwan, then that little green plastic leaf, and then the bun
and finally the thin plastic cover. As they were completed, the bentos
were stacked in boxes, which were placed into the reefer ready for
distribution that afternoon. It was a sight to behold: 60,000 bentos in
production.[34]

---

[31] By comparison, only 5,000 were released at a typical Hula Bowl event at Aloha Stadium.

[32] Tickets were sold not for admission but for a bento and a drink—all for just $2.50.

[33] Chew Hoy and I would enjoy a long-term relationship, culminating in our work together at
Amfac. Later on, his brother Sam Lee, Sam's wife, Marilyn, and I would also have a longtime
relationship when I was at the legislature.

[34] For a video of the packing see http://uluulu.Hawaii.edu/titles/528.

If getting 50,000 people into the stadium was difficult, getting 50,000 people to the stadium seemed next to impossible. Bill Milks and Alan Ramos set up a bus pickup service at Keolu Elementary School, Castle High School, Kailua Intermediate School, Kahuku High School, Wahiawā Recreational Center, Nānāʻikapono Elementary School, Ilima Intermediate School, Waipahu Recreational Center, Farrington High School, McKinley High School, Wilson Elementary School and Koko Head Elementary School. In those days, the H-2 and H-3 freeways were still in the planning stages. Roads to Wahiawā and Waiʻanae were narrow two-lane affairs much of the way.

To make things even more interesting, we got word through the grapevine that the Protect Kahoʻolawe ʻOhana activist group was planning to storm our event. Bob Fishman and I met with stadium personnel to discuss what to do if they tried using the north entrance, which offered a direct route to the stage. We considered dropping the north entrance's heavy steel gate. We also discussed the possibility of protestors draping a sign over the loges—and what would happen if others tried to pull the sign down and the accompanying sign holders with it. We consulted with stadium security about handling such an occurrence. Because people would be allowed to bring stuff in, we also needed to inspect coolers and bags for glass bottles, or anything else that could be thrown at someone else. And I had thought my only issues would be making sure everyone had a good time!

The entertainers were to be provided their own secure place in the north end, where they were supplied with their own stash of beer and snacks. These provisions were to be guarded by my good friends Ben Kudo and Gerald Kibe.

As the time drew near to open the gates, I walked out of the press box and peered out over the still-empty south end parking lot. My mind began to wonder whether anyone would show up. After all, despite the entertainment, it was still a political rally. Would folks show up for such an event? And for George Ariyoshi? I began to wonder what would happen if we threw this party and no one showed. I realized that not only would my career be jeopardized, I would become the focal point for the ire of many people. But it was too late to think about that now; all I could do was finish preparing for the event and then let it happen.

The entertainers had all been secured by longtime Ariyoshi friend Larry Mehau—Uncle Larry to many. Thankfully, this was a real burden lifted from my shoulders. I needed only to focus on the rally logistics, not on the stage production. Larry had every major act in Waikīkī pledged to perform that evening and it was truly an impressive list: Clay and Al Naluai of The Surfers; Don Ho with his singers Angel Pablo, Patti Swallie, Tokyo Joe and Sam Kapu; Country Comfort; Sonny Chillingsworth; Frank De Lima and Na Kolohe; Ed Kaahea; Keola & Kapono Beamer; Al Lopaka, Cyril Pahinui's Sandwich Isle Band; Blah Pahinui; Moe Keale & Anuenue; Danny Kaleikini; Nina Keali'iwahamana; Jimmy Borges; Bobby Enriques; Ledward Kaapana and Na Leo Kane O Punahele; Nephi Hannemann; Dick Jensen; Al Harrington and Iva Kinimaka. Yvonne Elliman, Zulu, Cecilio & Kapono,[35] The Brothers Cazimero and Marlene Sai were also tentatively scheduled.

As the afternoon flew by, cars finally began appearing in the parking lot. It was like watching a tub of water fill. In the beginning it seemed there wouldn't be much traffic at all; by 3 p.m. the lot appeared almost full; by 4:30 p.m. it was a full-fledged traffic jam. We began to get word from our CB radio crew that Red Hill traffic was backing up; that folks who thought they'd stop and pick up their bentos and leave were stuck in the stadium because there weren't any exits available. Then we heard that when one of the reefers holding the bentos was opened, the workers discovered to their horror that the bentos were crushed in the boxes. No one had thought to consider the tensile strength of a box of bentos. We asked the stadium's concessionaire to open up all its concessions to sell food, and we passed out credit chits to everyone who couldn't get a bento. Then another snafu: The drink volunteers had thought to pre-pour the night before, but that afternoon when they opened the chillers, they found fruit punch all over the floors. The wax cups we used in those days had soaked through and collapsed—all 60,000 of them. So now we were running out of both food and drink. What else

---

[35] On Thursday, September 21, just three days before the event, C&K took a stand. They decided to sing at the stadium as their right. Frank Fasi had made allegations that the entertainers were appearing because of Ariyoshi's ties to organized crime. Fasi argued that entertainers that had helped him in his campaigns before wouldn't support him this year, and yet they were now helping Ariyoshi. Through their manager, Mel Mossman, C&K said that Fasi's remarks had prompted them to perform. They noted they had previously turned down such requests and were planning to decline this one as well—until Fasi made the issue political.

could go wrong?

About 5 p.m. we got word that the governor and his family were stuck on Red Hill, and the police escort couldn't do much because the traffic backup outside the stadium was impenetrable.

Randy Iwase started handing out his 17,000 balloons, only to discover that the balloons couldn't be seen. It was like floating a single pea in the Pacific Ocean; you need a lot of peas to make an impression. Randy noted later that the balloons that got away from his crew stayed in the high rafters of the north entrance for days afterward, clearly visible but unreachable.

With the Surfers' Clay and Al Naluai handling the emcee duties, each of the entertainers got the chance to perform in front of the growing crowd, which finally peaked out at 50,000. (There is some dispute about this as the north entrance turnstiles broke and a number of people jumped over them to get in.)[36] But the photographic evidence captured by Jim Dote proves how big the crowd was. I sincerely believe we had 50,000 people there.

As 8 p.m. drew closer, I telephoned the stage to tell them my fireworks permit was about to expire. I first spoke to someone on stage, who said, "Larry [Mehau] wants the entertainers to keep going. They're having a great time, and the governor is up there shaking hands." I responded that I needed to blow all the fireworks before 9 p.m. Finally, Larry got on the phone himself. I repeated my problem, Larry argued with me, and in my naïveté I hung up on him—after telling him I didn't care what they wanted, I was blowing the fireworks. I called the fireworks guys on the north side and told them to let it rip. They did, just as the Naluais were performing. And like real troupers they were, they began singing along to the fireworks. What was to be a thirty-minute fireworks show was condensed to ten minutes.

Later, in a saner moment, I wondered what I had done. Hanging up on Larry Mehau was not one of the smartest things to do. In hindsight it was just plain stupid. Larry and the George Ariyoshi were close friends from the governor's days as a young attorney defending Chinatown gamblers, when Larry had been a vice cop. So much for my career at

---

36 Jerry Burris reported in *The Honolulu Advertiser* the next day that we had surpassed the stadium's previous attendance record of 48,197. The *Advertiser* headlined it "The Ariyoshi Bowl."

the AG's office.

As the last fireworks went off and the song ended, and the crews prepared to tear down the stage and assembly stations, I wept. It was a huge load off my shoulders,[37] and I done my bit for "the cause."[38] ❧

---

[37] In the September 24, 2008, edition of *MidWeek*, promoter Tom Moffatt would credit Larry for producing the rally. That was partially but not entirely true. The truth is that it was the sparrows who put this on. But Larry did secure the entertainers. "This week in 1978," Moffatt wrote in retrospect, "the biggest political rally in Hawai'i's history takes place at Aloha Stadium. Organized by Larry Mehau and emcee'd by Don Ho, about 50,000 attend the six-hour event for Gov. George Ariyoshi. For the $10 admission price, attendees get a freshly made bento and entertainment that includes Keola and Kapono Beamer, Dick Jensen, Cecilio and Kapono, Nephi Hannemann, Nina Keali'iwahamana, Ed Kenny, Zulu, Jimmy Borges, Brothers Cazimero, Ledward Kaapana, Moe Keale, Iva Kinimaka, Frank DeLima, Al Lopaka, Sam Kapu, Rap Reiplinger, Al Harrington and The Surfers. What a lineup!" Note: The actual price was $2.50 for the bento, and admission was free, not $10. http://archives.midweek.com/content/columns/utg_article/uncle_toms_gabbin134/.

[38] For a shortened clip of Governor Ariyoshi's inauguration see http://uluulu.Hawaii.edu/titles/524.

CHAPTER SEVEN

The Cause

⚬

"A great cause may gather such wide, intense, and persisting support
that it overwhelms the leadership structure of one or both parties."
—James Macgregor Burns, *Leadership*

If you'd left Hawaiʻi in February 1978 and arrived back in October,
you'd wonder what had happened. At the beginning of the year, Frank
Fasi was leading George Ariyoshi in the polls. It looked inevitable that the
firmly entrenched Burns-Ariyoshi team, a dynasty stretching back over a
decade, was about to be overtaken. Fasi was the ultimate campaigner—
charismatic, brash, outspoken. He appealed to a disenfranchised base—
which in many cases meant the haole voter. Ariyoshi pulled from his AJA
constituency. It looked like the collision would finally happen that year,
and Fasi was predicted to be the winner—except, of course, among the
loyalists of the Burns-Ariyoshi group.

For these loyalists, early 1978 felt like a dark and gloomy time—like
being in a deep pit and trying to claw your way out. It required an enormous amount of energy to gain even a single percentage point in the polls.

But as in all campaigns, once you began to overcome inertia, all
things were possible. The year 1978 was to be phenomenal from that
standpoint. But first we needed a ground game to get some traction.

Walter Dods and Phil Wood, who at the time worked as a creative
director for adman Jack Seigle, came up with Ariyoshi's trademark ditty,
"Quietly and Effectively." Walt later told me that the theme and slogan
came about through research done by pollster Peter Hart. The surveys
showed Ariyoshi falling behind because people didn't know what he had
done as governor. Thus Walt developed the "Quiet and Effective" message.

Phil found the music, which as I recall was a product of a Canadian campaign adapted for a Hawai'i audience. Quiet and effective: That described George Ariyoshi. And it counter-positioned Fasi as a boisterous and defective candidate—e.g., one who couldn't work with people.

Much has been written about that side of the campaign, so let me instead focus on the grassroots end with which I was involved.[39] Bobbie Crowell was the warm-up act to the governor's presentation. He and RCO were the guys who would inspire folks at coffee hours and rallies to get emotionally charged and committed to the man running for office.

It wasn't always easy to identify people who had a gift for getting groups of people excited. RCO was clearly one of them, but Bobbie was a truly remarkable find. He had a gentle Hawaiian character with an ability to rally the crowd. I wish I had kept some recordings of his presentations, but suffice it to say he was a key ingredient in an Ariyoshi event.

Central to this warm-up was "the cause"—the "why" of any campaign. Bob always spoke emphatically about the cause. Without it, why would anyone become engaged in a campaign? For example, Bob believed that if you got involved solely because you were expecting something from the campaign after a victory, you would be sadly and sorely disappointed, possibly even angry. I know many who entered a campaign with the anticipation of some kind of reward—a job, influence, appointment to a board or commission. In the end, such involvement comes down to an exercise of power by the volunteer. Bob warned against this, and he did so right up front. As a result, none of his "kids" ever held such a view, or none that I knew of.

Bob's feelings about campaign structure gave rise to our slogan, "There are no chiefs, only Indians." If you got involved in a campaign it was to do a job, do it well and help others achieve a goal collectively. Thus, a win was the win of the collective, not of individuals. No one was entitled to claim that he or she was the reason a campaign was successful. Credit and blame were equally shared. This is a very Asian concept, more Japanese than Western, in which recognition is an integral part of an organization. Bob focused on collective responsibility, sharing and group acknowledgement.

In such an environment, then, why would individuals even get involved? There was no opportunity for individual glory, as in the Greek sacrifice at Thermopylae, where Spartans claimed glory. There was no

---

[39] See Dods' book, *Yes! A Memoir of Modern Hawai'i.*

Caesar, no Themistocles. All of us were committed not so much to a man or a woman, but to a cause, an ideology, a thought, a belief. These were concepts that went well beyond the candidate. In fact, the candidate was just a part of a stream of change, not the end itself.

One would infer that this made the candidate less important and the cause more so. It also meant that the candidate was really just the vessel through which change came. Bob often mentioned that the candidate was the crucible, the expression, through which the hopes and aspirations of men and women were formed and created and implemented and realized. In an April 22, 1978, memo to the campaign leadership, he wrote:

> A political organization can be said to be an ecosystem of the symbiotic relationship of human beings. It does not have logic. We are talking about dynamics and dimensions. Accordingly, we have to develop the organization, keeping in mind, as I've said many times, is people. A human being with the following elements.
>   1. Psychological. Self-respect. Work is an extension of personality. It is achievement. It is one of the ways in which a person defines himself, measures his worth and his humanity.
>   2. Work is social and community bond. Man's need for belonging to a group and for a meaningful relationship to others—fellowship.
>   3. Work is "living."
>   4. Power relationship implicit in working within a group and especially in an organization. Work has to be designed, structured and assigned.
>   5. In organization there is a need for authority. Apportioning economic rewards; in politics—recognition.

Bob also had a checklist for the campaign programs, and this too has stood the test of time:

1. DESIGN—What is the function and mission of this program?
2. CLEAR OBJECTIVES AND GOALS
3. PRIORITIES:
    a. Select Targets
    b. Standards of Accomplishments and Performance

c. Deadlines
d. Work on Results
e. Accountable for Results
4. MEASUREMENTS OF PERFORMANCE
5. FEEDBACK
6. AUDIT OF RESULTS

If you use this framework in your campaign, you will operate successfully, but you still need that cause. What then was the cause behind the election of George Ariyoshi? In many respects his election was part of a bigger movement, the one first led by Jack Burns. It was the elevation of Hawai'i's people from being thought of as "second class"—both by themselves and by others. It was our subtle inferiority of spirit that manifested itself in such local notions as, "No make A." Local style was not to stand out, to be humble, even while seeking to be considered equal.

It was a long-standing belief nurtured by such dramatic events as the Big Island lynching of Katsu Goto in 1889, the infamous Massie rape and murder trials in 1931 and the Hilo dock strike and massacre in 1938. For Hawai'i's people, much of modern history had centered on the desire to be treated like the rest of America. It found its inspiration in the men and boys who went to war with the 100th Battalion and the 442nd Regimental Combat Team. It found further expression in the leasehold conversion act, which took residential land from the big estates and made it available to the middle class. It found itself in the election of Jack Burns, the non-college graduate, who walked with the people, and not with the plantation owners and businessmen who controlled the lives of common folks. And it found its way into the growth of the Democratic Party and the gradual diminution in the ranks of the GOP.

The ascension of Hawai'i's people in the social and political arenas was perhaps best expressed by Sammy Amalu in his 1974 book, *Jack Burns: A Portrait in Transition*:

But sparrows do not spring to life out of nowhere. They are not by miracles fashioned nor out of only air created. Somewhere, they have nests of their own—perhaps in some lost valley beside a laughing brook, or high in the topmost branches of a lonely tree, or nestled beneath the eaves of a deserted house. They build their nests, mate, bring forth young. They labour long hours searching through field and forest for sustenance to feed their babes. They pass their few short years, and then they die—leaving behind them hardly even a mark that once they, too, had dwelled upon this earth. Obscure they came upon the earth. And in that same obscurity, they leave and are seen no more. No pillar of granite is raised to mark their graves; no temple is reared to their memory. It is almost as if they had never lived at all.

Yet even sparrows dream, have hopes, aspire. They raise their eyes and see the eagles soaring the skies and the falcons flying with wings outspread, cleaving the wild winds and bracing the storms. Has never a sparrow dreamed of being an eagle? Or of flying with the wings of a falcon? Yet how many sparrows would dare essay the impossible to fly beside an eagle or to dive where the falcon dives? He quails instead with fear lest the eagle look upon him and see him only as prey, lest the falcon fall upon him and slay him on the wing. But the dream continues; the hope never dies, and even a sparrow can aspire.

Providence in His divine wisdom has provided for miracles. Were this not so, we would be dreamless and hopeless and without aspiration. Even the humblest can dream of a throne and even the naked for sables to cover his flesh. And, lo, when miracles are born, the throne appears; and sables come to shield the dreamer from the winter's blast—for the stuff of dreams can be woven into the web of reality if the weaver but have the heart and the will, and if God provides the miracle.

So the miracle was done. The sparrows flew as eagles fly where never before a sparrow had dared. They sailed the highest skies where only falcons sail those skies. They spread their wings, and they flew as no sparrow had ever done before. And the eagles saw them and recognized them not for what they were. They were soaring where only eagles soar, so they must by that definition be eagles. The falcons looked upon them and called them brother for who else but a falcon would fly the highest skies?

The sparrows were our code name. All of us were sparrows—not falcons, not eagles, but lowly sparrows. Our governor was also a sparrow, not an eagle or a falcon. Our humble, common roots would no longer be a constraint to what we could achieve.

An AJA could be governor of the state of Hawai'i, and "the cause" would also pave the way for the first governor of Native Hawaiian ancestry; the first governor of Filipino ancestry; the first female (and Jewish) governor and the first governor of Okinawan ancestry. The cause would open the doors for our native sons to become the first African-American president of the United States, first US Senator of Chinese ancestry and the first of Japanese ancestry, and for our native daughters to become the first congresswoman of Japanese ancestry and the first congresswoman of the Hindu faith.

Hawai'i's sparrows have indeed soared with the eagles. ~

CHAPTER EIGHT

Stepping Out

⤳

"The evolutionist…saw strategy as a natural consequence of scarce vital
resources and the struggle for survival. But it was not just a question
of the survival of the fittest, in terms of raw strength and instinctive
aggression. The survivors would also need to have outthought their
opponents, to have shown a better grasp of social relationships and
how to manipulate them. From the start of time, success could
come as much from being smart as being strong…"

—Lawrence Freedman, *Strategy*

After 1978 what was there to do? We had run a complex organization
and accomplished something historical, but how could I follow that
act? My career was blooming. After Governor Ariyoshi was re-elected,
my boss, Tany S. Hong, moved to the Department of Regulatory Agencies (today, it's the Department of Commerce and Consumer Affairs).
The new AG, former "Reg Agencies" director Wayne Minami, became
my boss. Wayne was an incredible attorney—bright, intelligent and
humble—but he didn't let his humility shadow his decisiveness. He was
a great boss, and he gave this twenty-eight-year-old the assignment to fill
Tany's shoes. Could I?

The division covered a lot of state departments: "Reg Agencies,"
Department of Agriculture, Department of Health, Department of
Planning and Economic Development (now known as the Department
of Planning, Economic Development and Tourism), Department of
Hawaiian Home Lands and Land Use Commission. Unlike the other
divisions, the "Reg" division had more than one department and a multitude of agencies under it. Our team handled everything from DEA

drug forfeitures to leasehold conversion cases in federal court, from environmental issues to nuclear waste ships entering Honolulu Harbor, from mental health commitments to land use matters. It was a wide-ranging set of issues and I loved every moment of it. It was made all the more enjoyable by my deputies, some of the best in the division—old-timers like Maurice Kato and Larry Lau, newcomers like Phil Moon and long-time friends like Russel Nagata and Randy Iwase. It was a great crew.

Politics was always lurking around the corner, but with one gubernatorial election just completed and the next one four years off, by all accounts I would be out of the political arena for some time.

As luck would have it, my former colleague Clyde Sumida, who had worked at Alexander & Baldwin's general counsel office, had recently moved to Amfac, the largest conglomerate in Hawai'i. He and his boss were looking for additional attorneys. Clyde told me later that I wasn't his first choice. That was our good friend Darryl Choy, who later became a circuit court family judge. But not knowing that at the time was fine with me. Clyde and I had a number of talks and I was close to deciding to go.

Then fate put on a jovial smile and offered a bend in the road on my career path. The John A. Burns Foundation had decided to honor RCO that year. Sandy Ebesu had already begun the process, and Bob had Shirley call me to discuss the fundraiser details. Bob and Sandy hadn't worked together much, and I gathered from our discussion that he wanted to have one of his sparrows involved. If Bob asks, all I say is "How high?" so as usual I dove into this new assignment.

Bob asked me to meet two individuals, Herb Cornuelle, the head of Dillingham Corp., and Castle & Cooke CEO Malcolm MacNaughton. Mr. Cornuelle was the gentleman he appeared to be, and we had a productive discussion in which he agreed to be the event chair. I met him in his airy office in the Ala Moana Building, with a great view of Honolulu's Kapi'olani district. Rarely did I get the chance to see the city from this perspective. By contrast, my meeting with Mr. MacNaughton in the Bank of Hawai'i office tower downtown was a different experience. With what I recall to be red drapes, oak paneling and a red shag carpet, it was decidedly darker than Herb Cornuelle's spacious, open office at Ala Moana. Malcolm MacNaughton was an imposing figure, and our discussion was basically a talk about "Bobby" and how much Mr. MacNaughton admired him. It was my first introduction to

Merchant Street, the business side of town.

I was calling on people around town handing out tickets to the event when I got a call from Andy Chang who, along with Josh Agsalud, was working with Eileen Anderson on her possible run for mayor against Frank Fasi. The thought was intriguing. The Ariyoshi camp's political calculation was not necessarily to beat Fasi, but to drain his capital in hopes that in three years he wouldn't run for governor. Eileen was also an imposing person, not physically but because she was the State budget director, with an office was on the fourth floor of the capitol, *makai* side. And she was always viewed as one tough lady.

My office was near Eileen's at the middle of the fourth floor's Diamond Head end. So late one afternoon Andy arranged for me to meet her. I thought she was going to ask me to help put on a rally like the one we'd organized at Aloha Stadium. I was prepared to tell her in no uncertain terms that another such event was insane, but that I would definitely help otherwise. No matter what the outcome, I felt it would be good for the budget director and I to get to know each other, because in the end such a relationship might be useful for the AG's office.

But when we met, Eileen asked me to run her campaign. That came as a shock. I didn't have to think much about it before saying yes.

I met with Bob later that week and he gave me some pointers.[40] First, go into the community and meet the leaders and get to know where they are. During a campaign, you don't have the luxury to call everyone to ask what they think; you needed to know intuitively, innately, how your team of supporters would fall in. This was crucial to making decisions. Those who have been in politics understand that timing is everything. So I took a tour of my friends in all the districts, recruiting as I went along.

Bob also told me that I had to get a loan to pay my "salary," instead of being paid by the campaign. After all, how can you decide between food on the table for your family and/or paying your mortgage, versus paying for a mail-out that could win the election? It was hard to fight that logic. So I called Walter Dods, whom I had met briefly in 1978, and he set me up with Gary Fujitani, who ran First Hawaiian Bank's main branch and

---

[40] Bob also mentioned that he wanted me to run the next gubernatorial campaign in 1982, as he clearly wanted to avoid doing it himself. But he understood why I was doing this and did not discourage me. Maybe he wanted this sparrow to leave the nest and fly.

secured me a signature loan of about $15,000. This sum represented my net annual take-home from my AG position. With the loan secured, I went to see Wayne Minami and asked for leave without pay to run the Anderson campaign.

I then called Clyde and told him of my decision. Amfac had all manner of permits with the City and County, and I knew he'd be crazy to agree to keep the offered position open for me, but I asked anyway. No guarantees, he said, and I watched my opportunity to leave state government and move into the private sector fly off into the sunset. But this was the right thing to do, or at least I thought so.[41]

That October of 1979, I headed off to the biggest adventure—and gamble—of my life. ❧

---

[41] Bob asked me to deliver the prefatory remarks before his keynote speech at the John A. Burns Foundation dinner. Here's what I said: "From my first meeting with Bob back in 1970, I have felt awe and indeed a deep admiration for this man's extraordinary abilities and achievements. But much more than his achievements, there were his lessons on life and humanity. Bob always spoke of 'uplifting people.' He strove to show others that they can accomplish anything that they set their minds to do, that nothing is impossible or unattainable. And more than just a result, Bob always stressed the means to obtain a result. It was always the 'how,' not the 'what,' that mattered. In every political campaign he has stressed that one must be clean and positive. He has constantly emphasized that every person must be treated with equal dignity. For Bob, this was not campaign rhetoric—it was reality. Bob also spoke of 'the cause,' which to many people had a special personal meaning, but in essence always had as its basis the advancement and betterment of Hawai'i and its people. The cause represented the driving force behind Bob in every endeavor he undertook. The cause became all-consuming at times, leading to the cessation of his law practice. That this man had dedication is surely an understatement. Bob also spoke of the future. He was always seeking new challenges and ever greater dreams. To this end the young and idealistic were drawn to him. These new and younger faces brought with them an interest and concern for service to Hawai'i's people. Bob brought to each of them the aspirations of a new Hawai'i, wherein the sparrows would continue to multiply and indeed aspire, dream, hope and finally attain all their impossible dreams."

CHAPTER NINE

Eileen Anderson:
Great Expectations

❧

"Whether you prevail or fail, endure or die, depends more on
what you do to yourself than on what the world does to you."

—Jim Collins, *How the Mighty Fall*

The 1980 election was Frank Fasi's to win or lose. He seemed virtually
unstoppable, like the pink Energizer bunny. No one would argue
that he wasn't the best politician of the time. He was charismatic, had
political timing, was scrappy and had effectively carved out his niche:
Fasi was for the little guy, not those in power. In many ways his populist
message struck a nerve amongst the "outs" and those who hadn't shared
in the Burns-Ariyoshi largesse. It wasn't so much that they were revolutionary, far from it. He and his campaign were no different from the
Ariyoshi campaign. In fact, the two mirrored each other, but Ariyoshi's
was specifically borne aloft by the memories of the AJA community and
the legacy of Jack Burns. As long as these memories lingered, that voting
block of AJAs was immovable. Fasi's wife, Joyce, an AJA herself, poked
some holes in that monopoly, but after all, Ariyoshi was still an AJA and
the Mainland-born Fasi was not. Not coming out and saying any of this
was a good thing, but it was what it was.

Nineteen eighty was also the year for the Burns faction of the Burns-
Ariyoshi team to try one last time to win an election. Dan Aoki and
Don Horio were supporting Hiram Kamaka, by all accounts an honest,
respectable and loyal member of the team. In a *Honolulu* magazine article
entitled "The Making of the Mayor, 1980," writer Dan Boylan told the

story. Francis Yamada, the president of Hawaiian Finance, approached his friend the governor in early 1979 and asked Ariyoshi if he would have a problem if he supported Kamaka for mayor. Ariyoshi reputedly told him to go for it, but then warned Francis that Kamaka couldn't win. Ariyoshi maintained that position consistently thereafter, even when he met Kamaka himself that December. Dan, Don, Francis and Hiram all knew the basic math: If there were two opponents in the race against Fasi, the effort was doomed.

Dan also wrote that Ariyoshi didn't recruit Eileen Anderson, his budget director, to run for mayor. Instead, Ariyoshi is recorded as advising his team to "stay loose." But, Dan wrote, "On March 10, 1980, Eileen Anderson announced her resignation as director of the Department of Budget and Finance for the state of Hawai'i and declared her candidacy for mayor. Suddenly the anti-Fasi vote appeared irrevocably split."[42]

By the time of that March announcement, I had already been working with two of the biggest names in local politics: Jack Seigle of the local ad agency Seigle, Rolfs and Wood[43] and Walter Dods, then First Hawaiian's VP of marketing.[44] It was a friendship that would span decades.

Many considered me to be Bob Oshiro's surrogate, and who could blame them? I was all of twenty-nine. Who would ask this kid to run a campaign against a popular two-term mayor for a candidate with no name recognition, in an uphill battle to raise monies and an organization? The fact is, the loyalty of a campaign organization is not transferable. Just because you supported George Ariyoshi didn't mean you supported Eileen Anderson. I did meet with Bob, who shared his earlier advice to me, but after that I was on my own, sink or swim. I received advice along the way from mutual friends, but Bob wasn't there at headquarters and neither did I bother him. I was sensitive to his displeasure in being called up and having to put his practice on hold for several months to run a campaign. In some ways this was my gift to him, to honor his previous sacrifice, and to employ his lessons and advice, shared over the

---

42 Dan Boylan, "The Making of the Mayor, 1980," *Honolulu* magazine.

43 Although I'd met Jack Seigle before, he had been working for the ad agency Lennen & Newell out of New York, which produced John A. Burns' thirty-minute TV special, "Catch A Wave," when I was Burns' "supply sergeant" ten years earlier.

44 For a good description of the times, see Walter's book, *Yes! A Memoir of Modern Hawai'i.*

previous decade. The fledgling was leaving the nest and the only options were to fly or die.

Dan writes, "Like all campaign managers, (Tsujimura) projects confidence. And on the first of July [1980], he has got reason to. On a blackboard behind him in Anderson's Kalihi headquarters are the results of a recently conducted poll: Anderson twenty-four percent, Fasi twenty-eight percent, Kamaka seven percent, Undecided forty-one percent. 'This is only a telephone poll. There's a wide margin for error,' he says. 'I think it shows Eileen doing well. We're going to check it during the next few days.'"[45]

Anderson headquarters was in the Safety Loan building, just down the street from Kamehameha IV Road in Kalihi. There was limited parking in the rear of the building and we were on the second floor. The office was empty when I first arrived and Eileen and her family, especially Cliff, her husband, his brothers and Randy Iwase, my good friend, set about repainting the walls. Soon huge metal desks arrived and I arranged them in some order.[46] Someone obtained movable Canec[47] pin boards, one of which had a blackboard. It was beginning to look like an office; the missing element was a staff. But for the time being, in late 1979, it was just me. Eventually our staff would include Myrna Ishii,[48] Michael Hee,[49] Neal Okabayashi,[50] Ed Hasegawa,[51] Jim Dote,[52] Sophie Sheather,[53]

---

[45] Dan Boylan, "The Making of the Mayor, 1980," *Honolulu* magazine.

[46] I screwed up my back doing this. The condition would plague me for decades.

[47] Canec was the local product made from compressed fibers left over from the sugar processing, typically it was used for ceiling tiles, but sometimes used as a substitute for pin boards.

[48] Myrna at the time was married to my good friend, Dan Ishii. Unfortunately they later divorced, and she is now married to another close friend, Andy Chang.

[49] Mike is the son of Jensen Hee, deputy director and later director of the Department of Budget and Finance.

[50] Neal is one of my oldest and closest political friends, who was a Bank of Hawai'i attorney at the time. He is now with the legal offices of First Hawaiian Bank.

[51] Ed, a former school principal, is one of those folks who has forever been in politics. I am proud and honored to call him a friend. He has been there for candidates and the party, but I treasure him mostly because when I was in need, he was there.

[52] Jim and his wife, Char, are among those rare individuals who spoke softly but contributed greatly. There wasn't anything Jim wouldn't do to help us win. The photos in this book of the 1978 stadium rally are Jim's work. Had he not memorialized that event, most people wouldn't even believe it.

[53] Sophie—What can I say?—she was a gem. She was everyone's auntie, mother and sister. She was the face of the campaign and kept the headquarters humming and smiling.

Pat Brandt,[54] Aurelio Arnobit,[55] Les Paraz, Mike Tokunaga,[56] Wayne Yamasaki,[57] Bob Nagao,[58] Bob Watada,[59] Pat Tanaka,[60] Craig Nakamura,[61] Tany Hong,[62] Patty Mau,[63] Terrance Young, Muriel Anderson,[64] Patty Dauterman,[65] Lori Anderson[66] and Jeff Agader.[67]

The campaign organization was themed *Hoolaulima Ana No Eileen R.*

---

[54] Pat headed the women's group, which was critical to the campaign. We needed the women of Honolulu to support Eileen if we were to turn the corner. A longtime politico, she was another of those go-to people.

[55] Aurelio was one of the leaders who helped us maintain a connection to the Filipino community. This was critical, as Fasi had tremendous support in that ethnic group. We didn't need to win there, but we couldn't cede it without a fight.

[56] Mike Tokunaga was the deputy director for the Department of Accounting and General Services and later Reg Agencies, but he was much, much more. He was a veteran of the 100th and the 442nd. I remember Mike as one of the most gracious men I ever knew. He never lorded either his position or his legacy over anyone. He was one of those guys who put his nose down and plowed ahead. I treasure the times we had together over the many campaigns, but not more than this one.

[57] Wayne was a close ally in 1980 and a true friend in life. We worked together many times until his retirement. He served as a deputy director at Personnel Services and the Department of Transportation, eventually becoming DOT's director.

[58] Bob was a stalwart. We first met in 1976 and became close friends in the trenches. A Jaycee, Bob was always active in giving to the community, always a go-to guy. He now heads the Hiroshima Kenjin Kai. He served for many years with the Department of Agriculture.

[59] Bob and I knew each other for years. He was the political guy for 'Aina Haina, where I grew up. He knew me and my parents well. In later years we would be on opposite sides as he became executive director of the Campaign Spending Commission, but in 1980 he was an ally and close friend.

[60] Pat was one of the political operatives within the Judiciary, and one of the members of Tom "Fat Boy" Okuda's political action group. Vilified later in life, Tom was a stalwart supporter and reliable political asset for any politician.

[61] Craig was deputy AG and active politically. He now resides on Maui, and has still been active in local politics.

[62] Tany was the director of Regulatory Agencies department and my former boss at the AG's. Reliable and trustworthy, he always delivered.

[63] Patty is now the head of the Bar Association, but this was all before her stint at the legislature.

[64] Muriel was Eileen's sister-in-law, who continued in government service for many years at the State Department of Business and Economic Development (now Business, Economic Development and Tourism) and later the Hawai'i Tourism Authority.

[65] Patty was Eileen's older daughter, and she was a gem.

[66] Lori was Eileen's youngest daughter.

[67] Jeff was the finance chair for the campaign. I didn't know Jeff before the campaign. But he earned more than my respect, keeping us on the straight and narrow.

Anderson, or "Many hands working together for Eileen R. Anderson."[68]
Here's how I explained it at a rally:

> The term has cultural significance for it represents the coming to-
> gether of friends and relatives to perform the task of planting and
> harvesting. This is why we have asked you all here tonight. To help
> us plant and harvest the seeds of victory for Eileen R. Anderson.
>   Why Eileen R. Anderson? Because she is an individual commit-
> ted to the people of Hawai'i. Secondly, she will persevere for the peo-
> ple of Hawai'i. Thirdly, she will give of herself to the people of Ha-
> wai'i. The late governor John A. Burns, in his message of *mahalo*
> and aloha, noted: "Kamehameha and Damien tell the whole story
> of Hawai'i. They stand as shining inspirations. *They have taught us
> that leadership means service to others.*" (Emphasis added.) In Eileen
> we have just such a leader. We have a leader with a basic love and
> concern for the people of this great city. We have a leader who is
> more concerned for people other than herself... Eileen is a very
> concerned citizen. She believes in good, clean, honest and effective
> government. Her sincerity, honesty and personal commitment to
> serve you as mayor of the City & County of Honolulu cannot be
> attacked. She shares the same goal as you do: The betterment of
> life for ourselves and our children. Come and join us in that goal:
> working together for the future.[69]

In January 1981, *Hawai'i Business* magazine declared Eileen to be its
Woman of the Year. In their supporting article, "Eileen Anderson: Great
Expectations," editors Bill Wood and Paul Addison wrote:

> A year ago, Anderson was politically a virtual unknown and was
> herself a neophyte at the hustings. Yet her come-from-behind win
> over Fasi was engineered and carried out in textbook style. She
> made no mistakes and forced errors on her far more experienced
> rival. Candidate Anderson was clearly not only an apt and willing

---

[68] My first speech for Eileen occurred at the Central Intermediate School cafeteria. Luckily the text of my speech was saved by my inner pack rat.

[69] Ibid.

pupil for some skillful coaching, she also enjoyed the behind-the-scenes organizational support needed to do what no candidate had been able to do before—beat Frank Fasi in his own backyard.[70]

The article correctly noted that Eileen was a great pupil. I know because I was there. We had an agreement early on: I ran the campaign, and she had complete control over the policy issues. It was a good agreement.

We did have our tussles though. Eileen always thought we were running her ragged, and she demanded time off to gather herself. Myrna, who handled the calendar, took the brunt of that criticism and anger. One day Eileen just dropped off the face of the earth; we later discovered she had gone to the hairdresser.

She wasn't like George Ariyoshi or Jack Burns, and it wasn't because she was a woman. Burns and Ariyoshi had been through these wars before; they knew and appreciated time and how limited it was. Eileen was still learning. To beat a guy like Fasi would take an extraordinary effort. The candidate had to give the most. As observers before and since have noted, a candidate without a "fire in the belly" can't win. Burns and Ariyoshi always had that fire, Eileen's was growing but it was still a flame, and not yet a blaze.

Despite these shortcomings, she was a natural politician. Political ad guru Joe Napolitan, the one-time John Kennedy and Hubert Humphrey confidant who is actually credited with coining the term "political consultant," said as much in a memo to Eileen dated September 11, 1980:

First of all, let me congratulate you on running a superb campaign. For someone who had never run for office before, you certainly handled it like a pro. It has been a real pleasure working with you, and you are one of the quickest-learning candidates I've ever worked with... Best of all, and astonishing in view of the fact that you had never run before, is the fact that I don't think you made a single mistake in the campaign. No goofs, no off-the-cuff Reaganesque statements that needed explaining afterward, no charges that Fasi could turn to his advantage. Not many candidates go through a long, hard campaign without shooting themselves in the foot at least

---

[70] Paul Addison and Bill Wood, "Eileen Anderson: Great Expectations," *Hawai'i Business*.

once, and I think you have come out unscathed... Good luck! Win or lose, you're a hell of a candidate.

Eileen wasn't the only pupil. I was learning a lot from Walt and Jack. I waited for those meetings to listen and learn. They were the deans of media, and I was a willing student. But the most important relationship I built was with Joe Napolitan, who was the dean of political advertising. I fondly remember just watching him ask Eileen and the team a few questions and then disappear into a back room; the next day he'd have short, one-page instructions on what to do. I really admired Joe's perceptiveness and keen mind. I was fortunate to have had the privilege to work with him.

Eileen was a good student, the perfect candidate.

Fasi was an excellent opponent, the perfect foil.[71]

Just a note on demographics to put this all into perspective: In the grossest of terms, George Ariyoshi's tacit if not open support brought us the AJA base so critical to winning any election. In the past the Democratic primary[72] was ceded to Fasi. He was that strong. In 1964, Masato Doi challenged Fasi and lost. He had been City Council chair for the previous four years. This may have been an attempt to unseat Frank by the Burns forces, supported by followers of former mayor Neal Blaisdell, who had lost to Fasi in 1960. Four years later, the Democrats would field no one, but the Republicans led with D.G. "Andy" Anderson. There was a large Democrats for Anderson group, but Andy lost as well. Fasi seemed unstoppable. In 1972, State Senator Mason Altiery ran for mayor. Altiery was a former broadcaster turned politician. He had worked for Patsy Mink before becoming a state senator. He was unsuccessful. In 1976 the Democrats fielded no opposition, but the GOP put Dan Clements, a councilman, into the fray. Dan did not win. Where the Burns-Ariyoshi AJA group fell in this story is hard to say, but it's unlikely that the AJAs

---

[71] Fasi was quoted in the October 1, 1970, edition of *The Honolulu Star-Bulletin*: "When you want to discredit your opponent, create a lie and keep repeating it... Sooner or later, a certain number of people will believe it though it's not true." In the June 1972 issue of *The Beacon* magazine, he was quoted as saying, "I guess I prize honesty as much as any other quality in a person. By that I mean honesty in the sense that a guy who frankly admits he's a crook is honest."

[72] In those days the race was not a non-partisan election but decidedly partisan.

Governor George Ariyoshi and wife Jean, ca. 1970.

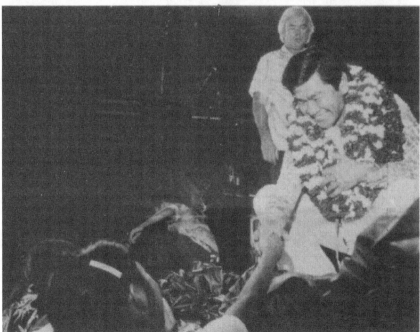

Top: Robert Oshiro and Jack Burns attend a Democratic National Convention in the 1960s. Above: George Ariyoshi greets the crowd at his 1978 rally at Aloha Stadium (opposite), the largest political rally in Hawai'i's history.

Top: Robert Oshiro is honored at a John A. Burns Foundation fundraiser in 1979.
Left to right: Dan Ishii, Bob Nagao, Alan Tamayose, Ron Yokota, Mike Hee, Sandy Ebesu,
Herb Cornuelle, Bob Oshiro, Ed Correa, Shirley Kimoto, unidentified, Jerry Kimoto,
the author and Brad Mossman. Bottom: Vice President Al Gore, Kirk Caldwell
and the author at a campaign gathering in Nashville, Tennessee,
during Gore's run for president in 2000.

Top: Bob and Ruth Oshiro upon his receipt of an honorary doctorate from the University of Hawai'i. Bottom: Craven rally ticket, 1976.

Hui books were an important campaign tool for candidates in the pre-computer era.
Eileen Anderson (opposite) used them to her advantage in her successful run for
Honolulu mayor in 1980.

Top: The author and his sons (William, left, and Jonathan) pose with Governor John Waihee on the occasion of the author's confirmation to the Hawai'i Community Development Authority. Bottom: Sign-waving political supporters turn out for Mazie Hirono in Honolulu.

alone were strong enough to topple Fasi, as demonstrated by Doi's loss. You needed much more. Eileen had the extra kick. She was appealing to the business types with her conservative fiscal approach; she led with the AJA support from being Ariyoshi's budget director and having his behind-the-scenes support; she appealed to the haole voter since she too was from outside but became inside. The stars were aligning this year.[73]

This was a shoestring campaign financially. Despite what a layperson might think, just because an incumbent governor is supporting you doesn't make the fiscal spigot flow. You have to demonstrate you can win. Money was in short supply, so I started making the rounds of the Ariyoshi cabinet and subcabinet to get a $2000 loan/contribution from each of them. Luckily my prior experience running the 1978 stadium rally for the governor opened doors, which would otherwise have remained closed. We picked up a fair amount of contributions this way. So we were off to the races, but just barely. At one point in the campaign we had to decide which of two mail-outs could be taken to the post office. Once I'd discovered the wrong brochure had been taken and had to run down the stairs to stop the truck from leaving.[74]

Mike Amii brought day-old bread daily for us to feed our volunteers. In previous campaigns we'd had hot meals; in this one we had tuna sandwiches. But this didn't deter the volunteers. They began to believe in "the cause." We continued to grow incrementally.

We designed a shell brochure for canvassing, or "walking," plus different color inserts announcing stew-and-rice events or coffee hours in various districts. On the back of each insert were Eileen's remarks about

---

[73] There is a sidebar worthy of note because it will prove important in a later chapter. Most sitting Democrats except for Governor Ariyoshi took a bye in the primary battle, save and except for a young Filipino senator by the name of Ben Cayetano. He broke with tradition and maybe logic to endorse Eileen. I always felt a debt of obligation to Ben for doing that. Not only was it courageous, it was a real sacrifice. I would later repay this debt. I should also note that I was in discussions with Andy Anderson as well his operative, Doug Eagleson, who mentioned that Andy was willing to endorse Eileen in the primary as well. Since Andy had run previously against Fasi and had had the backing of the Burns-Ariyoshi group, he was a likely endorser. We arranged to meet at John Dominis, one of Andy's dining establishments. I drove to the restaurant and waited a while, and when Doug and Andy appeared, we talked pleasantries, but Andy had decided not to endorse. I was disappointed, but that's politics.

[74] We also had our share of hilarity and "oops" moments. We had worked on a friend-to-friend card. Several eyes looked it over before it was sent to the printer. When the cards returned, someone discovered a disastrous mistake, "public service" was misspelled as "pubic service." Needless to say, the cards were reprinted and the ones with the errant message destroyed.

what she wanted to do for that particular neighborhood. It was a way for us to save money on printing.

We had a telephone bank from which volunteers called up the names on our hui book submissions. Everything I had learned from Bob was being turned into a program.

Some notes about organization: In its basic form a campaign has three, possibly four, distinct elements. There are grassroots volunteers, media and finance and headquarters. I think the first three are self-explanatory, but the last one deserves a little more detail. HQ was really a coordinating function. In some campaigns the organization ran top-down, like a pyramid. Bob's concept of "no chiefs, only Indians" suggested a "flat" organization. How did we do that? First we had a calendar of events, scheduled to allow the campaign to peak at the right time before the primary. Everything from media to financing to grassroots were on this timetable. Peaking early meant you needed more money to sustain the peak until the primary; peak too late and you lose. Getting the timing right is and will always be an art, not a science. But like seasoned seamen, if you do this enough times; you get a sixth sense, an intuitive feeling about how and when that peak happens.

Once established, the timetable allowed us to schedule grassroots events. Usually you begin with your strength and move to your weakness. This time it was a free-for-all. The districts that were ready went first; those less organized followed. This "organic" methodology meant that HQ needed to be prepared to help the district prep for the event: printing walking brochures, purchasing the food, securing the location. The district sought the volunteers. For the most part, the program worked well. Each district was empowered to stage whatever function it wanted. If a district wanted a stew-and-rice dinner, we said OK; if they wanted a coffee hour, that was OK; if they wanted a *pau hana* event, that was OK too. The idea was to bring the district together in whatever way they thought they could raise and secure support. We just facilitated. This delegation of authority was the innovation which separated this campaign from the previous ones and from the following ones as well.[75]

---

[75] In 1982, I was told by the Ariyoshi campaign that I had spoiled the districts. They enjoyed their independence, and when they were told what to do it didn't sit well.

I had district coordinators, each of whom did not actually live in his district: Bob Nagao, Les Ihara,[76] Wayne Yamasaki and Ed Hasegawa. The idea was they were coordinators, not leaders. Again this harkens back to the "no chiefs, only Indians" concept. HQ wasn't the "leader," it was the coordinator/facilitator. The districts became the "leaders." In many ways this decentralized concept of politics is both novel and old. Logically if we all know what we have to do, and trust each other to do it, we really don't need a leader in the traditional sense. We do need a coordinator—you could say "manager," but that implies that the manager makes all the decisions. This was partially but not completely true here. This campaign was my first attempt to test the "flat" organization theory. To my pleasant surprise it worked, and remarkably so. Districts began to make decisions on sign holding and events on their own, coordinated through the HQ schedule. We all began to appreciate our strengths and weaknesses, our duties and responsibilities and this mutual understanding allowed us to shrink the "management" team and deploy resources at the grassroots. In some respects, this was necessitated by our small HQ. We couldn't have these mass meetings; our premises were just too small. By redirecting efforts, we took advantage of what should have been a liability, and instead made it a strength.[77] (I would test this concept some years later in another mayoral campaign.)

Therefore, to say that I ran the Anderson campaign would be overstated egotism. The volunteers ran this campaign. To a large extent my responsibilities were to coordinate on a bigger scale with media activities. Once they set a schedule we would begin asking the districts to sign hold over a certain span of time, and we would tell them why—we were running radio ads or TV ads. For the layperson, the combination of an aural message in the car coupled with a visual message, sign holding, was exponential. People relate better if all senses are stimulated, not just one. This is why TV is so influential; it stimulates the aural and the visual at the same time. We were very successful at this. And that is a testament to the districts and the grassroots.

---

[76] Now a state senator; but back in this day he was with the litter control branch of the State Department of Health, working with Clyde Morita.

[77] My good friend Randy Iwase handled our only big mass rally at Moanalua High School. We wanted to avoid an outright connection to the old campaigns, so we split the difference between the stadium and McKinley and chose Moanalua. It was a well-attended rally with the usual accouterments.

Time sped by. An *Advertiser* poll showed Fasi with a lead, but not by much.

Fasi	41%
Anderson	36%
Kamaka	4%
Beck	1%
No choice	18%

But then came the newspaper endorsements. It was no secret that the papers disliked Fasi. And on September 11, the *Advertiser* endorsed Eileen in a full-page editorial:

> Churchill saw politics as an honorable calling. People like Fasi have cheapened it. People like Eileen Anderson can help restore our faith in the institutions of government. We need that as much for our own self-respect as Americans as for our community good... If we want honorable and responsible government, instead of a City Hall atmosphere of wheeler-dealing and favoritism for cronies, then we have to look past Fasi.

The following day, the *Star-Bulletin* ripped another one with an editorial entitled, "The Case Against Mayor Fasi."

> "We need a two-term limit on the tenure of mayor. People in office too long—and I mean anybody in office—tend to become arrogant and forget the public interest." Wise words indeed. This was Frank F. Fasi talking to an interviewer early in 1967 when he was younger, 46, and still two years away from becoming mayor. Now having turned 60, he ignores those early words—probably thinks he is wiser... Just yesterday at a press conference, the mayor invoked Hitler and the Nazis to smear his chief opponent. Campaigners ought to be able to disagree with their opponents without such name-calling tactics... Eileen Anderson wouldn't try to be a solo performer. She would emphasize teamwork and share credit. She could both get things done and lower the political temperature considerably.

By September 27, 1980, our primary polling was wrapping up. The results were really encouraging.

Anderson	30%
Fasi	34%
Kamaka	3%
Unsure	32%

These numbers demonstrated, first, that this was a two-person race; but more importantly the Unsures were more likely AJAs who typically never answered polls. If you assume that more than fifty percent of the Unsures were going to break our way, then we were neck-and-neck.

We were fortunate that Fasi and his team didn't think we had a snowball's chance in hell, so they paid almost no attention to us. They stuck to their playbook. That is a good strategy. You never start to respond to the opponent's strategy, because then you play their playbook, not yours. But your playbook had better have the right plays in it, and your intelligence on your opponent better be on point. We were lucky—Fasi didn't respond to us. We hit with the tag, "If the Mayor isn't responsible, who is?"[78] The problem with incumbency is that you have to run on a record. Challengers only have to pick holes.

Eileen was also the first woman candidate that Fasi faced. Female candidates during this time created a conundrum for their opponents. If you hit too hard you'd be thought less a gentleman. If you didn't attack you were letting her message get out unchallenged. What would Fasi do?

Fasi had eight years and several campaigns worth of statements and activities. He also had those who loved him and those who hated him. We had to get those who disliked him to join with those who liked Eileen, and we would turn the corner. How do you do that?

Fasi took credit for a lot. But there were many things that weren't right. So give him his due for TheBus and his other ideas; but hold his feet to the fire on other stuff. Our brochure, in black and white, did just that. Let me tick off the headings:

"Oahu's growth must be controlled before our 'paradise' becomes

---

[78] This, by the way, had also been Burns' tagline.

'paradise lost.'"

"Crime statistics don't mean a thing. But crime does."

"There is no higher priority than managing our money properly."

"Waikiki: It isn't just for visitors."

"Adequate housing—at prices people can afford."

"When politicians fight, it's the people who suffer."

Each of these questioned Fasi's accomplishments and cast doubt on whether Fasi really "got it done." [79] The last bullet was aimed at his combativeness; the first at what many felt was Honolulu's runaway growth. Waikīkī at the time was considered by many to be honky-tonk, with porn houses scattered along Kalākaua and Kūhiō Avenues; it was also becoming a place that many locals didn't want to frequent. Housing was "unaffordable" and the responsibility was being laid at the mayor's feet for not doing enough. These messages were powerful. Add to that the fact that Eileen was a former budget chief who had been watching your state dollars—and she would do the same for the city. People felt comfortable that a non-politician would be controlling the purse strings. [80]

In an interview with Jack Seigle published in *Honolulu* magazine, Dan Boylan captured the essence of our approach:

"We expected Fasi to respond eventually. The only questions were when and to what degree. From the standpoint of strategy, I am delighted. In every campaign, Frank Fasi, reaches a point where he takes over. He stops listening to advisors and says things he shouldn't say—things that will hurt him." … "Anderson didn't look like a rollup-the-sleeves and get-the-job-done type. But she

[79] One of Fasi's most effective catchphrases was "Fasi Gets It Done."

[80] Fasi was also facing a scandal involving the Kukui Gardens residential development in downtown Honolulu. In an October 12, 2003, article in *The Honolulu Star-Bulletin*, reporter Rick Daysog wrote, "During the Kukui Plaza scandal that plagued the Fasi administration, separate state and federal grand juries indicted the engineering company's former head, Richard Towill, for allegedly filing a false corporate tax return. The 1975 federal indictment, based on an investigation by the Internal Revenue Service, charged that Towill awarded $13,850 in bonuses in 1969 to employees who were required to make political contributions with that money to Fasi and other local politicians. Two years later, a separate Oahu grand jury, prompted by an investigation by Special Prosecutor Grant Cooper, indicted Towill, Fasi and former Fasi campaign treasurer Harry C.C. Chung on related charges. The federal jury acquitted Towill in 1979 and the state dropped their cases against Towill, Fasi and Chung."

spoke to issues which concerned the voters. Frank was right. Crime *was* a phony issue, but it bothered voters, and Anderson milked it for all it was worth…"[81] At 7:04 Bob Sevey announces the first returns, based on 20 percent of the total vote: Anderson 18,817; Fasi 16,616; Kamaka 1,288; Beck 87. Suddenly the crowd grows quiet—very quiet. A few moments later pollster Dan Tuttle guardedly predicts Anderson will win…[82] When the final returns were announced, showing Anderson's 89,224 to Fasi's 87,547, the Democratic nominee spoke again to her supporters. She offered thanks to Fasi and his family for the good things they had done for Honolulu over the past 12 years. She thanked her supporters, and then called upon her campaign manager Rick Tsujimura for special mention.

She told a story of a get-acquainted meeting with Tsujimura at the campaign's outset. Anderson told him that she had graduated from the University of Hawaiʻi in 1950. Tsujimura said he was born in 1950. Anderson smiles, "I've never forgiven him."[83]

That election night was to be my swan song, my last foray into the campaign game. I was hoping that Amfac would still have a place for me, so that I could get back to my career.[84] Like Bob, I too was growing weary of the political arena, and although nowhere near the sacrifice he had made, I felt that mine was enough, at least for the present, and I deserved to enjoy the next few years away from the fray.[85] ❧

---

[81] Dan Boylan, "The Making of the Mayor, 1980," *Honolulu* magazine.

[82] Some time that evening while I was sequestered on the second floor of the HQ watching the returns, I saw Walter Dods motioning to me as I peered out our second-floor windows. He was making a motion with one hand slicing across his other upper arm. I couldn't figure out what he was trying to say. Later Walt said he was sending me a message that Senator Inouye was there. I had missed him.

[83] Dan Boylan, "The Making of the Mayor, 1980," *Honolulu* magazine.

[84] I was fortunate to be offered the same position at Amfac, which I joined in mid-January 1981.

[85] A few weeks after the general election, I made an appointment to see Bob in that familiar second-floor office on California Avenue. I told Bob that this win was for him, that it was a tribute to all he had tried to do in 1976. We had overcome power, money and organization for an unknown candidate with little funding and no organization of her own—just a faithful core of believers. All Bob and I did was look at each other; no further words were necessary.

CHAPTER TEN

Ma Perkins

～❧

"Be careful that victories do not carry the seed of future defeats."
—Ralph W. Sockman, senior pastor, Christ Church, New York City

In the January 1981 *Hawai'i Business* article entitled "Eileen Anderson: Great Expectations," writers Paul Addison and Bill Wood quoted Eileen as saying:

> I attribute my victory not to Governor Ariyoshi's support, but to the fact that we put together a good campaign organization and that Eileen Anderson as a candidate sold herself to enough of the community. I don't think anybody should discount the amount of hard work on my part and my husband's part to get out and meet the people. We worked 15 hours a day for seven months. We did two to three coffee hours every night. We did a breakfast every morning. We walked residential areas. I wrote speeches. I gave speeches. I didn't win this election because the governor supported me. I didn't win it because I had a lot of money so I could go on television, although those were parts of the whole picture. To a very large extent I won because I was able to sell myself to the people in the community. And nobody should ever believe that if you've got enough money, any Tom, Dick or Harry can win. Regardless of anything else, the City of Honolulu needed a new mayor and people said to me, "You're a viable candidate." I decided for myself that I was.

Now contrast these remarks with the following quote from Jim

Collins in his book, *How the Mighty Fall*:

> The best leaders we've studied never presume that they've reached ultimate understanding of all the factors that brought them success. For one thing, they retain a somewhat irrational fear that perhaps their success stems in large part from luck or fortuitous circumstance.

It was unfortunate that Eileen chose to distance herself from—or felt compelled to proclaim she was outside of—Governor Ariyoshi's sphere. Obviously this issue bugged her deeply.

But even more disturbing was her inability to recognize the sacrifices of those who worked so hard to get her elected. Yes, she worked hard too, but so she should: In the end she was the one who would be mayor, and who would be rewarded both personally and financially. The volunteers, however, could only count on their own satisfaction in the victory. Theirs was not a triumphant parade, but a chance to be on the sidelines watching it, or producing it, or cleaning up after it. Their enjoyment was vicarious, not direct. This is true in all elections.

Yet in a way, these people deserve that recognition more than the candidate does. I believe Bob put it best—that the candidate is the manifestation of the people's hopes and aspirations, and the politician needs to understand this and appreciate their sacrifices. Too often that recognition is not forthcoming. Too often the candidate believes that he or she is the sole reason for a victory. Too often those who the live and die for politics receive little, if any, recognition for their efforts in making our city and state a better place.

Eileen did ask Andy Chang to be her managing director.[86] Bob Nagao became one of Andy's assistants, primarily to work the political issues and be the contact with the grassroots. Andy brought with him Larry Koseki, a gentleman who would also become a close friend of mine. Larry was an acquired taste, but like Ham Nee he grew on you, and I enjoyed our collective discussions on politics and life. An eye affliction had given Larry tunnel vision—yes, real tunnel vision, not the psychological kind. He couldn't see peripherally, and many took this for snobbishness,

---

[86] Andy was appointed to replace Alvin Pang as US Housing and Urban Development area director, but he resigned to join Eileen. That was a sacrifice.

but in truth Larry couldn't see you if you were right next to him and he didn't turn to look at you directly. But physical limitations aside, Larry's philosophical bent was always fodder for discussion, and I appreciated every moment we had together.

Eileen sort of tolerated us, rather than use us for the expertise we had. Similarly she was trying to draw away from Jack, Walter and me, or at least me.[87] Jack coined the nickname "Ma Perkins," an ironic reference to the kindly matriarch from the popular radio show of the 1940s and '50s. In November 1982, mid-term in her administration, I sent Eileen a memo. In it I analyzed a recent poll that we had taken. At the top was the necessity for her administration to establish an "accomplishment" record.

As 1984 approached, employment would become a more important issue, I pointed out. In the early 1980s we had suffered, and were continuing to suffer from, an economic recession. The economy was a top-of-mind issue. Ronald Reagan had just defeated Jimmy Carter for the presidency, and Reaganomics was on the horizon.

I recommended that the piecemeal release of City and County capital improvement projects be done in a coordinated and single package, after private discussions with union and business leaders. I urged her to toot her own horn, to avoid the need for a "quiet and effective" type of campaign. In so doing, she could reach out to the grassroots, to continue to take the pulse of the public, to gauge that whatever she was doing was what touched the public.

Because of the possibility of revenue shortfalls, I recommended that budget and service cutback contingencies be put in place. Better to have a strategy before the cataclysm strikes, I advised, so that the strategy is a result of objective decision making, not emotional responses to urgency.

I warned her that our poll results showed Frank Fasi to be a significant and viable threat, and that she needed to have accomplishments at least equal to a third of what Fasi had accomplished. Fasi would always be a political challenge for her. He had been a very successful mayor for many

---

[87] Jack and I were working on the H-Power project in which Oahu Sugar Co. would burn its own waste instead of outsourcing to an independent facility. Jack was retained by Bob Oshiro, who had been retained by Henry Walker. Bob then recruited me, as I worked for Amfac, and he likewise enlisted Bob Ozaki, who would become one of my best friends at that company. Jack and I were asked to meet Eileen to share and explain the Oahu Sugar rationale on H-Power. Eileen's comment to us was that we were hired guns, and our voices were therefore unpersuasive.

years, after all, while she was still new to the scene. Her support was soft. Much of it was anti-Frank, and she needed to move this to pro-Eileen.

I urged innovation in financing, in jobs, in employment opportunities, and I asked Eileen rhetorically, "What haven't we looked at?" I urged self-reliance and volunteer programs at parks and recreation centers, along with decentralizing city services, urging her to take government to the people. I also made suggestions for relocating and renovating existing facilities.

I urged her to invite foreign technology investment in Honolulu. "Hawai'i can be at the crest of the wave of the world's conversion to an information based society," I wrote. "Our global position makes Hawai'i a natural for international business. That should be our next great leap… The administration should be at the forefront of alternative energy production. Real property tax credits for solar installations, heat pumps, windmills, photoelectric cells, hydroelectric power, should be explored." I also urged recycled water for "gray water" usage in new homes.

Meanwhile, whenever Joe Napolitan would come back to town, we'd discuss Eileen's next campaign. On October 7, 1982, Joe wrote me a memo headed, "Looking Ahead to 1984 and 1986." In it, he outlined his thoughts on the future:

1. It's never too early to start looking ahead to the next election. I have been told that Eileen plans to run for re-election in 1984 and for governor in 1986.
2. I think it would be a mistake to assume Eileen is a shoo-in in 1984, and there is no doubt in my mind that 1986 will be a real battle.
3. Let's look at 1984 first. Assuming Ariyoshi wins re-election, this will mean that Frank Fasi has faced the voters five times since 1974 and won only once, against Nelson Doi in 1976. Ordinarily, this should finish any candidate, but Fasi is so persistent and so tenacious that I think it would be a mistake to write him off in 1984.
4. He will be in a much weaker position, of course, and probably will have a hell of a time raising money, but he somehow maintains a strong base of support and some really loyal followers.
5. And while we have never publicized this (I don't even know if Eileen is aware of it) in a couple of polls we took earlier in the year we asked who had done a better job as mayor, Eileen or Fasi, and Fasi won each time. Presumably he has been asking similar ques-

tions in his polls, and has the same information.

6. There might well be another primary challenger, although I couldn't name him at the moment. The most dangerous would be a credible, respectable Japanese candidate. In a three-way race, Eileen could be vulnerable, considering Fasi's residue of strength and the possible erosion of Japanese support if such a candidate emerges.

7. On the Republican side, I see two possibilities: Pat Saiki or Charles Marsland. Of the two, Saiki might be the more formidable candidate, but Marsland is vicious and I would not underestimate him.

8. All of which goes to say that in my opinion Eileen would be making a big mistake if she thinks she can drift through 1984 and then gear up for 1986. There will be a temptation, probably not by her but perhaps by some people on her staff who are more involved in government than in politics, to think 1984 can be won with a minimal effort.

9. My feeling is that Eileen should plan a full-scale campaign for 1984 for several reasons:

    a. It may well be necessary.

    b. There is no penalty for winning big if the threat I envision does not materialize.

    c. The 1984 campaign serves as a prelude for 1986.

10. I believe you should talk soon with all the key people involved in the 1980 campaign—i.e., Walter Dods, Jack Seigle, Frank Hata—and begin planning early for 1984. This means selecting a pollster, talking with Mique Quenzer about television production, determining strategy and writing a campaign plan.

11. I have always felt that the longer the gestation period of a political campaign, the better the chances of success. The Ariyoshi campaign this year is a perfect example. I think the best thing we did in this campaign was to produce and run early the 30-minute documentary on Ariyoshi's accomplishments. We could do this because we started working on the campaign in January, 1981. Had we not started planning until January, 1982, there is no way we could have produced and aired the documentary as early as we did. And by running it we deprived the opposition of one of their main weapons, the claim that Ariyoshi hadn't done any-

thing as governor.

12. My recommendation is that sometime between Election Day and the end of the year, you, Eileen and whatever other key people she has in her organization should sit down with Walter and Jack and talk about 1984. The earlier you start, the better off you will be.

13. So far as 1986 is concerned, there is little doubt John Waihee will run for governor. Head-to-head, Eileen can take him, perhaps without too much trouble, but it is much too early to make that kind of projection. There also is the real possibility Cec Heftel would get into the race, and that could be troublesome. Or, again, this faceless respectable Japanese might show up, and in a three-way race with a haole and a Hawaiian might be a factor.

14. Actually, I wouldn't worry much about 1986 until you get through 1984. I am writing this before we talk, so I don't know your feeling on the situation, or Eileen's, but, if I were you, I certainly would recommend starting early and not take any risk of treating the campaign too lightly.

Further to this is a paper by Joe headed, "Some Thoughts on the Importance of Strategy in a Political Campaign," dated November 1, 1982, and a more specific paper entitled, "Preliminary Thoughts on Strategy for Mayor Eileen Anderson's Campaign for Re-election," dated February 24, 1983. In the latter, Joe outlines the potential candidates in 1984, which included Patsy Mink, Frank Fasi, Cec Heftel, Jean King, John Waihee, George Akahane, Charles Marsland, Pat Saiki and Andy Anderson. Joe correctly noted that except for Fasi most of the remaining potential candidates would wait and watch, and if Eileen stumbled and became vulnerable, then they'd jump in. Joe noted, "If no major problems or scandals develop within the administration, and if the Mayor shows continuing signs of strength as the year goes by, the less likely they will be [able] to take her on." Joe went on to recommend early polling; and adapting a direct mail and telephone targeting campaign. A thirty-minute documentary film was posited but never went much further. He noted, "There is no question in 1982 that our early use of the Ariyoshi accomplishments film was a major factor in our campaign; in fact, I would say it was the turning point... What worked in 1982 is not necessarily what will work in 1984. My only recommendation is that we keep all our options open."

But Joe saved the toughest for last: Would Eileen run for governor in 1986? He parsed out the possible responses: no, yes and maybe. He argued that "maybe" was the best answer and went something like this: "I intend to keep all my options open. None of us knows what may happen in 1986. I would be less than honest with you if I made a flat statement that either I was or was not going to run. Right now I am running for re-election as mayor, and I don't want to look beyond this election." Every mayor seeking to run for governor has used this same language in slightly different words.

Finally, Joe wrote one of the most insightful statements on politics that I've ever read: "The best politics is the best government." This was true in 1983 and it is doubly true today.

In July of 1983, plans for Oahu Sugar's H-Power facility in Waipahu had hit a roadblock. Veteran politician Patsy T. Mink and Eileen were in a fight. Anderson argued for a broader city view, while Mink argued that her Waipahu community should have a stronger voice. *Star-Bulletin* editor A.A. "Bud" Smyser noted:

> The mayor takes and is expected to take, a citywide perspective. Mink represents her part of the Island, and seems to be doing it quite effectively. The true art of politics lies in trying to find through such adversary positions and different interests a path, which serves the common good.[88]

On one of his trips to town, Joe asked what had been done since his last visit and Eileen basically said nothing. Joe was more than a little upset, and wrote a scathing memo, which was uncharacteristic of him. But I understood. When I was given a preview of the memo, I suggested to Jack and Joe that we get it in front of Eileen before the meeting. That was a mistake. She summarily canceled the meeting and Joe left town.

The upcoming 1984 mayoral campaign had no campaign manager, and Eileen needed to find one. We went months without anyone. Finally, she chose a gentle soul, Stanley Lum. He was a good person but had no

---

88 A.A. Smyser, "Political Process Problems," *Honolulu Star-Bulletin*, July 8, 1983.

political experience. But Stan was a trooper nevertheless, and if Eileen asked him, what could he say?

In the meantime, we were all meeting in a small group that included Eileen, Andy, Larry Koseki, her chief of staff Bob Awana and me. We talked lots of policy and politics, but truthfully nothing ever happened, or at least I didn't sense anything happening. I suspect I was seen as an Ariyoshi surrogate, even though I was now at Amfac. Maybe that was the problem. In any event I did not know, and I never would. All I knew was that in a couple years Eileen would be up for re-election, and it was my duty to be helpful if she asked for her support. She did, but when I joined Amfac, my new boss, Dan Curry, required as a condition to employment that I not get involved in politics. Consequently, I declined to run her 1984 campaign.

Watching a train wreck happening from a distance is no better than being there, even if you wanted to help. Eileen rejected the base of Ariyoshi supporters that got her elected. Repeated attempts by that group to reach out to her were rejected. She seemed to believe every single word she'd said in that 1981 *Hawai'i Business* article.

What's more, the business leaders who had supported her were now having second thoughts. For example, in response to Eileen's controlled growth policy, Tim Chow, her planning director, denied a number of permits, which angered and frustrated the development community. That well, and the support it generated, was drying up quickly. The political base we'd worked so hard to cobble together to beat Fasi was quickly disintegrating.[89] By the later days of the campaign, the end began to look inevitable.

I was at home that evening when the election results were announced. She had lost to Fasi. The result was predictable but nevertheless disappointing, since so much effort was sent down the drain, and so much hope was evaporating. In the end she lost to Fasi 117, 841 to 132, 375—a margin of 14,534 votes. She had beat him in 1980 by 1,617 votes (89,224 vs. 87,547). We always knew Fasi was a strong candidate, and 1984 demonstrated his ability to marshal votes even without a position of incumbency. Even as

---

[89] One rumor I heard when Eileen was first elected was that city employees didn't like Frank Fasi. But within a span of three years, Eileen was the person they disliked, and they yearned for Fasi's return. One of the most critical support bases in the city are its employees—not the union, the employees. By 1984, they had had their fill of Eileen and wanted Frank back.

the incumbent, Eileen couldn't capture enough votes to win. Could the Ariyoshi supporters have made a difference? We'll never know.

Of course, defeats like our Anderson and Craven campaigns are chances to contemplate what went wrong. As the old saying goes, victory has a hundred fathers, defeat is an orphan. The post mortem on the 1984 election was one of blame. The word I got (because I wasn't involved) was that Eileen blamed a lot of folks for her loss, and never took responsibility for any of it herself.

That campaign taught me a lesson. A person's character is the key to success—the sole key. Narcissism has no place in a candidate's political repertoire. If one acknowledges that he or she is but a reflection of the hopes and aspirations of society, then the life of that politician should reflect the true nature of public service. The American statesman Andrew Oliver got it right some 200 years ago:

> Politics is the most hazardous of all professions. There is no other in which a man can hope to do so much good to his fellow creatures…and neither is there any in which, by mere loss of nerve, he may do as much widespread harm. There is not another in which he may so easily lose his own soul, nor is there another in which a positive and strict veracity is so difficult.

For all its faults, I still believe that politics is a noble profession. But like any profession, its reputation is measured by the acts of its professionals. It is unfortunate for us as a society that good people rarely seek to serve in public office. I admire those who do; I sympathize with those who do not. But in the end we, society, are the losers if capable and honorable people avoid politics because of the hardships it forces them to endure.

If you, as I do, feel like throwing stones at politicians, I ask you to ask yourself before you pick up that rock, "Are you without sin?" [90] Sometimes we criticize what we really see in ourselves, throwing rocks at someone who just reflects who we are. If I might suggest a better solution: Get involved and offer a better alternative. Don't throw rocks; use them to build a foundation for a better society. In the end we will all benefit. ❧

---

[90] John 8:7, "When they kept on questioning him, he straightened up and said to them, "Let any one of you who is without sin be the first to throw a stone at her."

CHAPTER ELEVEN

John Waihee:
A Very Short Chapter

❧

"That is all I have to say, my brother. It is not that I know more
about politics and elections than you, but I realize how busy you are
and I thought I could more easily set out these simple rules in writing.
Of course, I would never say that these precepts apply to everyone seeking
political office—they are meant just for you—but I would appreciate
it if you have any additions or suggestions just in case, for what
I want this little handbook on elections to be complete."
—Quintus Tullius Cicero, *How to Win An Election*

Eileen's defeat in 1984 sort of set me free. I had been away from
government now for four years, one election cycle. Ariyoshi was in
his last few years as governor. I was finally able to focus on my career.

The truth is that politics is never far from anyone's occupation. Some
may think they can avoid politics, but it is to their peril. My Amfac clients,
many of them real estate development executives, saw me as the perfect
entrée to the political system. But I honored my agreement with Dan
Curry and never took an active political role after joining the company.

I did receive one call in 1989 from supporters of Governor John
Waihee. RCO had run Waihee's first campaign for governor. Bob,
Hawai'i's Cincinnatus, had emerged from his Wahiawā domicile yet again
to run another campaign. By 1989 he was growing weary of this, and
the governor's supporters knew it—hence this phone call. By this time,
I was a junior Amfac corporate executive, but I still reported to Dan
Curry, who was still my boss. The first inquiry came from Sandy Ebesu,

and I met with her and Jimmy Yasuda. I stated that my agreement with Amfac allowed no more campaigns. But they were un-persuaded, so they arranged a meeting for me with Governor Waihee in his office. We had a very cordial conversation, and he did ask me to help, but I told him about my commitment to Amfac. I knew that if I asked Dan Curry, he probably would have said yes, but I didn't want to go there. Not because I didn't like Governor Waihee—far from it, he was a very personable guy. But because I was now assigned to the Amfac division responsible for the development of Maui's Kā‘anapali resort, as well as residential and commercial developments around the Islands, I felt that my employment might prompt me to ask the governor for favors. I just didn't want to be in that position. Business is business, and if I found that my political connection provided an asset, I would probably try to tap it. And so I declined the governor's invitation. In hindsight, maybe it wasn't the smartest thing to do, but Governor Waihee was a gracious man. He also went on to win his second term handily.[91]

Being on the sidelines was a welcome respite for me. I had a luxury few in town had—the ability to just say no to politics. I am sure Bob would've wanted to play that card too. So for the next few years I was virtually "retired" from the political system—that is, until I got the call to become involved in Ben Cayetano's quest for governor in 1994. ❧

---

[91] My biggest regret about this decision was that I missed an opportunity to work with Dan Aoki, who passed away during the Waihee campaign. Hawai‘i lost a political giant that year.

CHAPTER TWELVE

Ben Cayetano:
The Farrington Governor

❧

**"For those who don't like you without good cause, try to win them over by
being kind to them or doing them a favor or by showing concern for them."**
— Quintus Tullius Cicero, *How To Win An Election*

In 1980 only one sitting politician came forth to endorse Eileen against
the formidable Frank Fasi. Tradition was that no sitting politician
ever endorsed any candidate in the primary election. It just wasn't done.
Today you see much more of it, but in 1980 it was decidedly uncommon.
Ben Cayetano's endorsement of Eileen in 1980 was thus not only unusual
and extraordinary, but it demonstrated a courage that most politicians
didn't seem to have.

Ben was lieutenant governor during Governor John Waihee's two
terms, the man who had defeated Eileen Anderson's LG run in 1986.
The story of that campaign is best told in Ben Cayetano's own memoirs,[92] but I will note that by 1986 Jack Seigle and Joe Napolitan weren't
helping Eileen Anderson, but Ben Cayetano. Eileen had almost no one
from her original 1980 campaign except a few diehard loyalists.

George Ariyoshi had become Hawai'i's longest serving governor, with
both acting and gubernatorial roles from 1973 until 1986. A generation
grew up knowing only Ariyoshi as governor. If you added the time that
his predecessor, John A. Burns, was in office, starting in 1962, it was a
period just shy of a quarter of a century. If you added John Waihee's term

---

[92] Benjamin J. Cayetano, *Ben: A Memoir, from Street Kid to Governor*.

to that total, it was thirty-two years.

Ben Cayetano was not a successor to the Burns-Ariyoshi-Waihee tradition; in fact, he was quite the opposite. He was one of the state senate dissidents, along with Clayton Hee, Dante Carpenter, Charlie Toguchi and Neil Abercrombie, who pushed the envelope on public service and challenging the status quo. They were seen by the old guard as threats, but something new usually is. The real question was: Where did the public stand? That too was changing.

In 1954 the fight had been with the long-standing economic and political monopoly of the Big Five companies—Amfac, Alexander & Baldwin, Theo H. Davies & Co., Castle & Cooke and C. Brewer & Co. In 1994 it was over tainted milk, corruption and alleged corruption and political cronyism. Ben Cayetano appeared to many people as the right answer to the issues of the time.

Once I became involved with the Cayetano campaign[93] we met regularly, a group including Ben, Lloyd Nekoba, Charlie Toguchi, Carol Takahashi, Colbert Matsumoto and others. We started early planning for the election. The hardest decision was determining who would make the sacrifice to run the campaign. It would be Charlie Toguchi, a man of gentle tenacity and loyalty who I am proud to call my friend.

On the media side it was Jack Seigle, Walter Dods and Joe Napolitan. I was home again with the same team from 1980. And much of what I will recount here comes from an archive of Joe's memos. On November 6, 1993, a year out from the elections, Joe wrote to Jack, "From here Cayetano looks like a real long shot if [former Republican Congresswoman Pat] Saiki is the candidate, but we've been in this position before, although under different (and more unfavorable) circumstances."

Jack noted that, according to an Omnitrak survey of 750 likely voters, conducted between Thursday, September 30, and Saturday, October 16, and analyzed by Ray Soon, Ben was trailing Saiki significantly. He was losing to Saiki in a three-way race (including Frank Fasi) to AJAs by

[93] At the time I was in a real estate partnership with Bill Milks, Everett Dowling and George Ariyoshi. I was attending meetings in Tokyo with Governor Ariyoshi, and in a taxicab one day we had a conversation about my participation in Ben's campaign. He was clearly not happy with my involvement. I recalled the many confrontations between Ariyoshi and Cayetano, especially over the nomination of my friend Mike Lilly to become AG. Ben opposed the nomination furiously, and the governor had to withdraw it. I had asked Ben for some consideration for Mike, only to be politely rebuffed. Clearly, Ariyoshi still remembered those days.

nineteen percentage points, to union members by fourteen points and on the Neighbor Islands by nine points. Although Ben led in the Filipino column, he only garnered forty percent of that vote.[94] Joe summarized the poll's results:

a. Right now, Ben Cayetano's major problem is himself. Like it or not, Ben is considered part of the establishment in Hawai'i, and the people don't like the establishment and where they think it is taking the state. Ben's personal profile, while not bad, can stand a lot of improvement, and this is what he should be concentrating on in the next several months.

b. Go positive at the beginning. In my opinion this campaign has started on the wrong track, attacking Pat Saiki and the Republican state chairman... Right now, Ben should concentrate on showing voters he has the competence to be governor, and giving them some solid reasons to vote for him. He must try to get voters to like him. He must identify himself with some of the major problems people are worried about, and design some realistic approaches to those problems. He must demonstrate his vision for Hawai'i's future. He must offer hope and be optimistic about the state...

c. This campaign can't be won only with the media... [U]ntil [Democrats, AJAs, Filipinos, and labor unions and their families] feel more comfortable with Ben...efforts [to create a favorable image of Ben] will not produce maximum benefits.

d. Ben must establish some independence from the Waihee government... If voters are left with the feeling that a Cayetano government will mean "more of the same" or that Ben is just a warmed-up Waihee, he will have difficulty...

---

94 When I told my old Ariyoshi contacts that I was helping Ben, the response wasn't always kind, thanks to the nature of the relationship between Cayetano and Ariyoshi. One AJA old-timer even told me a Filipino couldn't be governor. I was appalled. After all, that was similar to what people had said about Ariyoshi in 1974. This notion that ethnicity was a bar to the governorship was both strange and contradictory to all I had campaigned for; for an AJA to say this openly was to my mind the antithesis of what it meant to be a Democrat. I could tolerate a person who disagreed with Ben's politics and views, but not one who based his opposition on Ben's ethnicity. Note: On a trip to Manila, I learned that Spanish colonists once oppressed the Filipinos by denying them an education; it was only when Americans colonized the Philippines that universal education was promoted. Upon reflection, that AJA old-timer's statement seemed to represent those old Spanish values.

e. <u>Ben must firm up his own vote.</u> Usually a candidate in Hawai‘i starts with a hard, unshakable base; Ben seems to be lacking such a base... [H]is support is very soft.

f. <u>Don't underestimate what George Bush calls "the vision thing."</u> Voters need to have a clear view of what Ben Cayetano will do for them. They want to know what he will do differently than Waihee has done or is doing.[95]

On January 5, 1994, in another memo, Joe had more to say about Ben's campaign:

It has long been my belief that strategy is the single most important element in a political campaign. The right strategy can survive a mediocre campaign; the wrong strategy, no matter how brilliantly executed, will fail.

But there is a lot more to developing a strategy than just putting thoughts down on paper. Just as a football coach in designing a game plan must take into consideration a variety of factors, including the talent on his team and his opponents, then a political strategy must be designed and adapted to the individual candidate in the unique environment of a specific election.

A strategy evolves as the campaign progresses and sophisticated intelligence becomes available. Right now we are relying on a four-month-old poll, gut instincts, media commentary and personal knowledge.

The first step in defining a coherent strategy for Ben Cayetano is identifying the problems he faces in this campaign. Once we have identified the problems we can begin developing solutions.

Some of the problems are obvious and clear-cut, and these will be addressed first.

Unfortunately, we are starting a little late. In previous campaigns

---

[95] During a meeting I had with Ben about "the vision thing," it was clear he was having difficulty grasping the concept. One way to address it, I said, was to ask yourself: After four or eight years what will be my legacy? What will be my accomplishments? And what makes these things so important to the state and to you? Vision is sometimes less "visionary" or prophetic, but more decisive, more directed. For example, you could build a building, or you could build a *building*!

for governor that I have worked on in Hawai'i, we usually began having meetings like those we are having this week the year <u>before</u> the election.

There's nothing we can do about that now except recognize that there is a lot to do and not much time to do it in. This means we cannot agonize over minor decisions or keep second-guessing ourselves. The best people available to Ben should use their best judgment in arriving at a decision and then sticking to it.

No one outside the inner circle is going to be happy with every decision but unless there is clear proof that a decision is wrong then we should stick with it. Otherwise the campaign will flounder and fizzle and a lot of time and money will be wasted.

Despite his terms in the legislature and the LG's office, Ben was not well-known, and what people knew of him was often negative. So Joe Napolitan and Jack Seigle both argued for a thirty-minute film to tell his story. I was a fly on the wall during this discussion, including a presentation by Jack and Joe to Ben, Lloyd Nekoba and Dennis Mitsunaga, Ben's money man. Until the price came up, everyone seemed agreeable. But when Jack mentioned that it would cost somewhere between $300,000 and $400,000, the room turned cold. Ben wasn't Senate Ways and Means chair for nothing. He was a tight-fisted fiscal conservative. The three decided not to do the film. No amount of arguing could change that. We all left the room.

Dennis, Lloyd and I regrouped at campaign headquarters at the corner of Pi'ikoi and Kapi'olani. We were sitting around the old campaign table that had seen many such meetings in its history. Dennis and Lloyd knew I wasn't happy, and they tried to justify their decision by saying we needed the money for the general election. "Then put the money in a twelve-month CD," I said, "and spend it on a farewell party in October after we lose the primary!"

No sooner had I said this when Neil Abercrombie, now a US Congressman, walked in. I couldn't believe what happened next. Neil began lambasting Dennis and Lloyd, demanding they do the film. They were not happy, and Lloyd later accused me of arranging Neil's visit. I hadn't done that, nor did I speak to Ben about it, though I suspect Neil did. In any event, Ben recanted and they did produce a film called "Reach for the Moon."

Did the film push Ben over the top? That can always be debated, but I believe it did change people's opinions about Ben. The dramatic story of the Farrington alum from Kalihi helped explain his combative style. His caring for his stepfather and his fights on behalf of common folks resonated with people. He may be a son of a bitch, they figured, but he's *our* son a bitch. Ben became seen as the people's advocate, especially those who weren't getting a fair shake.

And it was true. Ben was that dedicated public servant looking out for the public interest, and that's what you wanted. But there were still many roadblocks to hurdle. In January 1994, Joe Napolitan wrote:[96]

Ben faces some other problems. These seem to be the most serious:

In the minds of most voters he is linked with Governor Waihee and the unpopular Waihee government.[97]

The Democratic Party is in disrepute. (Actually, this is somewhat inaccurate: there really isn't any significant Democratic Party in Hawai'i, just a whole lot of Democratic officeholders, candidates, appointees and job holders.)

Voters don't know as many of the good things about Ben Cayetano as they should. He is well known but not known well.

Like every candidate, Ben has some personal areas of vulnerability which may or may not become issues in the campaign.

But the situation is not all bleak.

Ben does have a good record. He is an independent spirit who has not hesitated to differ with the governor when he felt it was necessary to do so. He has served in the legislature and eight years as lieutenant governor, and he knows how the state works.

---

[96] The excerpts reproduced here are only part of a whopping twenty-one-page memo.

[97] Governor Waihee was facing controversy over the appointment of his AG's wife, Sharon Himeno, to the Hawai'i Supreme Court. In a *Honolulu Star-Bulletin* article dated February 22, 1993, state senate president Jimmy Aki stated that thirteen senators were prepared to vote no to her confirmation. Senator Richard Matsuura questioned Himeno's ability to be independent. Senators Kobayashi and Taniguchi had raised the issue at a public meeting in Mānoa. The attendees all voted no, and told them to take that message to the capitol. Ben distanced himself by suggesting the nomination process was flawed. Waihee's budget director, Yuki Takemoto, was also embroiled in allegations of issuing non-bid sole-source contracts to political friends.

He is intelligent and articulate. I thought he expressed himself well in the Honolulu Weekly interview.

Ben also has some liabilities beyond those we discussed at our meeting Tuesday. He is so deeply involved in the campaign that he sometimes forgets he is the candidate and not the campaign manager or media director and spends time worrying about problems better left to those on his campaign team... He does not do as well as he should among fellow Filipinos and his strength on the neighbor islands is less than what is necessary for a Democrat to be elected governor. Although labor unions apparently are poised to endorse and support Ben, it is important that this support be vigorous and persuasive among members of those unions.

Finally, unless Ben can make some serious inroads into the traditional Democratic AJA vote, it is difficult to design a scenario which will produce victory.[98]

Our opponents that year were also making our job more difficult. Pat Saiki, the grand dame of the local GOP, would surely appeal to AJAs. The question was whether we would feel any defection, with voters staying out of the race and not participating at all. We needed to give AJAs a reason to stick with Ben and the party. Frank Fasi decided he wasn't going to be in anyone's party and ran on an independent ticket he called the Best Party. Joe wrote:

Before we can persuade people to vote for Ben we've got to get them to like him and trust him. If they like him and trust him, he will win their confidence and his credibility will rise.

Then, when it becomes necessary to attack Saiki or Fasi, Ben will be dealing from a much stronger hand then he holds now. Ben doesn't have to prove he is feisty or a fighter; he does have to prove to people he has the intellect, the moral character, and the vision to be governor.

---

[98] Joe also weighed in on Ben's mustache and whether it should go or stay. Shades of John Craven and his falling socks! Were we really that concerned about Ben's mustache? Was it really that important? Maybe not in hindsight, but it was definitely an issue for the campaign at the time. In politics, appearances do count.

In January of 1994, things had still not fully jelled, and there were concerns about whether Ben and this team could pull it off. To advise us on this situation, Joe wrote a memo with the following points:

1. Produce an "Insiders" newsletter
2. Let the supporters know the organization is shaping up
3. Ben is working hard
4. Consult the grassroots
5. Make specific assignments for the workers
6. Send the supporters material
7. Outline the reasons why Ben will win
8. Ask for feedback
9. Let them know they are appreciated
10. Quietly spread the word that Ben has a plan to win the election

This confidence building and operational plan was right in line with RCO's operational plans laid out decades earlier. Political operations don't really change. The methods may, but the operations and actions are basically the same. Winning or losing depends on how well you execute. Do it well and your candidate will win. In his memos, Joe outlined why and how he thought Ben could win. Let me summarize them here:

1. Don't be afraid of your opponent's early lead in the polls. Others have come from behind; others have led before and lost.
2. The big guns of the Democratic Party are behind you. Both locally and nationally the Democratic hierarchy will be in support. In many ways they have to; they can't afford to lose the governor's office.[99]
3. Money is coming in.
4. The candidate must focus on the issues and programs that will help ordinary people.
5. The main effort should be on building the organization.
6. Unions will line up behind the candidate.
7. The candidate should:
   a. Build the organization

---

[99] As we will see, this will prove to be a problem eight years later.

b. Travel the state

c. Develop attractive positions

d. Complete his/her duties as an elected official

e. Film for media

f. Sharpen his/her issues

In a focus group in March, we found that Ben was getting "clobbered," to use Joe's term, by Caucasians, who were choosing Saiki over both Cayetano and Fasi. The focus group count was nine for Saiki, one for Fasi, none for Ben. Among AJAs Ben got two and Saiki got seven, with one person undecided.[100] But Saiki's support was soft, meaning they liked her but didn't know her. In a portent of things to come, some in the focus group liked Saiki because she was—wait for it—a Republican woman, and she could bring change. Unless she attacked, Saiki was getting a free ride. Even though her politics were diametrically opposite to those of the focus group participants, they didn't know that. Once they knew, they switched. The danger, Joe noted, was Ben prematurely launching a frontal attack. "Ben was practically everyone's *third* choice," Joe emphasized.

Our biggest weapon, our weapon of mass influence, was the thirty-minute film, which showed a side of Ben that few people knew. His advocacy became a reason to vote for him, not against him. His caregiving of his stepfather specifically addressed the AJAs, who respected and admired caring for the elderly. It was the culturally right thing to do, and Ben was doing it. So while some people still didn't like *how* he did things, Ben was beginning to be appreciated for the *why*.

In June 1994, Omnitrak reported on a new poll taken after the film started rolling out. The top line results were that Ben was going to beat state health director John Lewin in the primary with forty-seven percent of the vote to nineteen percent for Lewin. Tony Hodges and George Nitta, meanwhile, would each receive just two percent.

Saiki was still leading the general election poll. Forty percent of those surveyed said they'd vote for her, while twenty-seven percent would vote for Ben. Fasi would hang onto twenty-one percent. Ben was going up and Saiki was coming down; Fasi was flat. The end lines were in our favor, but when would they intersect? Would there be enough time, enough effort?

---

[100] It wasn't that we didn't know we had a tough race, we just didn't appreciate how tough it was.

The film was definitely affecting voters. More than half (fifty-three percent) had a favorable opinion of Ben after they viewed it. Of those who saw the film, Saiki would receive thirty-five percent of the votes in the general election, with Cayetano in a close second with one third of the votes. Fasi dropped even lower among voters who watched the film, with nineteen percent.[101]

So did the film lead to Ben's victory? I believe it did, and I think both Dennis and Lloyd were relieved that their investment paid off better than a twelve-month CD in a local bank.

The three met in the general. The Democrats rallied behind Ben. He won with 134,978 votes to Fasi's 113,158 to Saiki's 107,908. ❧

---

[101] "Hawai'i Governor Tracking Study," prepared for Starr Seigle McCombs Advertising, Inc. by Omnitrak Group Inc., June 1994.

CHAPTER THIRTEEN

Arnold Morgado:
An Unexpected Journey

❧

"What sweetness is left in life, if you take away friendship?
Robbing life of friendship is like robbing the world of the sun.
A true friend is more to be esteemed than kinsfolk."

—Marcus Tullius Cicero

In 1996 I worked on Arnold Morgado's mayoral campaign at the request of Bert Kobayashi Jr. and Walter Dods. The campaign was having issues—I didn't quite know what, but I was asked to come in and run it. This did not sit well with the existing campaign staff and supporters. After all, they had been with Arnold from the beginning, two years prior, and I was just an "interloper," a "carpetbagger."

But I was doing this for Bert and Walter, as a personal favor to them. I found Arnold to be a great guy. He could be stubborn, but so are we all. The problem seemed to be with an organization that had managed a city council district race and was now facing a run for a countywide seat.

The scale of a campaign changes the way you run it. The smallest elected office (except for a neighborhood board seat) is a house of representatives seat, followed by a senate seat and finally a councilmember seat. In relative numbers there are fifty-one representative seats for the entire state, thirty-four of which are on Oʻahu; twenty-five senatorial seats for the entire state, of which seventeen are on Oʻahu; and on Oʻahu just nine councilmember seats. State legislators are not term-limited but councilmembers are. Councilmembers have a larger and wider constituency than a state senator, but can only serve a maximum of eight years;

a senator can be re-elected ad infinitum. A councilmember thus is much more capable to run for mayor than a state senator. But just focusing on the numbers would be folly. The nature of a campaign on an island-wide scale is far larger. It requires a certain level of logistical sophistication, voter identification and organization.

A good councilmember campaign committee can challenge an incumbent mayor, but the incumbent has the advantage of networking, money and in most cases, organization. Eileen Anderson's campaign stood for the proposition that a challenger could pull off a win against an entrenched incumbent.

Since I had helped a relative unknown beat a well-known sitting incumbent mayor, what was so hard about this? Or that is what I believe Walt and Bert thought.

But first there were some critical housekeeping issues to resolve. The following memo will give you an idea of some of the day-to-day matters that must be addressed in a new campaign, and how a campaign manager must interact with his or her candidate.

MEMO TO: AM
FROM: RBT
RE: First Thoughts, Suggestions for Action

1. The campaign must hire a full-time secretary/office manager for the HQ. Your campaign manager shouldn't be answering phones; he should be out in the field.
2. The campaign HQ must be moved to a more visible location, and the current location used for storage and/or sensitive data processing or assembly of materials. The problem is that the location is so obscure that no one can see the activity (or lack thereof) of the campaign. In order to build steam we need to create public perception that there is a campaign.
3. Scheduling needs to be brought back to the campaign and not left with you. This is to ensure that you are attending the events which will bringing you into contact the most people. Secondly, you need an advance person and someone to take you around a group, moving you through the crowd.
4. Also on the issue of scheduling, I fully recognize the demands of

family and especially children. I know you want to be the best father to your kids and spend time with them. However, if this campaign is to be won, there must be hard sacrifices and this will include time with your kids. We can save Sundays for you, but generally all of your available time must be spent on campaigning. This will directly impact attending sporting events for your kids, but it is necessary.

5. You must articulate and establish a statement of your legacy after being mayor of the city. This is necessary to inspire the troops. Why should they follow you? State now what you are going to be held accountable for, what you intend to do. Don't get esoteric and talk planning (which is a nebulous, ill-defined and hard-to-grasp issue). Rather, talk about your concrete proposals. Reclaim the issues you feel Jeremy Harris has stolen from you. Make it clear that those are your issues and claim them.

6. I do not believe it is wise for you to participate in fundraising directly or to know how funds are being raised, in case of a controversy.

My comments here are intended to be constructive. There is so little time remaining that I am unable to couch some of my phraseology in a more deliberative manner, and have been much more direct than usual, however I believe these things need to happen and quickly.

The primary election required the winner to get fifty percent plus one in the primary to win outright, so the strategy was to get to the general. Jeremy Harris, Arnold and Frank Fasi were in the mix. If you think about it, Jeremy and Frank should have split the vote, with Arnold therefore a shoo-in. But the circumstances weren't what they seemed. Jeremy was ahead and likely to win on the primary ballot. Time was too short to win outright in the primary. The question was how to get to the general. Jack Seigle, Joe Napolitan and Walter Dods were once again involved. It was like being at an old familiar club, and my involvement in the campaign was worth it just for that. We all concluded we needed a thirty-minute film. Like Ben, no one really knew Arnold—except, in Arnold's case, in a sports setting. We really needed to tell his story. Unlike our experience with Ben, Arnold said OK and we started filming.

Arnold's story is an emotional roller coaster. His dad was in the service in Japan, where he met Arnold's mom. But back in Hawai'i, life was tough for the Morgado family. The story of his father's decision to send Arnold to the Mainland, *hanai*-ed to family there to help make ends meet, broke your heart. When I saw the rough cut of the film, it was emotionally moving even without the music and fades that were added in later. The high point for me was the part about Arnold being sent to live on the Mainland—just the raw emotion that came through. The experiences of Arnold and his mom just tugged at your heart. I teared up. You wanted to reach out and hug the guy and tell him things would be all right.

He went to Punahou School on an athletic scholarship and made the most of it, later turning pro as a running back with the Kansas City Chiefs of the National Football League. Here was a real Horatio Alger story—a local boy made good. He was a great father and a great husband, and the Morgados were a great family story. Their struggles were your struggles. You could relate. I knew at that moment we had a chance to pull it off. Like Ben's "Reach for the Moon," Arnold's film grabbed the hearts of those who saw it. I believe the film injected the Morgado campaign with fresh blood.

On November 1, 1996, *Star-Bulletin* reporter Gordon Y.K. Pang wrote:

> Polls through the Sept. 21 special election showed Morgado trailing Harris badly. [Harris] came close to winning it all—he got 49.3 percent when he needed 50 percent plus one vote. Morgado's strong showing rejuvenated the campaign, and the latest polls show him surging and in position to capture his goal... Morgado considers himself an underdog, a role he's used to.

When you're the challenger, it's tough to raise money and organize. The incumbent has the cards on his side. I think we did a good job of pulling all the necessary pieces together, but I'm convinced that, like Ben's film, the thirty-minute film changed the game.

Once I'd helped produce his film, I left Arnold's campaign, after the primary. Even though I'd helped organize it, I was still an outsider. The grassroots had continued to perform as they had before I joined. And there were issues with my continued presence in the campaign (or at least I felt there were), so I called Walt and Bert and told them I was getting out. No one said I should stay in, nor was I asked to reconsider. I was politely allowed to walk.

The theme of the campaign was "Local roots, local values."[102] Maybe it was the wrong theme. To be sure we were going after the local vote; the film was clearly aimed there. But did we leave behind the haole vote? Did we cede that population to Jeremy? This dichotomy always plagues candidates who need the AJA vote as well as the Caucasian vote. But Mufi Hannemann, for one, would later use this theme to his disadvantage.

Arnold did attack Jeremy's record to good effect, but it wasn't enough. When asked, Arnold made the distinction between running negative ads and simply comparing the candidates' records. *Star-Bulletin* reporter Gregg Kakesako wrote:

> Responding to criticism that the waning weeks of the campaign may have appeared to be a lot of negative attacks, Morgado said he didn't believe that 'comparing records' could be perceived in such a manner. I think it's a mistake at this point to say it was a negative campaign. Our position all along has been to prove to the people of the City and County of Honolulu that the current administration has not lived up to their promises. Our campaign did all of these things above board.[103]

Arnold was absolutely right. Comparing the record and holding an incumbent to his or her record is a legitimate comparison. Indeed, the public deserves to see such comparisons. However, many times it is the tone of the comparison, rather than the substance, that people react to as negative.

And the media itself bears responsibility for how campaigns are conducted. Many may have forgotten Jeremy Harris' unwillingness to participate in any debate, as well as his move to have a local news station provide him equal time after he turned down one such televised event. The League of Women Voters made much of this, and rightly so. Again,

---

[102] Gordon Y.K. Pang, "Morgado: A focused fighter who pushes the envelope," *Star-Bulletin*, November 1, 1996, http://archives.starbulletin.com/96/11/01/news/story2.html.

[103] Gregg K. Kakesako, "Morgado to take a break after tough mayoral race," *Star-Bulletin*, November 6, 1996, http://archives.starbulletin.com/96/11/06/news/story1.html.

reporter Gregg Kakesako wrote in the *Star-Bulletin*:

> The League of Women Voters of Honolulu today expressed its outrage at the *Advertiser*/Channel 2's arranging in advance for Mayoral Candidate Jeremy Harris to have free time to rebut Arnold Morgado and Frank Fasi after the debate he refused to participate in on September 18. His rebuttal followed immediately upon the end of the debate. Obviously, cameras and reporters were waiting in Harris' office to conduct the interview. Reacting to the storm of protest which followed, Channel 2 offered time to Morgado and Fasi on the September 19 10 o'clock news to answer Harris' September 18 statement. This in no way, the League alleges, was adequate, as the viewership for the advertised debate was in all probability far greater than for a routine news broadcast. *This is an example of situations that can occur when the media venture into creating news in addition to reporting news which is their true role and responsibility.*[104] (Emphasis added.)

Had the media properly reported this action, would Jeremy have made it into the general? Was he given a free pass? Had the *Advertiser* and Channel 2 overstepped the bounds of propriety?

Arnold did make it into the general election but could not overcome Jeremy's strength. It was unfortunate. I truly liked Arnold and still do. He is a gracious, upstanding gentleman, and I wonder how things would differ today had he been elected. The lesson to be learned is that a challenger can bring himself within striking distance. But the home stretch in the general election is a whole other matter.

I was later told by Peter Char that the film got us really close. Who knows what might have pushed the Morgado campaign first over the proverbial finish line—or possibly whether the debate fiasco should have been pushed even further than it was.

The best political team that I knew, Walt and Jack, were on the job, so by all rights Arnold should have won. Senior Senator Dan Inouye, Governor Ben Cayetano and former mayor Frank Fasi had all thrown their support behind Arnold. So how could a campaign with so much

---

[104] http://www.lwv-hawaii.com/alohavoter/av9610-press.htm.

going for it lose? The role I played before stepping away from the campaign was coordinating the media with the grassroots activity. Maybe the lack of this coordination when I left contributed to the loss, but I can't believe that no one stepped in to fill those shoes.

I do believe that the coordination function between media and the grassroots is critical. Media is like an air force; you can soften the ground, but it can't take the territory. You need grassroots to do that. Politics is all about relationships—that's how you take and hold the ground. Maybe a better analogy is the idea from Japanese gardening called *nemawashi*, "an informal process of quietly laying the foundation for some proposed change or project, by talking to the people concerned, gathering support and feedback, and so forth."[105] Media prepares the ground; allows the public to accept the idea of the candidate as leader. The campaign is the instrument through which the idea is transplanted and nurtured. The campaigners are like the drops of water and nutrients necessary to keep the plant growing.

Much is made about media in politics. It's the exciting part of a campaign. In our increasingly visual society, media has become more and more integral to electioneering. But I remain committed to the notion that politics is all about relationships. If you rely solely on media contacts to win, you run the risk that media will poison the well or erode support, either through negative campaigning or smears. ❧

---

[105] https://en.wikipedia.org/wiki/Nemawashi.

CHAPTER FOURTEEN

Jeremy Harris:
The Other Side of the Tracks

~&

"You want to be a consul and everyone agrees you have the
ability to do the job, but there are many who are jealous of you.
You are not part of the nobility, yet you seek the highest office in
the land. Serving in this position would confer on you a tremendous
distinction, especially as you are courageous, eloquent,
and free from scandal, unlike so many others."

—Quintus Tullius Cicero, *How To Win An Election*

Jeremy Harris was born on December 7, 1950, in Wilmington, Delaware. I was born on December 18, 1950, in Honolulu. Jeremy and I shared the same years of experience growing up. Each of us was an only child. But we did not share the same politics. He grew up on Kaua'i's northeastern shore. I grew up in Honolulu's urban core. He was considered by many party regulars as radical. He and political activist JoAnn Yukimura were always at the forefront of curbing growth and pushing environmental restrictions. I was at Amfac developing resorts and residential communities. Jeremy and I were on opposite sides of the fence.

But in 1998, I found myself supporting the guy I had worked so hard against just two years earlier. Hard to understand, maybe, but I was looking toward the future, and I knew Jeremy had the potential to be governor. Ben Cayetano was in his second term, and Mazie Hirono was his LG and likely successor. No offense to Mazie, of course—we'd known each other since she was a law clerk at the AG's, when I worked there.[106] Her husband, Leighton, was a former colleague and a friend. But despite all this, I felt that Jeremy was the best candidate and the most formidable. In the wings was Maui mayor Linda Lingle, the most likely GOP candidate. Lingle would be tough to beat. She'd already run against Cayetano, and Ben had barely squeaked by. I thought the Democrats needed their best shot and in my mind, Jeremy was it.

Why Jeremy? Why the change? Good questions. He wasn't the most loveable guy; in many ways he was aloof and stubborn. But so was I. He knew politics as well as or better than many others; after all, he had run Frank Fasi's campaign. I can't say I ever really got close to the man, but I saw something in him. For all his faults, and we all have many, Jeremy had the interests of the people of Honolulu and Hawai'i at the top of his mind. If you scraped beneath his veneer, I believed there was a similar spirit—an almost naïve soul—who believed we could bring needed change to the Islands. Was he perfect? By no means, but who is?

For example, consider the improvements in Waikīkī during his term as mayor. For decades, Waikīkī had been deteriorating. Except for intermittent private sector redevelopment, the area had changed little since the demolition of the Waikiki Biltmore to make way for the Hyatt Regency Waikiki. The infrastructure was basically unchanged. Jeremy started the long process to change all that. Waikīkī Beach was improved; the Kapi'olani Park Bandstand was rebuilt. The streetlights were changed from those awful cobra lights, and baskets of flowers were hung on new vintage-themed light posts. Outside of town, Jeremy took an idea that Randy Iwase had championed for years and finally made it happen—Central Oahu Regional Park. Jeremy was a builder. But he stepped on toes to do it. He rubbed Mufi Hannemann and Donna Kim and Ann Kobayashi and who knows who else the wrong way, to do what he thought was right. This single-mindedness was his biggest strength—and also his Achilles' heel. Jeremy was not known as a collaborator unless he got his way. But what is leadership? Isn't it partly leading others to do things they didn't or wouldn't do?

So I got involved, hoping to help the media side of the campaign,

---

[106] I did have my battles with Mazie when she served as House Consumer Protection chair. She was decidedly pro-trial lawyers and I represented an insurance company. One day as we passed each other on the street, she raised two fingers in the sign of the cross, not saying a word.

where I thought I'd be more useful and could contribute. But my good friend and colleague, Norma Wong, had other ideas. Norma and Jeremy were close. She asked me if I would consent to be a co-chair. I brushed it off as one would lint from a pant leg. That wasn't what I wanted to do. I thought I could deal with it with silence, but in a meeting at Harry Mattson's office downtown she sprung the offer in front of Jeremy and the rest of his crowd. What could I do? Say no to the mayor? I reluctantly became one of Jeremy's co-chairs, along with someone who would become a lifelong friend, Audrey Hidano. Life and fate took an unexpected turn.

Working on Jeremy's campaign was a different experience. He ran the campaign, he called the shots, he edited the commercials, he decided everything. We could all kibitz but he made the decisions. Being campaign chair was more show then do. But as in all my other campaigns, I learned a lot from this one.

My first observation was the loyalty of his cabinet and appointees. I'd always thought the Ariyoshi cabinet and appointees were the best until I encountered the Harris team. When Jeremy decided to do the Sunset on the Beach free movies program following the start of the first Gulf War, when Waikīkī seemed almost empty of tourists, his appointees set up the tarp, the tables and the chairs. In Ariyoshi's time, it would have been the appointees directing volunteers. That happened here too, but the appointees were there at dawn and stayed past dusk, right along with everyone else. These were committed guys. They were impressive.

My second revelation involved Ben Lee. Ben and I had had a checkered relationship up until then. Not long before, he was the guy telling me I had to pay for the privilege of building a golf course in He'eia Kea for a client of mine. This was when Mayor Fasi was requiring every golf course to pay a price or you couldn't build. My project already had residential zoning along the highway facing the ocean, and no one, including the landowner, wanted to pay this extra cost. The alternative—homes built next to the roadway fronting the ocean—was not acceptable, and thus the local community supported our desire to build the houses further back, with the golf course along the highway. And so Ben's demand had fallen upon my deaf ears. That was our first encounter.

But when I next met him, he was Jeremy's managing director. I came to appreciate Ben in a different light. He was a loyal soldier. Many blamed him for certain things and sought to complain to Jeremy, but I knew Ben wasn't acting independently, but rather with the full knowledge and assent of his boss. No matter how many times you'd tell people that, they disagreed. It was as though no one could bring himself to blame the mayor. But I knew, and that was good enough for me. From that moment on, Ben was a friend, a good friend.

Jeremy had a great team: Norma Wong, Harry Mattson, Peter Char and his wife Lynette, Ben Lee, Don Clegg,[107] Chris Parsons and Mike Amii.[108] The mayor had brought Harry and Norma from the Ariyoshi and Waihee campaigns together with Don, a longtime Fasi supporter and pollster, and Mike from the Burns, Ariyoshi and Waihee campaigns. It was the first collaboration between these former competing interests. But if you think there'd be contention or competition among us, think again. Like any professionals, we had a goal and a job, and our focus was on getting that job done. What's more, the confluence of Don, Ray Soon and Harry Mattson, all pollsters, made for some interesting and lively discussions. In the end, the gathering of so much talent on this component of the campaign resulted not in chaos but in a greater intellectual understanding of the political scene among voters. It was a pleasure to find such camaraderie in an arena that sometimes sees too much competition and back stabbing.

Scheduling Jeremy was a big deal. Peter, Lynette, Jeremy and I would go through the schedule, often making decisions about where he should

[107] My relationship with Don was, to say the least, interesting. After years on opposing sides, when he supported Fasi and I backed Ariyoshi, we had never worked together. The first time we actually met, Don was back in town after Fasi beat Eileen Anderson, and we were at a conference at HISAM, a state facility in Nuʻuanu, working on some policy issue with about a hundred people. Don nominated me for something, which I can't recall, but it was an olive branch. My relationship with Don was forever changed by that gesture. It suggests that enemies can be friends, if you conscientiously build a relationship. And Don and I did. So it was a welcome sign that we were now working together. I also first met longtime legislator Susie Chun, before she became Susie Chun Oakland, at that same conference, when she was still a legislative aide.

[108] I should point out here that in 2003 Mike pleaded no contest to a misdemeanor charge of having his secretary file campaign spending reports on City time, when he was a Harris cabinet member. He was given a year's probation and required to pay a small fine, but remained on the job. I bring this up in the interests of full disclosure, for despite the charges against Mike, he is still a friend. I believe you can forgive such indiscretions even if you don't condone them; in our island culture, you can grow up with a tolerance for the person, not his actions. I knew Mike's wife, Jan, and could only feel her pain as this became public. But she was a trouper. It's unfortunate that Mike couldn't retire under better circumstances, but of course we all pay the price for our actions, both inside and outside the political arena.

go. Clearly you want to meet the most people in your target group of voters. Second, you want to avoid sending the candidate to different parts of the island, thus spending more time traveling than meeting voters. Third, you want to avoid sending a candidate to the same set of voters multiple times. Finally, you want to provide the candidate as much information about the group as you can.

Scheduling is an art form. And the more you do it, the more instinctual it becomes. That said, every scheduler has biases. Obviously you're more inclined to respond positively to a friend who calls with a request, rather than someone who's been bugging you for weeks. The key is getting the many people watching the candidate's schedule to agree on the right decision. The four of us met twice a week or so, deliberated on all requests both official and political, made a judgment call and implemented it. I have no recollection of any disagreement among us.

Of course, canvassing is always an important campaign activity. Going door to door has been the classic way to campaign, and many politicians make multiple rounds of their district each election cycle. House members usually do this multiple times in the two-year cycle. In large part, the representative districts are smaller are more conducive to this activity. Moreover, the representative has a better pulse on the community this way, and consequently is much more regionally focused and sensitive to his or her constituency.

But as one climbs the political tree to state senate and councilmember, the ability to canvass the district becomes more problematic—not because of inaccessibility but because the district is simply larger. Determined senators and councilmembers can still do this multiple times, but not to the same extent as representatives. And when you run for mayor or governor, this becomes practically impossible. The best you can do is assign surrogates do most of the walking and have the candidate do spot canvassing.

Such targeted canvasses were focused on the low-hanging fruit—the areas where a candidate's supporters lived. Mass canvasses, on the other hand, were shows of strength—in other words, getting the message out was secondary to showing the public, opponents and news media, that you had an organization and it was large enough to do this. Mass canvasses also bolstered morale because you saw so many people congregating together. Typically, a mass canvass has a single place to start and stop.

The logistics of canvassing wasn't merely the walking. It also included people who mapped the districts. This was an art form as well. In the days before widespread computer technology, these folks copied the senatorial maps, cut them into pieces and highlighted each house to which a canvasser was to deliver brochures. Hundreds of these tiny maps were handed out, and when the distribution had been completed, they were handed in to be tallied.[109]

Counting and bundling the brochures was the task of another group. Every map had a count and every group had a bundle with the map. If that sounds simple, multiply that by the number of homes in Honolulu and you begin to appreciate the magnitude of this effort.

What would you do if no one was home? Many canvassers stuck the candidate's brochure in the mailbox—that is, until the postal inspector called HQ and warned us that this was illegal. I don't recall any local campaign actually being fined by the postal service, but I'm sure some came close. Another delivery method was sticking the brochure through a chain link fence, especially if you heard or saw a dog inside.[110] Eventually someone got the bright idea to hole-punch the brochure in one corner, then slip a rubber band into the hole and loop the other end onto a doorknob, fencepost or anything else handy.

Jeremy came up with his own unique angle. His idea was to hand out fish. Fresh fish! The rest of us all reacted the same way, of course. It was a logistical nightmare, but Jeremy wanted to do it. He had done this years before on Kaua'i when he ran for the county council. He'd catch invasive species on the reef and hand them out to households with instructions for preparing them. That may be a great idea on Kaua'i, but not in urban Honolulu. We gave him a long memo on why it wasn't doable, not the least of which was the problem of spoilage and of people getting sick from food poisoning or even ciguatera. The fish had to be chilled and that required lots of ice—not in a regular cooler but an industrial-strength container. We'd also have to wrap the fish in plastic bags. We imagined a two-ton truck equipped with a mega cooler rolling

---

[109] In the Burns-Ariyoshi days, for instance, the mappers were the Watson family, including brothers Dave and Ed and their father.

[110] You were always wary when a house had a chain link fence or a gate. Typically dogs bark, but some wait stealthily under the house or around a corner until you enter the yard, then come charging. As a political campaigner in Hawai'i, I've had more than my share of such experiences.

through the streets of Honolulu, with volunteers running to every house with bagged fish with recipes. Needless to say, that idea was dropped, although not the idea of handing out edibles. We shifted to fresh vegetables—eggplant, zucchini and so forth. The HQ had a whole room devoted to storing veggies to be distributed. And it was a hit! Jeremy had the concept right; we just needed to find the right stuff to hand out.

If Jeremy went to a *kenjinkai*[111] picnic, he'd take along volunteers bearing veggies. If he walked a neighborhood, he'd bring veggies. It worked extremely well. People remember a mayor who gave them something personally. It was a powerful image and message.

We did receive unconfirmed reports that some canvassers were picking up the brochures and vegetables and, once away from HQ, dumping the flyers and taking the produce themselves. These rumors persisted but were never confirmed, nor did they put a stop to the giveaway program.

Jeremy and managing director Ben Lee also comprised the audit patrol—my description, not theirs. If they were driving down a street and Jeremy spotted a pothole, he'd call the City maintenance department and wait for them to come and patch it before leaving. If something the City was supposed to handle wasn't being done, he'd call and wait for the crews to come do it. He was the "everywhere mayor." Even on election night 1996, instead of being at headquarters watching the results, Jeremy was out surveying flood damage in 'Ewa. Here's how the *Star-Bulletin* reported it:

> At 12:05 a.m. today, when mayoral opponent Arnold Morgado was giving his concession speech, Jeremy Harris was wading through 13 inches of muddy water in his rain boots. Reports of flood evacuations at the old plantation villages of Varona, Tenney and Renton villages, sent Harris, his two top lieutenants and wife Ramona from the victory celebration at the mayor's campaign headquarters on Kapiolani Boulevard... Soon after the third printout showed

---

[111] "Issei immigrants often organized and joined prefectural associations called kenjinkai for mutual aid in time of illness or death, as well as for various kinds of misfortune. *Ken* denotes the Japanese prefecture from which a group's members emigrated. Particularly during the early years of immigration, when most Japanese were single men, the kenjinkai provided collective assistance to individuals from the same ken. In Hawai'i and on the Mainland, kenjinkai provided aid, fellowship and a sense of community for immigrant workers thousands of miles from Japan." Densho Encyclopedia, http://encyclopedia.densho.org/Kenjinkai/.

him with a comfortable 14-point lead, Harris—the "everywhere mayor"—was at it again, out in the field rather than celebrating his win over a game and tenacious Morgado. Assured by Civil Defense and National Weather Service officials that the worst of the storm had passed, Harris and his retinue returned to headquarters about 1 a.m. where only a handful of diehards remained.[112]

I don't know how City personnel felt about all this, but it surely kept them on their toes. Jeremy was a different kind of candidate. With me personally he was quite distant, but I knew he had a vision much like Burns and Ariyoshi before him. In a September 19, 2000, *Star-Bulletin* article entitled, "Goal-oriented 'perfectionist,'" reporter Tim Ryan wrote:

"A fellow marine biologist with UH's Sea Grant program is not surprised at Harris' political life. Some people have an aura about them to take charge of things, and that was always my impression of Jeremy," Bruce Miller says. "He was always hardworking, goal-directed, personable and attended a lot of community meetings on Kauai." Harris went on to create "a huge" environmental education program for kids, Miller says. "He always had some kind of reef walk and limu lecture going. He's always been involved in making things work. *People do tend to like him. He got things done.*" (Emphasis added.)

Getting things done. That surely described Jeremy, despite the criticism you might hear about his micromanaging. Peter Char and I once envisioned a commercial where a young Jeremy is playing with his blocks in a small bedroom. As the camera zooms in, we see a full-sized city with monorails, buses, bikes, parks and open spaces with futuristic residential towers. Another commercial idea we had was one of a young Jeremy on his bike headed to school. He's hitting all kinds of potholes, dips, uneven surfaces and bad traffic, and he says something like, "When I grow up, this will all be fixed." But no matter how whimsical or entertaining these ideas were, in real life Jeremy was a no-nonsense workaholic who got

---

[112] Gordon Y.K. Pang, "Harris' victory over Morgado is not as close as expected," *Honolulu Star-Bulletin*, November 6, 1996.

things done. In many ways he was "out-Fasi-ing" Frank Fasi.

But like Hermione in the Harry Potter stories, being seen as a know-it-all wasn't the best way to garner AJA votes, which he needed to succeed politically. Jeremy needed to be liked. He was charming, but he was also driven. This combination led to criticism about his nature. He was this haole kid who always had an answer, and sometimes you just didn't like kids like that. I am sure that played into the objections that many locals had to Jeremy's style.

Getting to know Jeremy close up suggested that some of the criticism wasn't deserved. Like anyone, he had a good side and bad side. The balancing of these two is what distinguishes a great politician from a poor politician. Politicians need to have a bit of "larceny" to play the political game; some hide it better than others, but all of them have it to some degree.

In his *Star-Bulletin* piece, reporter Ryan noted as much:

> [JoAnn] Yukimura also isn't surprised at Harris' political successes. "It was hard enough for a young person like me, who grew up there, to break into the old boy's political system," she says. "And here you have this haole guy going for it. That's a pretty audacious thing to do." Harris is a "tireless campaigner" who is "smart and articulate," Yukimura says. The boyish-looking Harris "uses conflict to his advantage," she says. *"Sometimes he wanted to be involved in controversy because it helped make the issues very clear. He ended up being elected as a mechanism for change and didn't work with a lot of arrogance."*[113] (Emphasis added.)

For Jeremy, the tireless campaigner wasn't just an image; it was true. I thought Governors Burns and Ariyoshi were hard campaigners. Jeremy was on steroids. You'd get tired just listening to him. But you appreciated his campaign acumen. It was both a joy and a pain at times, because he knew more about it than most. Add to that his intelligence and articulateness, and he was unstoppable—or at least appeared to be. By way of illustration, here's another *Star-Bulletin* excerpt from Tim Ryan:

> Harris, seeking another term as mayor against former City Council-

---

[113] Ibid.

man Mufi Hannemann and former mayor Frank Fasi, is described by current and former workers as "a hands-on manager," "micro-manager," "perfectionist," "easily convinced by the last person who grabs his attention" and "fanatic for detail." Several people who worked for or are currently employed by the city agreed to talk about Harris only if their names were not published. City workers say they would be reprimanded even if they spoke in support of the mayor. People who have worked with Harris on other projects say they fear reprisals to friends or family members working for the city. Several years ago when he was working on a Fasi campaign, Harris was in charge of setting up sign waving along a section of Nimitz Highway. According to a fellow campaign worker, Harris staged a rehearsal, sending sign holders out well before pau hana traffic began. "Then Jeremy drove around the block several times in 5-miles-per-hour increments until he decided how far apart sign holders should be spaced," this campaign worker says. "He drives everybody nuts with his micro-managing and burns a lot of people out."[114]

Whatever he did, though, earned him public support. Jeremy was always focused on accomplishments, and whatever it took to make them happen:

"I am a perfectionist," he says. "I strive to get it right; you have to take care of the details if you want the end product to be good... I can't stand it when people don't take pride in their work, or when politics interferes with a goal..."[115]

You had to give the man his due; he was a productive mayor in the Frank Fasi tradition. He got it done. His constant desire to get things done contributed to this visceral reaction to him. But there were detractors, notably his successor, Mufi Hanneman, and his former boss, Frank Fasi, who criticized the ways in which he accomplished his goals.

One of Jeremy's most memorable campaign-related liabilities was the allegation that he was involved in a "pay-to-play" scheme of awarding

---

[114] Ibid.

[115] Tim Ryan, "Goal-oriented 'perfectionist,'" *Honolulu Star-Bulletin*, September 19, 2000.

contracts to major donors. The *Star-Bulletin* listed the details in its June 14, 2001, edition:

> Honolulu Mayor Jeremy Harris has raised nearly $750,000 in political contributions from people linked to companies that have received business from the city, including waitresses and a Maryknoll School student who donated thousands of dollars each. Since 1996, the Harris campaign has collected $748,837 from individuals connected to dozens of local construction companies, engineers, architects and law firms that were awarded substantial city contracts, according to a computer-assisted examination by the Star-Bulletin. The amount is more than a quarter of the $2.98 million that the Harris campaign raised between 1996 and 2000. During the same span, the companies received more than $200 million in city work, which ranged from simple playground repairs to the consulting contract for the $300 million expansion of the Sand Island Wastewater Treatment Plant."[116]

Both managing director Ben Lee and Peter Char, representing the campaign, denied there was any pay-to-play scheme. Peter specifically denied the charge: "We approach anybody who is willing to give a contribution. Do we specifically target somebody? No."[117]

But once the allegation by the *Bulletin* was made, the environment became toxic, campaign-wise. People began to question whether Jeremy was in fact honest, or whether he was indeed engaged in campaign spending violations.[118] Soon, the allegations were being portrayed as true.

---

[116] Rick Daysog, "Harris funds questionable," *Honolulu Star-Bulletin*, June 24, 2001. Rick and I had been close friends since the days I had represented Gannett Corp. in Hawai'i and he was reporter working for that company.

[117] Ibid.

[118] It's interesting to reflect on this phenomenon. During Fasi's long tenure, many people, myself included, believed he was less than honest, maybe even "crooked" (the Kukui Plaza scandals, for example). But most of the public overlooked this because Fasi "got it done." He was seen as the gadfly in the old-boy system, who helped keep the establishment politicians "honest." In Jeremy's case, though he appeared to fulfill the same function. He never had the same tacit support on the issue. Could it be he was just "respected" but not "liked?" Many respected Harris for getting things done, and some liked him personally as I did. But other people harbored an unstated, elemental dislike of him, which only needed the right catalyst to stir them up. Thus, I believe, the torrential downpour that occurred once the Harris campaign spending allegations began to flow.

Jeremy was being judged in the court of public opinion, not in a court of law, and the "prosecutor" was making bold public statements to influence the jury, the public at large. This would never have happened in a criminal case. But this wasn't a criminal case; rather, it was an attempt to convict Jeremy in the court of public opinion, to end his political career.

Consider this article in a January 15, 2002, article in the *Star-Bulletin*, in which reporter Rick Daysog wrote:

> Honolulu Mayor Jeremy Harris' 2000 campaign recklessly violated state campaign spending laws and should be the subject of a criminal investigation by the city prosecutor's office, the head of the state Campaign Spending Commission said. But an attorney for Harris said the charges are part of a plan by commission executive director Robert Watada to single out the mayor's campaign and besmirch its reputation with "innuendo-filled statements..." The complaint did not provide specifics on the alleged campaign violations, but Watada, whose staffers and private investigators have interviewed scores of contributors under subpoena during the past six months, said that several people told the commission that they were listed as donating money to the Harris campaign when they did not. "Certain individuals, identified as contributors, reported that... they did not personally provide the funds for said contributions, had no knowledge of making contributions to Harris, or provided funds to other individuals for the purpose of making contributions to Harris,' the complaint said."[119]

I had never experienced such actions by governmental officials, save and except for Attorney General Ron Amemiya's bribery case against Frank Fasi in 1976 involving the Kukui Plaza project. When I joined the AG back in 1975, I had known little about it, except that there were allegations of bribery by the mayor and Harry C.C. Chung, Fasi's money man. Many people, especially Fasi, believed the investigation was politically motivated. But of course I believed, as a staunch Ariyoshi supporter, that Fasi was indeed crooked and there must be truth to the allegation—

or why would my boss, the AG, bring the action? Chalk it up to naïveté, or unbridled loyalty, but I believed this to be true. Now fast-forward a quarter-century, and history was repeating itself.

In a January 17, 2002, article in the *Advertiser*, reporter Johnny Brannon quoted Jeremy:

> "I do think I'm the victim of a massive smear campaign to hurt my gubernatorial race," Harris told *The Advertiser*. "I think a warning sign should go up around the state, that if they can treat these men of unquestioned integrity this way, anyone could be next. I am still running for governor. I have not dropped out, and I'm not dropping out."[120]

One could hardly fault Jeremy for thinking there was a vendetta. First there were the accusations by Russell Blair, a former senator and judge, who had taken Mayor Harris to court for not resigning when he began his run for governor. The resign-to-run law was aimed originally at Frank Fasi to strip him of his mayoral campaign and his position as mayor if he wanted to run against then-governor Ariyoshi. That law, which was politically motivated, was now being used to attack Jeremy as if there was some moral justification. In fact, it was and is a political sword. Blair lost.

State campaign spending director Watada sent boxes of materials to then-city prosecutor Peter Carlisle, who would neither confirm or deny that he was investigating Jeremy or the campaign. In the event nothing ever came of this, but contrary to Governor Cayetano's claim that if nothing happened Jeremy would be seen as a victim, such sympathy did not find itself at Jeremy's door. I had no knowledge about any of these allegations. I can only say that Peter Char was an honorable man, and when I spoke to Peter, he insisted there never was a *quid pro quo*. I believe him. I have no reason to question his statement. And those who know Peter feel the same way.

Some will say this was all eyewash, and that surely deals are struck behind the scenes. If any were, I was not aware of them. No one came to me to ask for special dispensation. Nor did I ask the mayor for any dispensation for anyone so accused. Nevertheless, I was subpoenaed by city prosecutor Peter Carlisle to appear before the Honolulu grand jury.

---

120 Johnny Brannon, "Mayor calls criminal probe 'massive smear campaign,'" *Honolulu Advertiser*.

If anything will get your attention, it is being subpoenaed in a criminal case. I never did appear, and nothing ever happened, but I still wouldn't wish such an experience on anyone. Essentially, my counsel told the prosecutor's office that I knew nothing—the "Schultz" defense. In the end, nothing came of this except, I believe, that the attacks began to wear on Jeremy. And it showed how far the powers arrayed against him would go.[121]

The lessons here are not to avoid getting involved in a campaign. Nor are they about the character of your candidate. Rather, it is to expect the unexpected, to realize that the forces opposed to your candidate may come after you as well. And even if you're doing everything by the book, if those forces are determined to bring you down, there is nothing to limit what they will do, including damaging your candidate's reputation and the reputation of others. In this case, I believe that Peter Char's reputation was besmirched. But despite the allegations, he remained above the fray, not because he was putting on a show, but because the campaign did nothing wrong.

Standing with Peter, Lynette, Don, Chris, Ruth Ann Becker and Ben in the Harris campaign trenches made us comrades in arms. I trusted them unqualifiedly and without any doubts. I continue to do so today.

Peter Char's passing in 2003 was all the more difficult because of these events, which were still fresh in our memories. In many ways I lost a personal friend, one whom I hoped to be closer to, and he was taken away too soon for me. If I sound like a big fan of Peter, I am, unapologetically.

Jeremy Harris ultimately decided not to run for governor in 2002. The animosity against him contributed to this decision, I believe. On the day before his scheduled appearance at the state Democratic Party Convention, Peter, Lynette, Ben and I, among others, were with him. We huddled together, we talked, we shared our viewpoints. I told Jeremy I had never been in a gubernatorial race where my candidate was ahead. It was always the other way around. I recall urging him to continue the fight. I reminded him that he could win, despite all the negative stuff. The others also shared their positive views about his chances. But I had

---

[121] Anecdotally, there's a certain sense of irony in all of this. Ron Amemiya's nephew, Roy Amemiya, currently Mayor Kirk Caldwell's managing director, was Jeremy's budget chief. I was a former deputy AG when Ron was AG and prosecuting Fasi's Kukui Plaza case. And now we were the ones being prosecuted.

a gnawing sense that he was going to pull out. It wasn't that he said anything, it was the way he acted—more subdued, more contemplative. He left with Ramona for their hotel room. We would have to wait until the following morning to hear his decision. I thought it was fifty-fifty whether he would stay in or drop out.

Early the next morning we all gathered together before the convention reconvened, and Jeremy told us he had decided not to continue the campaign. My heart sank. Here was a man who had borne the brunt of all these personal attacks for so long. He seemed broken—not in spirit, but in his feelings for the rest of us who campaigned with him. He knew that the allegations would continue, and that when he wouldn't bend, they would start upon all the rest of the campaign team. I believe Jeremy's decision was more about the rest of us than about himself. I never asked him why; in many ways that answer was inconsequential. I can say that was a tough moment for me, maybe even more difficult than losing John Craven's campaign.

Vision is always 20-20 in hindsight, of course, but to this day I wonder whether those who wanted to stop Jeremy fully grasped the result: It sent the local Democratic Party into disarray. But those who just didn't want Jeremy ultimately got their way.

And clearly, this was quite an assortment of people. Once I had encouraged him to establish a relationship with Al Gore, who at the time was the Democratic presidential candidate. Through various connections I had with the Gore campaign, I arranged for Jeremy to meet the chief campaign official in Washington, D.C. We traveled there together. We met with the official, and Jeremy committed to raising funds for Gore in Hawai'i. But upon our return, we were met with a firestorm of protestations. Alex Santiago, Hawai'i's Democratic Party chair, and Walter Heen were particularly upset that we had done this. Although civil, they were not happy that I had arranged the meeting, or that Jeremy had agreed to raise money and send it directly to Al Gore's campaign headquarters. The essence of the conversation was that the Democratic Party of Hawai'i wouldn't receive credit for raising that money.

I was so disappointed in Alex and Walt. I had thought more of them. It was clear to me, both in words and tone, that this was about Jeremy—that they wanted to discourage Jeremy and his campaign from helping Gore, except under their direction. I knew then the depth of their feelings toward Jeremy. I hadn't really experienced it before, but it gave me pause to reflect on all the years of campaigning—on Bob Oshiro's lessons, on Joe Napolitan's advice. Was politics all about power and control, or was there a higher calling? Of course, it should be the latter, so with no disrespect to Alex and Walt, I plowed ahead with our agreement with the Gore campaign. Hawai'i would be a better place, I reasoned, if Jeremy—who then had a chance to be our next governor—could maintain this personal connection to the White House. It was the right time to take a stand.

In hindsight, I believe Jeremy's decision not to run was the worst thing to happen to the local Democratic Party. It's a decision that still echoes today in our political psyche. Here's what *The New York Times* had to say:

> Democratic hopes for extending a 40-year grip on the Hawai'i governor's office have been dealt a major setback. The party's leading candidate in this year's contest, Mayor Jeremy Harris of Honolulu, unexpectedly pulled out late on Thursday, saying that "a year of bad publicity," including unsubstantiated accusations of corruption, had cost him at least 30 points in the polls. "I simply don't believe the race is winnable," he added. "But I do believe this is one of the most important races in the history of the state." ... Accusations of corruption are an old story in Hawaii politics. But it was Mr. Harris's lot to have the headlines, mainly involving the jailing of Honolulu employees and officials, appear just as he was beginning his campaign for governor. His name came up directly only once, when an investigation was begun to determine whether workers in his 1996 and 2000 campaigns for mayor had mishandled funds. He denied any wrongdoing and contended that the investigation was politically motivated. Mr. Harris said on Thursday that he had been hurt by a politically motivated lawsuit that caused him to suspend campaigning for two months early this year while it was being tried. The suit contended that under Hawaii law, a mayor must resign from office to run for another elective job in the state. The State Supreme Court held that since Mr. Harris was not officially a candidate at the time the suit was filed, the law did not apply.[122]

---

[122] B. Drummond Ayres Jr., "Top Democrat For Governor Of Hawaii Withdraws," *The New York Times*, May 31, 2002.

On the local level, meanwhile, while I don't always agree with *Star-Advertiser* writer Dave Shapiro, he got it right when he outlined the efforts Jeremy's opponents would take to keep him out of office. His was a lonely voice in a sea of opposition:

> You'd think Jeremy Harris' status as Honolulu mayor was settled when the state Supreme Court ruled that Harris needn't step down to run for governor until he files nomination papers by July 23. But some opponents continue to demand that he resign immediately— and suggest he's somehow unethical for following the same interpretation of the resign-to-run law that has guided other officials for nearly 25 years. Enough, already. This bogus issue has distracted the 2002 campaign for governor for too long. Let's steer the debate back to issues that matter—education, the economy and the proper role of our state government. For 24 years since Hawaiʻi's resign-to-run provision was enacted, officials making midterm runs for higher office stepped down when they officially filed nomination papers for the new office.[123] Nobody squawked.[124]

Shapiro's comments belied the fact that Mazie Hirono's on-again off-again run for governor and mayor—depending on what Jeremy decided—made her appear indecisive. Ed Case was even less the darling of the old guard, as would become evident in a few years. D.G. "Andy" Anderson was now running as a Democrat despite being Frank Fasi's managing director when he was a Republican. Andy's credentials as a Democrat were as deep as your epidermis. None had the machinery or the money that Jeremy had. In effect, the Democrats were going to be a day late and a dollar short. Mike Tokunaga's words in 1998 were prescient: "If you look at the history of the Democratic Party, I think it's coming to the end of the rule. Not so much in the House and the Senate, but the major positions." Mike was right.

Dave Shapiro, in his "Volcanic Ash" column in the *Advertiser* on June 5,

---

[123] This was always called the "Fasi rule" because it only dealt with Frank Fasi's constant attempts to be governor. The mayor was always out of sequence—that is, the mayor's term was always two years off from the governor's term. Therefore, a Honolulu mayor would always be in a midterm election for governor, if he or she chose to run.

[124] David Shapiro, "Get off Jeremy Harris' back," *Honolulu Advertiser*, May 15, 2002.

2002, observed that the "Democrats [were] lacking a 'titan.'" Dave again was right. But no one was really surprised that Mazie won the primary race. She was the only real Democrat from the old school. In the *Hawai'i Reporter*, writer Malia Zimmermann mused:

> What should voters expect next? An unexpected endorsement by the politically powerful Democrats at their convention this weekend… It won't be Mazie Hirono—she's a woman and she didn't have the support to pull it off. So who will the gubernatorial candidate of choice be for the old political boys? Names that have been floated: US Congressman Neil Abercrombie, former governor John Waihee, powerful Banker and Democratic Political Strategist Walter Dods.[125]

Well, Mazie did run, against Ed Case. She won that primary but then lost the general to Linda Lingle. Many thought that Mazie's wish-washy decision to run for governor, then mayor, then governor hurt her. It did, but I believe the party's actions towards Jeremy, and the efforts of the old guard to get Jeremy out, did far more damage. In practical parlance it was, in effect, *we don't want non-locals*, a theme that would permeate future elections. It was the antithesis of all that I had learned from the Burns and Ariyoshi campaigns. In those campaigns the ethic was Confucian—the best man or woman for the job. But was that so much eyewash? Were these elections only covering an innate discrimination? Would our better angels be forthcoming, or would we be awash in the seas of an earlier time, when your skin color or national origin mattered more than your ability to do the job? I believe this election cycle was the first step in Mike Tokunaga's prediction.

In any event, Jeremy Harris didn't run, Al Gore lost, Linda Lingle beat Mazie Hirono—and all the drama and trauma was swept under the proverbial rug. But in politics, you never forget. You forgive, but you always keep the memory of those lessons learned, some good, some bad. For the local Democratic Party, the trials and tribulations would leave a bad taste and taint the 2002 election.

---

[125] Malia Zimmerman, "Someone Got to Harris (Dem Mayor unexpectedly drops out of Hawaii Governor Race)," *Hawaii Reporter*, May 31, 2002.

Was the toppling of Jeremy worth the election of a GOP governor? I believe many had buyer's remorse after the general election. Maybe even before. Jeremy had been able to draw together the various factions and ethnic voting groups under one roof. But he was not beholden to the old guard in the Democratic power structure. They only acknowledged him because they had to, not because they wanted to. Jeremy had butted heads with too many of these old pols too many times in the past. They wanted him out. In the end, I wondered after Lingle won whether they had any remorse. I knew I had supported the right guy. And I believe the disgust of the public about the way Jeremy was treated, the accusations, which were made out to be true, said more about the powers-that-be than about Jeremy. Ask anyone and they'll tell you they think politicians are corrupt. To most lay people, the phrase "honest politician" is an oxymoron. Those who destroyed Jeremy laid the seeds of the party's defeat and Lingle's rise. The famous *Pogo* cartoon quote, "We have met the enemy and he is us," rings true.

John M. Broder, writing in *The New York Times*, October 19, 2002, edition, observed:

> "The Democratic Party is imploding," said Ira Rohter, a professor of political science at the University of Hawai'i at Manoa. "Right now, there is no Democratic Party here, just a lot of feuding factions. It's like watching a Three Stooges skit."[126]

The year 2002 was memorable as the end of Democratic rule in the governor's office, and the beginning of a walk in the wilderness for the party, as it was left without a titular head, who for many years had been the governor. It now lost the "rudder" it had had from the time of Jack Burns. Now it was a voyage into uncharted waters with uncertain currents, made even murkier by battles fought, not between Democrats and Republicans, but by "warlords" within the Democratic Party. It reminded me of China during its time of warring states, or the wars in Japan before Tokugawa unified the country. Democrats began looking for a way to undo what had happened, and they quickly began looking for a new candidate.

---

[126] John M. Broder, "THE 2002 CAMPAIGN: THE DEMOCRATS; Hawaii Democrats Reeling After Scandals and a Death," *The New York Times*, October 19, 2002.

Jeremy's political ambitions were still newsworthy three years later, as Democrats were still trying to field an election opponent for Governor Lingle. I believe it was part of the public's buyer's remorse after several years of GOP reign. I talked to *Advertiser* reporter Johnny Brannon for an article that appeared in the paper's January 2, 2005, edition:

> Party veteran B. Rick Tsujimura has been on both sides of Harris. As an attorney for a major Kaua'i property owner, Tsujimura campaigned against Harris when he ran unsuccessfully to be the Garden Isle's mayor in 1984, and opposed him again in a later race for Honolulu mayor. Tsujimura said he later became impressed by Harris' drive and determination to get things done. By 2002, he was the co-chairman of Harris' campaign for governor. It's true that some of the party's old guard never took to Harris, but the reasons are varied and it's not easy to gauge how deep the resistance was, Tsujimura said. "He wasn't in the old-boy network, and I think a lot of people viewed my working with him as an oddity, because if anything I knew all those old boys," Tsujimura said. "And I told them I'm supporting Jeremy because I think he's the way the future's going to be." Harris enjoyed strong support amid many old-style Democrats, but he rubbed others wrong with his headstrong personality, Tsujimura said... "This is a town where memories take a long time to go away, and sometimes it's generational," he said. "Political guys don't forget." After the past three years of controversy surrounding the campaign donation investigation, it seems unlikely that Harris will make a political comeback, Tsujimura said. "With this cloud hanging over things, I don't think so," he said. "But that's not to say he's out for the count forever. It's always possible to return. But why would Jeremy Harris want to come back? Is there a challenge that would bring him back? Maybe. I can't imagine him getting back into a political scene, at least not in the foreseeable future."

I still believe that Jeremy would have been a great governor, but why would he endure the scathing attacks leveled at him before? If anything, he was a smart man, and smart men don't do the same thing and expect a different result. As Einstein put it, that is insanity. Jeremy did not run in 2006; but an unlikely candidate and friend did. ❧

CHAPTER FIFTEEN

Randy Iwase: Ganbatte

❧

"You say you want a revolution
Well, you know
We all want to change the world
You tell me that it's evolution
Well, you know
We all want to change the world"

—The Beatles, "Revolution"

He came to tell me he had decided to run for governor. Would I help him? I replied that twenty-five years of friendship has got to count for something, so I said yes. The year was 2005. The friend was Randy Iwase.

After three years of a GOP governor, Democrats were searching for a candidate to take her on. The Demos had suffered a heavy blow in 2002. In many respects it was a catharsis that led to deep introspection for many of us. In my mind Linda Lingle's election owed much to the Democratic legacy. Had the GOP not been overthrown back in the 1950s, the notion of a female governor, let alone one of Jewish heritage, would be a pipe-dream. Lingle owed much to the governors and campaigns that preceded her. Rather than being an aberration, she represented the normal progression in our evolution as a society. This isn't to say that her programs were a straight line permutation of the Democratic tradition—far from it. By 2005 she had certainly established her credentials with many people, including marginal Democrats. The question was whether she was vulnerable politically, to the point at which a Democrat could run against her.

"I remember calling around to better-known people," Randy recalled, "and urging them to run against Lingle, but without success. What concerned me was leaving an open race for governor. Our party couldn't just concede the top office to the Republican incumbent. It didn't seem right. To simply concede without a whimper would dishonor our legacy—all the work and effort and sacrifice of those who were successful in the elections of the Democratic governors elected since Burns. Democrats now seemed willing to surrender the battlefield—on initiatives that sought to open our society, to provide fairness and opportunity to all, to take care of those in need.

"Moreover, I disagreed with her policies and her aim to run a show horse, rather than a workhorse. Other than her contention that the 'old boys' network was no good, she offered no vision, no hopeful initiatives to lay the foundations for our future, no plans to leave Hawai'i a better place for the next generation—all the things that prior generations had given to us."

KHNL reported on Randy's announcement of his run for governor in this way:

> Six years ago, Randy Iwase closed his campaign fund and gave Kaimuki High School $1,000 to repair damage left by thieves. Friday, the former state senator returned to his alma mater to announce his plan to resume a political career. A Democrat, Iwase said he wants to build more affordable housing, support public education and improve Hawai'i's economy. He is the first Democrat to publicly announce a candidacy for governor. "I believe that government must act. I believe that government is a force for justice," Iwase said. He accused Governor Linda Lingle of being more concerned with public relations than public policy. "As the gap between the cost to buy even a modest home and the salaries paid to us to buy that home grows, all we've gotten from the Republican incumbent is flavor of the month issues and slick public relation announcements," Iwase said.[127]

This was a really tiny election core. Randy had some loyal and hardworking friends, but this wasn't a big-name team. There was no money for polling and consultants, no widespread support from community

---

[127] "Randy Iwase Announces His Run For Governor," Hawaii News Now, http://www.hawaii newsnow.com/story/4422737/randy-iwase-announces-his-run-for-governor.

organizations, although his union friends were there from the start. It was all about relationships. If I seem to overuse that word, the fact is that it's a universal truth in campaigning: It's all about relationships. Bob Oshiro's test of availability, loyalty, trust and commitment are the keys to successful campaigning. Had Randy asked me if he should run, I would probably have advised him to keep his day job. But that wasn't his question. His question was, "Would you help me?" When a longtime friend asks—someone with whom you shared a daily ride from Mililani to town for years, who ate lunch with you nearly every day, whose family gets together with yours on weekends—how can you say no? Relationships count.

So on that day in 2006 at Kaimuki High, his close friends gathered to usher this lesser-known candidate into the battle of his life. And I mean close. Neil Abercrombie, the quintessential Democrat (though some would dispute this), was there to support Randy, but noticeably absent were the candidates and governors that Randy had helped over the decades. You'd think his sacrifice would be worth something to them, but no sitting politician appeared except for Neil. It wasn't an extraordinary crowd; in fact, it was a small gathering.

Honolulu Star-Bulletin reporter Richard Borreca wrote:

> Iwase, 58, is the first major Democrat to announce his candidacy. His announcement drew the immediate approval of party Chairman Brickwood Galuteria, who attended the news conference… "I believe that a governor must act to help our people. I believe that it is not enough just to take a stand. The governor must act to make things work. This is not the guiding light for the Republican incumbent," Iwase said… He also acknowledged that his campaign will not have anything close to the $6 million that Lingle estimates she will raise for her campaign. "We will rely on the grass roots," said Iwase, who served for 10 years in the state Senate and four years on the Honolulu City Council.[128]

Randy and I have a relationship that dates back to 1975. Our professional lives were literally in sync for the first five years of my career,

---

[128] Richard Borreca, "Iwase enters race to challenge Lingle," *Honolulu Star-Bulletin*, January 28, 2006.

and we drew close in those early days, sharing our views and discussions about political philosophy. Randy was a Jeffersonian and I a Hamiltonian. Along with a small group of others at the AG's, we did trial prep together. We also worked the political scene together. We shared a passion for public service. Randy would continue on at the state and city level. I went on to business and finally self-employment.

We became closer after Randy married Jan, and Ruth and I moved to Mililani and started our families. We'd have weekend dinners and barbecues. I got to know Randy in more than a professional way.

It came as a shock to me when he decided to run for City Council, but he quickly exhibited his talents and became the Council's finance and budget committee chair. He challenged Mayor Frank Fasi on a number of issues, most notably his vision for the Waiola District Park, which was contrary to Castle & Cooke's plan for a residential community.

"Frank wanted to put in about 1,600 housing units," Randy recalled. "It was the time when we were taking action to direct growth to 'Ewa, and this directed growth was set forth in two plans, one by the Department of Planning and the other, I believe, by the Office of Council Services. The Council moved to implement the plans by denying, in that year, a request to increase the General Plan population that would allow for more housing. The Fasi Administration proposed the project, and I opposed it. First, central O'ahu was filled with proposed housing projects to the detriment of the 'Ewa directed growth plans. Second, we were in the midst of implementing that plan by not approving the increase in the General Plan population cap for central O'ahu. The increase would have allowed for more housing projects. To be consistent, the Waiola project should not move forward. I remember several labor unions organizing opposition to our denial of the GP increase. They brought trucks and paraded around the City Hall block in protest. I lost the Council vote to disapprove Waiola—I believe by a vote of 5 to 4. But it then went to the Land Use Commission, where I expressed my opposition. Thankfully, the project was not allowed to proceed. Several months later, the Fasi Administration tried again. But the project didn't move forward because the City failed to meet the conditions set by the Land Use Commission.

"While I was no longer on the Council, I organized a petition drive to create a Waiola Regional Park encompassing the 270 acres. We submitted the petition with over 2,000 signatures to the LUC. While in the

State Senate, I got planning funds to develop Waiola. We sent the plans to the City. Thankfully, it caught the attention and support of Mayor Harris. He negotiated a land exchange with Castle & Cooke and today we have the Central Oahu Regional Park—a beautiful, well-used park amid a sea of houses."

Randy exhibited his commitment to a vision and a cause. He knew that the west side community deserved a district park equal to any in town, such as Kapi'olani Park or Ala Moana Beach Park. He stuck to his guns, and we are all the more fortunate that he did. If he hadn't, that park would be a tract of houses today. His concern wasn't just for more park space. During this time, in the mid-1980s, there was great demand for affordable housing. Most of this housing was being developed in central O'ahu, which further exacerbated traffic flow from the central/leeward region. There was also the necessity of preserving prime agricultural lands.

"There was the need for some semblance of planning," Randy recalled. "That's when my researcher, Brian Suzuki, found the two City studies—the one by Planning and the other by the Office of Council Services—and passed them on to me. I agreed with the conclusions and set out to push the Second City Plan, which addressed the housing issue, provided a growth plan to preserve more prime ag land, and addressed growing traffic congestion at the Waiawa interchange. If people could live *and* work in 'Ewa, we could reduce the amount of cars going into Honolulu. I talked to the state transportation director, who believed there was need for a seventeen-lane highway to accommodate the number of cars from future developments. There was, and still is, no easy solution. But the Second City Plan seemed like a sound plan to me back then. It still is, provided that 'Ewa is *not* merely a suburb. Job centers are needed as well."

If Randy's running for Council was a shock; it was an even bigger one when he decided he was going to run for mayor against Patsy Mink, Marilyn Bornhorst, Dennis O'Connor and the incumbent Frank Fasi. Randy didn't ask if he should run, he just decided to run. He came asking for kōkua, and as a longtime friend he deserved that, at a minimum. Ben Kudo ran his small campaign. It was a shoestring campaign. We didn't have money and had an even smaller organization, but Ben did his best. He was always good at analyzing numbers and strategy. But this effort needed more and we all knew it. We did have one shining moment in that campaign—the "swish" bumper stickers that someone designed.

They were done in a fluorescent aqua blue or striking pink with IWASE emblazoned on the front, and they went like hotcakes. We couldn't figure out where they were going, because we didn't see any on cars. Then we discovered the surfing crowd really liked the colors and were sticking them on their boards. School kids liked them too, and they were appearing on their notebook covers. Had kids been able to vote, we'd have won. One sidelight to this was that the pink and blue faded fast. The residue was a black Iwase swatch that stood out. In any event, Randy didn't win but he did beat a longtime acquaintance, Dennis O'Connor.

"In the Democratic primary," Randy recalled, "it was me, Dennis, Marilyn Bornhorst and Patsy Mink. Dennis came in last; I came in third."

After this run for mayor, Randy signed on with the Aloha Tower Development Corporation. But he couldn't give up the urge for elective politics and so got himself elected to the state senate. It was fortuitous for me because at the same time I was moving into lobbying as a full-time job. Thanks to Randy and Senator Donna Ikeda, I obtained my first client, State Farm Insurance Companies, which I continue to represent more than twenty-five years later.

Randy was part of a legislative faction that included Milton Holt, Donna Ikeda, Jimmie Aki, Malama Solomon, Marshall Ige, Norman Sakamoto, Joe Tanaka, Bobby Bunda and the two GOP senators, Whitney Anderson and Sam Slom. They were in control for a while until Aki got into political trouble and lost to Colleen Hanabusa. That left Randy out of the majority faction in the senate. But he was a leader in this "dissident" group.

My most memorable recollection of that time was Randy's bill on Native Hawaiian access rights. His bill enraged Hawaiian activists, who came to the capitol to "drum" him. One drum was so enormous that I couldn't believe they got it into the capitol rotunda. I was with Randy in his office. Malama Solomon and Randy went down to the rotunda and Malama tore up the bill, in a symbolic gesture to signify that it was dead. It took courage for them to do that in the face of such opposition. It was like Daniel entering into the lions' den. One has to admire that kind of courage, more so today, when a tweet or a press release will suffice. Here's how Randy remembers it.

"It was a twenty-four-hour vigil," Randy recounted. "Given the strong reaction in opposition to the bill, as evidenced by the vigil, I was concerned about the impact it might have on Malama and Whitney, who were both Hawaiian and had co-signed the bill. The morning after the start of the vigil, Malama and I spoke. We agreed that it was best to hold the bill, allow tempers to cool, and then try to address the question at another time and be more inclusive in searching for a solution. Malama felt that more than words were needed. Emotions were running high. There had to be a symbolic, physical end to the bill.

"So we agreed that it was best for her to go alone and announce that the bill would not move forward. She went down to speak to the crowd in the rotunda. They were giving her a hard time, making it difficult for her to speak. I was watching from the second floor. This was a bill I had initiated and I didn't want Malama to take all that grief alone. So I went down to stand with her—probably a mistake given the anger directed at me personally—but I had to do it. She announced the bill was dead and tore up the bill."

Randy was never seen as a show horse by his colleagues. He was always the "thinker"—the person who analyzed and worked through an issue and came up with the rationale. That was his forte and he had done that well at the AG's, then the council and the senate. But now he was running for the state's highest office.

Here's how *Star-Bulletin* reporter Mary Vorsino described Randy back then:

> At the start of his political career in the early 1980s, Randy Iwase was known as feisty and outspoken. He got onto the City Council with a special election and, after only 10 months, in the 1986 election, was running with the confidence of a veteran incumbent. One *Star-Bulletin* article on his City Council re-election called Iwase, whose seat extended from Waipahu to Kahuku, "abrupt, energetic and sometimes combative..." But when Iwase got into the state Senate in 1990, he mellowed, quieted and started to think before he spoke, former colleagues said. He took a public lead on few issues, rarely stepping into the spotlight. ...Iwase is known, perhaps thanks to his roots as an attorney, for thinking long and hard before he speaks.[129]

---

[129] Mary Vorsino, "Iwase known for quiet thoughtfulness," *Honolulu Star-Bulletin*, January 30, 2006.

So what compels a man to give up a good, steady paycheck to become a candidate against a juggernaut incumbent? Randy wondered about that too.

"As I spoke to people," he recalled, "some of them—only a few, I must confess—thought I should run. Me? A relatively unknown former state senator with a good job and a ten-year appointment [by Governor Ben Cayetano in 2000] to chair of the Labor Appeals Board. Moreover, being in politics was very tough on my family, both personally and financially. I had a decent paying job, and I was at home at a decent hour. My family didn't have to deal with harsh public criticism of a family member. *We were normal!* However, as I talked to people it soon became very evident that major Democratic figures weren't interested in taking on a popular GOP incumbent, whose approval numbers I believe were in the sixty-percent range. I felt that if no one wanted to run, I'd be a hypocrite not to consider entering the race, after giving my speech to other people, urging them to run. It wasn't something I really wanted to do. Having been involved in a number of campaigns, including Governor Ariyoshi's and my own, I knew it would be tough at best, and unwinnable if everything did not fall perfectly into place. After six years out of office, I was a virtual unknown. It would be difficult, at best, to get the financing needed to 1) get the voters to know me so that 2) they could determine if the liked me so that 3) I'd have the chance to garner their trust so that 4) they'd be willing to vote for me.

"I knew it was a huge decision. Moreover, in those six years out of office, I had come to understand that my family *must be first in my life.* They had sacrificed so much for me when I was in office. It was just wrong and unfair to make a unilateral decision. So, really for the very first time in my political career, I asked everyone—Jan and our three boys—for their thoughts. Jan's was the most important; she had sacrificed the most and was early in her dream career as a school administrator. Everyone needs to have dreams and goals, and I definitely did not want to disrupt her journey. But everyone said yes. What was so important to me was that my boys and Jan believed that I was qualified and would do good for our people and our state."

Randy's raison d'etre for running is best summarized in his announcement, which I believe still has relevance today: "Leadership is not just about one's own skills, it's also about the ability to bring out and utilize the strengths and talents of others... Our administration will be one of innovation, inclusion and openness... Traveling around the state, I have come to appreciate more fully the challenges, opportunities and vitality with which we approach living in Hawaiʻi. This election is about believing in ourselves, believing in each other, and believing that together, we can achieve anything upon which we set our hearts and minds."[130]

Despite his great and good intentions, Randy was an unknown. To political insiders he had a reputation and widespread recognition, but to the general public, he was the ship that passes in the dark. You need money to build recognition, and we didn't have money or access to such money. Lingle had the benefit of incumbency and name recognition. The difference in positions was staggering. In the *Advertiser*, Kevin Dayton wrote:

> Despite his political experience, Iwase is not well known, in part because he hasn't held elected office in six years. A poll by The Advertiser in June found 63 percent of the voters didn't know enough about Iwase to say whether they liked him. Relatively unknown candidates can rise to prominence during a campaign, but that usually requires money, and Iwase doesn't have much. According to his most recent campaign filing report, he had less than $17,000 on hand. By comparison, Lingle had $3.3 million on hand at the end of June to finance her re-election bid, and The Advertiser's June poll had Lingle leading Iwase by nearly 47 percentage points. And before Iwase can even face Lingle, he must prevail in a primary contest with Democrats William Aila Jr. and Van Tanabe.[131]

We had to use whatever we had, and use it to the max. I took the required classes to be a producer and place our promotional programming snippets on ʻOlelo community TV. The Internet was not yet accessible for campaign use as it would be just two years later. We used ʻOlelo for the "broadcast" part of our campaign, as little as that was.

---

130 Randall Iwase, "Randy Iwase Formally Files for Office of Governor," Votesmart, https://votesmart.org/public-statement/204192/randy-iwase-formally-files-for-office-of-governor.

131 Kevin Dayton, "Iwase says he entered governor's race to win," *The Honolulu Advertiser*, September 12, 2006.

I also cobbled together a video from family photos for the Democratic convention that year. Several stand out. A photo of Randy dressed in cowboy gear when he was ten or eleven was like those taken of many boys in our generation. But the one with a rocket, taken when he was at Kaimuki High School, was part of our generational psyche. It was the dream of space exploration and President Kennedy's goal to reach the moon. Randy and I, like many of us who grew up in the years following World War II, had aspirations of a better world—a world of Star Trek in which conflicts could always be somehow resolved. There was a shared sense of optimism.

But much of this was destroyed with the assassinations of John and Robert Kennedy and Martin Luther King Jr., when the safety and security of the 1950s collided with the shock of losing great leaders. Optimism for me gave way to a sense that one could never depend on what we were born into. Life was now unpredictable. Randy was engaged with space, and I believe that was one of the reasons he went to the University of Florida, after high school, but returned to matriculate at the University of Hawai'i.

According to Randy, he went to UH first, got bored, dropped out and went to work. Within a year he realized he needed a degree and his parents were so very supportive—told him they'd pay for the education. He went to the University of Florida, in part because Cape Canaveral was there, but also because it was on a quarter system, not semester, and he would get his bachelor's degree earlier—he had to catch up after being out of school for about a year. Finally, Florida was so far away; back then it was like going to another country. He needed to go away and grow up.

Randy never really had a relationship with his biological father, but he cherished his stepfather, Bruce Hamada. There was a genuine love there. His stepfather didn't treat Randy any different than his brother, Bruce Jr., and his sisters. And Bruce was a gem. His musical talents brought the family in touch with many of the musical greats in Hawai'i, including Rene Paulo, Jimmy Borges and others. Bruce was a musician with the Royal Hawaiian Band. His brother was an accomplished jazz musician. Randy, well, he could plunk a tune, but he wouldn't and couldn't give up his day job to be a musician. Randy's family and Jan's family were formidable assets.

Jan's dad, Keiji, was a well-known community leader in the Wahiawā-Mililani area. His story was the stuff we AJAs treasure. The eldest sacrificed his own education to have his brothers go to school. But Keiji was no slouch, he was not only extremely intelligent, he had a personality that one could only like. Ruth and I were fortunate to be a part of the family, and to be embraced by their fellowship. He and Jan's mom, Vivian, are treasures.

Another key person in all of this was Charlotte Nekota. Char has and always has been a real gem for campaigns. Not only is she a workaholic, she's a "do-aholic." She not only ran Randy's campaigns for the senate, she did almost all the work, including having meetings at her house and cooking the food. Many know Char from her current work at the Hawai'i Optometric Association, but when I first met her some twenty-five years ago, she was the boss of the Randy Iwase senate office. Her vivaciousness and personal touch helped Randy more than he probably knew. And she was a staunch defender of her boss. Like a mother defending her child, she never let people get to Randy unbidden.

But she also had a playful side. Once Char, staffer Herman Andaya (now working for Mayor Alan Arakawa of Maui), Mario Ramil (then a Hawai'i Supreme Court justice) and other colleagues came up with an April fool joke. Herman doctored a letter from Randy insulting the candidate for Miss Filipina. The insulted girl came to Randy's office to complain. Randy was flustered to the gills, and didn't know what to say. We all went to the senate president's office in the old YMCA building, since the capitol was under renovation. There, senate president Norman Mizuguchi and colleague Milton Holt berated Randy for his *faux pas*. Even Mario got into the act, asking Randy what he was thinking. Charlotte was beside herself and couldn't contain her laughter. Eventually Randy was told it was an April fool joke. He was a great sport, but I can tell you we all eagerly awaited his gotcha moment.

We had the benefit of many friends who donated their time for to campaign. One such person was videographer Robert Pennybacker, who agreed to produce a thirty-minute film about Randy and why he should be elected. Robert didn't use the traditional big crews for the production, just a small digital camera with which he filmed Randy and Jan.

The resulting film was a real gem that proved you can do a first-class production with few but dedicated resources. It begins on Waikīkī's Hobron Lane, where Randy is telling Jan where he grew up. Randy recalls how his mom and dad divorced, how his mom worked hard to support him, and how he was hanai-ed to his grandmother in Hilo. The film makes clear at despite rocky start, Randy was and still is a man of great character. The film also takes us to the modest Date Street neighborhood behind Kaimuki High School, where his family moved from Waikīkī. One shot shows Randy speaking about President Kennedy: "Politics can be a noble profession. That politics can be a force for good. You can inspire people. With that kind of inspiration you can move things. You can make the changes." If you look carefully at screenshots of the film, you will see a bust of JFK, which I received from my mom, and which I gave to Randy because of his admiration for the late president.

I believe that Randy's philosophy is one reason he and I are such long-time friends. I stated earlier that relationships matter. When one shares a common philosophy, differences are transcended. He often jokes about my evangelical background, often calling me Zachariah, but we are close friends despite our differences. And maybe that is the real lesson to be learned in politics. It is easy to try and put numbers and outcomes together and make politics impersonal, but I believe the biggest rewards are not in winning, but in having these kinds of relationships that transcend winning and losing. Do I wish Randy had beaten Linda Lingle? Of course, but not just to defeat her. She isn't a bad person. It's just that we differ in our philosophy, and my opposition is not so much opposition as it is support for my friend Randy, who I believe was capable of bigger and better things.

In the end, Randy's valiant effort was not enough. Despite all the heart he brought to the race, the power of the incumbent, the shortage of funding, the unwilling colleagues who couldn't get behind his cause and the political intrigue were all insurmountable. In the October 29, 2006, edition of the *Star-Bulletin*, writer Diana Leone reported:

Political observer Dan Boylan calls the election contest between Randy Iwase and Gov. Linda Lingle "a David-and-Goliath attempt." Although Iwase "was a fine state senator," he has been out of political office for six years and was not the Democratic Party's first choice to challenge the popular Republican incumbent, Boylan noted. Iwase, 58, "sort of came out of the blue to do service, and he will do it well. He's a passionate fellow and a smart fellow," Boylan said. "My guess is he will not embarrass himself..." Yet in Lingle, Iwase faces "probably the best-skilled person at getting across her message to the public and the media since statehood," Boylan said... "Lingle is not playing it like a runaway race," [Don] Clegg said. "It's the politician that takes it for granted that loses."[132]

Lingle's win four years earlier had been the result of Hirono's inability to get Ed Case's voters to go her way. A cursory look at the 2002 gubernatorial votes show more votes cast in the Democratic primary than for the Democratic candidate in the general. Just where those votes bled from is a good question. I was privy to some polling data in 2002, assisting LG candidate Matt Matsunaga. It was clear from the data I saw that the Hirono-Matsunaga team was bleeding AJAs. Why that was happening is open to conjecture, but it was happening. If in 2006 those same AJAs stayed with the Democratic candidate, then we had a chance. The odds weren't great but there was a chance. In his thirty-minute film, Randy's wife, Jan, notes that he went away to come back home to make a difference. Likewise, his run for governor was about making a difference. And by doing so Randy provided another lesson for would-be politicians. Sacrifice sometimes is much more worthwhile if you want to make a difference. Why should a candidate run for office? Is it for power? Glory? Adulation? Or is it to make a difference?

Moreover, with Randy as a credible candidate, Lingle had to stay closer to home, rather than assist the GOP's legislative candidates. In this respect we succeeded in helping the Democrats curtail Lingle's ability to help other GOP candidates. One Democratic senatorial candidate who benefited was Senator Jill Tokuda, now Ways and Means chair in the senate.[133] Would a Bill Aila have done better? I don't know. All I can say

---

[132] Diana Leone, "Goliath faces honorable challenger," *Honolulu Star-Bulletin*, October 29, 2006.

[133] Gordon Y.K. Pang, "Many parallels in Windward race," *Honolulu Star-Bulletin, October 11, 2006.* "Call it a mini-version of the Bob Hogue vs. Mazie Hirono 2nd Congressional District race. Republican Keoki Leong, a former Hogue aide, is squaring off against Jill Tokuda, one-time staffer to Hirono, for the 24th Senate District (Kāne'ohe, Kailua) seat that Hogue vacated. There are other parallels between Tokuda and Leong, both lifelong Kāne'ohe residents. Tokuda was once interim executive director of the Democratic Party of Hawai'i, while Leong served for a time as executive director for the Hawai'i Republican Party. The 24th District race is one of only two Senate contests on Nov. 7 not to feature an incumbent. The Senate is also fractured into different factions vying for control. Those two facts make the race one of the more closely watched battles in the general election. And with Leong only 26 and Tokuda just 30, the winner will also become the youngest member of the 25-person state Senate and be in position to become a force at the Capitol for years to come." Because Randy was a credible candidate, Lingle's largesse would not extend to these candidates. Tokuda would later thank me for Randy's candidacy.

is that whether he consciously knew this or not, Randy sacrificed himself on the public altar for the sake of the Democratic majority. To cite a respected old Japanese term: *ganbatte.* Randy did his best.

While his loss was a bitter pill to swallow, it was certainly no surprise. To win the race would have been, of course. But if there was anything to take away from this campaign experience, it was the sacrifices we made and that belief that we could emerge victorious. Like the story about the little engine that could, we believed.

"Of course, there were still plenty of believers who also came out to help," Randy pointed out. "Our slogan was the famous quote from the pitcher Tug McGraw: You Gotta Believe! For whatever reasons, people did come out to help. I am truly humbled by that. I can tell you that when we lost on general election night, the disappointment and pain that I felt was for them—those who believed, who worked their tails off. I was very sorry that I didn't do better for them. That sorrow is with me to this day."

In many ways faith may be much more important to winning than anything else. Our volunteers did believe, and they gave of themselves. That demonstration of faith kept us all going. The candidate became the embodiment of all of our collective hopes and aspirations.

The faith of campaign supporters cannot be underestimated. The campaign slogan we grabbed, "You Gotta Believe!" was our banner for that sentiment. If you don't believe you can win, why even start? All candidates believe they can win. The ones who actually win have a message that people can believe in. If people don't believe in you and your vision, the corollary is that they won't believe in you. It is this delicate relationship that matters.

There's a great Spencer Tracy film, *The Last Hurrah,* that I highly recommend for political junkies. It's the story of an old-time mayor of a New England city who is hated by the establishment because he ostensibly sides with the little guy against the powers that be. So his opponents get a simpleton to run, someone they can control, and then use the media to overcome the grassroots efforts of the old time machine. They lose. Tracy falls ill and dies. In his passing is the end of a generation and the end of relational politics; that is to say, the end of the old grassroots, backroom, less than "honest" system of cronyism. But you wonder whether some of that was all that bad. Not the corruption part, but like our paternalistic plantation era, the part about caring for the underprivileged and underserved.[134] I wonder whether in the mad rush to render all things objective and above board, we have thrown out the baby with the bathwater, as it relates to the caring we had as a community before. And that explains some nostalgia for the good old days, which phraseology most don't use. I too must admit to a hankering for those days, not because they were so good, because corruption is never good, but maybe this loss of what we often call the aloha spirit, that close-knit relationship we once had. Maybe this why I ultimately believed in Randy and what he could do. As he said, "This election is about believing in ourselves, believing in each other, and believing that together, we can achieve anything upon which we set our hearts and minds."

It is interesting to ponder, that if we are as much a liberal Democratic state as we claim to be, why do we have social problems, like homelessness or inadequate housing? Could we, as Lincoln once asked, call upon our better angels?

"People asked me if I were a *kamikaze* when I entered the race," Randy said. "In their view it was a hopeless effort. And in this town, being on the wrong side of a political campaign has consequences—mostly not good. So I wasn't surprised at the very lukewarm response I received from certain people I had hoped would help. Not surprised, but, of course, disappointed. This also played out in our quest for a running mate. We needed someone who had name recognition—hopefully much more than me. Prospect after prospect turned me down. Why risk the political office they already held? Or why jeopardize the businesses they were running?"

But many people did join the cause, regardless of the risk involved. Former state senator Malama Solomon deserves special mention. She came out of retirement for Randy. She didn't have to. She knew we were a long shot, but she readily agreed to help coordinate the Big Island.

"When Malama asked me about our LG options," Randy recounted, "I told her about our futile efforts to date and asked if she'd consider running herself. Malama had been out of politics for some time, having lost her state senate re-election bid. She was happy doing what she was

---

[134] The book *Machine Made* by Terry Golway (Liveright Publishing, 2014) about Tammany Hall may prove instructive on this point. Clearly corrupt, Tammany Hall stood for protecting "the marginalized and maligned immigrants" ignored by other New York politicians. Its power and influence was based on this attitude of caring, and the relationships built forged Tammany Hall's influence.

doing—running the family ranch and taking care of her mom and dad. But she cared deeply about our state and the future of our people. She had devoted much of her life to public service. She was tough, aggressive and blunt, and she could even offend people with her conversational style. But she also had a heart of gold and a passionate commitment to work to improve Hawaiʻi. She cared. And she agreed to run for LG. During that campaign, Malama was one example of the people who taught me the value of friendship."

But there were also critical mistakes made. Malama had run a campaign ad with an "edited" headline from a newspaper. It was reported in *The Honolulu Star-Bulletin* by Richard Borreca:

> Democratic Party officials are apologizing after Randy Iwase and Malama Solomon, the Democratic candidates for governor and lieutenant governor, ran a series of television ads with phony headlines pasted onto a copy of *The Honolulu Advertiser*. Mike McCartney, Democratic Party chairman, said he met with Solomon, whose campaign paid for the ads, and said she has apologized for the misleading ads.

This incident, coming just a few weeks before the general election, may have cemented the view of AJAs that we were just like all the rest of the politicians.

But what hurt even more was a newspaper report that Senator Dan Inouye had chastised Randy for "Monday morning quarterbacking," when Randy criticized Governor Lingle's emergency disaster response after a major earthquake. Coming from our highest ranking Democratic politician, this really stung. While the senator had cut some ads for our campaign, he had nevertheless been aloof in helping with our fundraising and grassroots efforts. He handed out his blessings as he saw fit, and apparently we weren't fit enough.

This seeming indifference to Randy's campaign wasn't an isolated incident. At a big rally for Randy, Governor Ariyoshi openly stated that Randy couldn't win. This from a man Randy had served for years in the AG's office and had supported in countless campaigns—and who, when the polls showed Ariyoshi couldn't win, still went out to campaign for him. I was personally shocked that Ariyoshi said such a thing. But reacting to his statement would just bring more attention to it.

Except for Neil Abercrombie, most sitting Democratic politicians went *kanalua* (doubtful) on Randy.[135] Few would take the risk to help a colleague and supporter, just because he "couldn't win." For me, that was a bitter pill to swallow. What about camaraderie and loyalty, about helping a comrade in arms as I had helped him once? It made me wonder if all those years of sacrifice for others had really been worth it. The lesson here was to expect disappointment, but also to relish the warmth of true friendship and camaraderie.

During that campaign, I learned that loyalty and camaraderie in politics can be a temporal thing. Too many candidates forget what a colleague or a volunteer has done for them in the past. I believe this is at the crux of the current dissatisfaction voters have with political parties and leadership.

The public must also bear part of the responsibility for accepting glib sound bites and easy-to-understand explanations. We may not trust politicians, but seldom do we do our own homework on the issues. We rely on politicians to tell us what the big issues are, but are they truly seminal issues or just great platforms for candidates themselves? To make this distinction, a citizen must invest the time and effort, or risk falling victim to what Frank Fasi called "soap salesmen."

I believe Randy Iwase would have made a good governor. Unfortunately, we never had the chance to find out. "I see a Hawai'i," he said, "where my children will have the same opportunities I have had. I see a Hawai'i where we retain those precious people values; 'islanderism' values that allow us to interact with respect for one another, to retain what some call the rural small-town values. I see a Hawai'i where leaders really want to make a difference for the better. It's not just about hope. It's about doing what we need to do to make our hopes become a reality, to achieve the dream."

Randy's words reflect a common thread going back to Governor Burns—that Hawai'i's values must not be consumed by the world outside. But it's not insularity—far from it. We in Hawai'i can embrace change but not lose our values in the process. ⚓

---

[135] Randy became one of Neil's co-chairs when Abercrombie decided to run for governor, in part due to Neil's selfless action of support when Randy had faced an unbeatable opponent. In much the same way, I volunteered to help Ben Cayetano because of his selfless act for Eileen Anderson. Maybe it's our "Japanese-ness," our belief in *giri*, that made us commit in this fashion. If Randy were to decide to run for an office today, would I be there? You betcha!

CHAPTER SIXTEEN

Neil Abercrombie: Coming Home

~❧~

"It was the best of times, it was the worst of times, it was the age of wisdom, it was the age of foolishness, it was the epoch of belief, it was the epoch of incredulity, it was the season of Light, it was the season of Darkness, it was the spring of hope, it was the winter of despair, we had everything before us, we had nothing before us, we were all going direct to Heaven, we were all going direct the other way—in short, the period was so far like the present period, that some of its noisiest authorities insisted on its being received, for good or for evil, in the superlative degree of comparison only."

—Charles Dickens, *A Tale of Two Cities*

Two thousand ten was to be Mufi Hannemann's year. He was the frontrunner for the governor's seat. He was a sitting mayor with all of the gravitas the office brings with it. By all accounts, running against him was foolhardy. But Neil Abercrombie decided to go for it.

My involvement was, once again, both serendipitous and unique. I had never been one of Neil's supporters. When my high school classmate Tina Yamamoto, a well-known political worker who worked for Neil, had once asked me to help with one of his congressional campaigns, I declined. For one thing, taking on a national election after the John Craven race just didn't interest me, even academically. For another, Neil and I disagreed on almost every substantive issue. I just couldn't get myself to like this guy.

I remember our first encounter, as my fellow deputy AG Randy Iwase and I were walking out of the old judiciary building, which at the time housed the circuit courts as well as the Hawai'i Supreme Court. We were somewhere between the entrance and the Kamehameha statue, when we heard a voice bellowing, "RAAAANDYYYY!" It was Neil up on the second-floor balcony. I thought, *What's with this guy?* In college he had been one of my TAs in political science, and I remembered him lecturing, moving back and forth on the stage. In my opinion, Neil had been more performer than educator, but I wanted an education, not entertainment. These were my initial images of Neil Abercrombie.

So when Bill Kaneko, Neil's longtime associate and political guru, invited Mitch Imanaka and me to lunch with Neil one day at the Prince Court, I knew something was up. If I had declined that lunch, my life would have been so much simpler. Previously I had supported Mufi Hannemann when he ran for the US Congress against Neil, in an election that set the stage for the animosity between the two.

At lunch, Neil asked us both to help in his 2010 run for governor. I didn't know what Mitch was thinking, but I was on the horns of a dilemma. Neil had been one of the few stalwart Democratic incumbents to help Randy Iwase in the last election. Mufi, on the other hand, had used his influence to make sure that Randy didn't make it. Bill Kaneko had been really helpful when Randy ran for governor. He didn't have to; he took a risk. Now Bill deserved to have that favor reciprocated. I had done it for Ben; why not now for Neil and Bill? So I said yes.

So here I was, a former Burns, Ariyoshi, Anderson, Cayetano and Iwase guy, helping Neil Abercrombie, who had caused me so much grief when I was a deputy AG under Ariyoshi.[136] Why would I help him? I'd never really liked the guy before.

A friend observed, "Neil was never really accepted by the powers that be. He was, really, the independent who made his own trail—getting elected to the legislature, winning a seat on the Honolulu City Council, getting elected to Congress failing once. In making his trail, there came a confluence—he was elected to Congress. With that election he was—indeed, had to be—tolerated, if not half-heartedly accepted. He did what

---

[136] Neil's campaign boasted considerably more diversity than even Jeremy's had. There were Bill Kaneko, Tony Takitani, Mitch Imanaka, Harry Mattson and Norma Wong (Ariyoshi, Waihee, Harris); Amy Agbayani, Charlie Toguchi, John Radcliffe, Marvin Wong and Lloyd Nekoba (Cayetano); Kate Stanley (Waihee, Cayetano); Walter Heen and Kelly King as campaign co-chairs along with Randy Iwase; and old Burns-Ariyoshi guys—Jimmy Toyama, Ed Hasegawa and me. We had Jim Loomis, Jim Boersma, Barbara Tanabe, Jim McCoy, Arnold Hiura, Tom Coffman, Laurie Wong and Alan and Carole Tang, as well as Natalie Cook from Olomana Loomis agency and a host of other media consultants. And there were the "young ones": Andrew Aoki, Amy Asselbaye, Tony Benabese, Neenz Faleafine and Kathleen Chapman.

he had to do for such 'acceptance.' He was a good soldier, good Dem, good second fiddle to Inouye. But I guess that wasn't enough."

As with Jeremy Harris, the powers that be didn't want Mainland haole Abercrombie to succeed; they wanted a local. For me "haole" wasn't about ethnicity; it was and always has been a state of mind. Friends like Jim Kirchofer and Bob Fishman taught me that long ago. Working with Jeremy taught me that there are no haoles, only those who think they are, and those who believe *they* aren't. In the final analysis we all share the same hopes and aspirations, dreams and desires. There are no haoles, only people. And if we truly want to be the people Jack Burns said we were, then this notion of "us and them" should be buried once and for all in our popular culture.

I discovered as I got to know Neil on a personal level that he was a genuine guy. Like my experience with Jack Burns many decades ago, Neil was a truly good person, dedicated to the people of Hawai'i. This isn't to say that Mufi wasn't, but I felt good about helping Neil because, like Burns, he was a man of conviction, not expediency. He was a dedicated husband and truly a person of repute. The only character fault I could see in Neil was his loyalty to his friends. But that was a failing that I could respect. Did Neil talk too much? Sometimes. You'd think a person with that much experience could control himself, so it was disappointing to hear about some of his rash statements. I understood what he was saying, but in Hawai'i, such self-expression was expected to be not assertive but restrained, especially if you were an elected official. Neil had been serving in the House of Representatives for nearly twenty years, and I think he'd just been away from the Islands for too long. In D.C. you could do that. It's a different culture in the beltway.

In many respects, he was much more down to earth than I was because he enveloped himself with the people, all people, no matter what part of society they were in. He would not repeat what had been done to his mother, who had once faced overt gender discrimination, or treat people as she had been treated. He might speak like a Mainlander and sometimes act like a Mainlander, but in his heart he was a local.

Neil didn't have to stay in Hawai'i; he chose to stay. And that choice was a life choice. As I got to know him better, the boisterous, blustery Neil gave way to a more loveable Neil, one I consider a friend today. There were many other campaign colleagues who were privileged to see that side of Neil, including Bill Kaneko, Amy Agbayani, John Radcliffe, Charlie Toguchi, Lloyd Nekoba and Barbara Tanabe.

By May, the race against Mufi was neck and neck. *The Honolulu Advertiser* reported:

> Hawaii voters are divided between former Congressman Neil Abercrombie and Honolulu Mayor Mufi Hannemann in the Democratic primary for governor in September, but prefer either Democrat to Lt. Gov. James "Duke" Aiona, a Republican, in the November general election, a new Hawaii Poll has found. Abercrombie, who trails Hannemann in fundraising and influential endorsements, attracted 36 percent of likely primary voters. Hannemann, who is expected to officially declare his candidacy this month, is at 32 percent.

We knew it would be a tough call. Although Hawai'i's senior senator in Washington was openly uncommitted, his ties to Mufi were definitely stronger than his ties to Neil. I suspected as much, given the cordial, but not necessarily warm, interaction I noticed when Inouye and Abercrombie were together. (Likewise, I believe Abercrombie's later appointment of Brian Schatz, rather than the Inouye-favored Colleen Hanabusa, to Inouye's US Senate seat, reflected this relationship—or lack thereof.) Meanwhile, it was unclear where former governor Ariyoshi stood politically, but one had to assume he was leaning towards Mufi, who had once worked for Ariyoshi. Among the former governors, only Ben Cayetano was a sure thing, because of his long friendship with Neil.

Given these alignments, one could easily conclude that Neil's candidacy would be a walk in the park. Like Jeremy, Neil was not seen as an insider. And although never stated out loud, Neil was considered haole in a somewhat pejorative sense by the old-guard locals. That said, Neil had a lot of local support. After all, he had good relationships with Clayton Hee, Charlie Toguchi, Ben Cayetano, Dante Carpenter and other influential political figures in and out of the legislature. Neil did have a more combative, Mainland style, but did that make him "haole?" He disciplined himself over the years to work with others, even those I believe harbored the Abercrombie-as-haole view. What I began to appreciate about Neil was that he said what he believed, embraced and acted upon it, and lived his life exactly as he proclaimed he was. Neil was not Januslike in this sense. What you saw was what you got. If anything he was too transparent; to a fault. Culturally, however, Hawai'i was still and maybe still is, constrained by its history. At the Democratic Party convention, both candidates expressed their views. And it is instructive to view this *Honolulu Advertiser* report in the light of the above:

Former congressman Neil Abercrombie and Honolulu Mayor Mufi Hannemann wooed delegates at the state Democratic convention yesterday, with Abercrombie framing his campaign for governor around values such as protecting public education and Hannemann vowing to serve as a collaborator who will get results... Hannemann took the opportunity to place himself, his family's immigrant roots and his childhood growing up in Kalihi into the lineage of Democrats who have dominated politics in the Islands since statehood. The mayor concedes that Abercrombie's strength is among traditional Democrats and union workers. But he reminded delegates that he, too, was inspired by and wants to build on the legacy of former governors such as John Burns, George Ariyoshi and John Waihee. The only former Democratic governor he did not mention was Ben Cayetano, an ally of Abercrombie. "There are those that would like to suggest that somehow we are this monolithic structure, a structure that perhaps has grown too tired, too weary, too old," Hannemann said. "We beg to differ. Ours is a party of diversity. Ours is a party that welcomes all people. Ours is a party of a big tent."[137]

These last words would later be contradicted by Hannemann, and in the end were the very reason for his defeat.

The election of 1986 was still resonating with the two veteran politicians. Neil and Mufi had had a bitter fight that resulted in the election of Pat Saiki to Congress. As Dan Aoki had lectured me many decades earlier, you've got to count the votes. The rancor between the two gave Saiki a leg up. In Oshiro's terms, the election came down to division and subtraction. Saiki was an inevitable winner then. Would the events from

---

[137] Derrick DePledge, "Hannemann, Abercrombie sum it up," *Honolulu Advertiser*, May 30, 2010.

1986 revisit the campaign in 2010?[138] More from the *Advertiser* on the morning after the convention:

> Abercrombie, speaking to reporters, warned of the dangers of a contentious primary. He said it was Hannemann who turned their 1986 battle for Congress so negative… "In terms of instruction for civics, you can look at that election and you see what happens when you run a negative campaign," Abercrombie said. "You see what happens when you concentrate on trying to tear people down rather than trying to concentrate on issues that will build people up."[139]

But this surface battle was only part of what was to be a scandalous campaign. The full flavor of it is difficult to experience without a complete sense of the tenor of the times. One unfortunate aspect of our forgiving Island culture is our remarkable ability to forget, or ignore, the events of only a few years earlier. But the actions of a few political types in the infamous Atomic Monkey scandal are instructive for those who think that unattributed character assassinations are acceptable. Much has been written about this ugly incident.[140] But few may recall the acts

---

[138] This same division between Democrats Colleen Hanabusa and Ed Case would give Charles Djou his congressional experience in 2010.

[139] Derrick DePledge, "Hannemann, Abercrombie sum it up," *Honolulu Advertiser*, May 30, 2010.

[140] Andrew Walden, "Could force Hannemann out of race: Admits AtomicMonkey site produced by Mufi campaign worker," *Hawaiʻi Free Press*, July, 1, 2010. "For months the now-defunct AtomicMonkey.blogspot.com site has skewered Neil Abercrombie as a 'flailing gasbag' and his wife, Nancie Caraway, as 'a witch.' One posting portrayed former governor Ben Cayetano as an evil scientist secretly controlling Abercrombie's brain. Now the Hannemann campaign has admitted that this site was operated by 'a campaign volunteer' who works at Honolulu Hale. *Hawaiʻi Free Press* on May 19 exposed the anonymous site as an operation run by Mufi Hannemann supporters. Our expose drew an immediate response from the blogger—identifying himself under the pseudonym Bob Wiesel—behind the site who stated: 'Some of us work for the City… we proudly stand by our description of Abercrombie as 'flailing gasbag." Wiesel—who the Hannemann campaign has now acknowledged is Keith Rollman—claimed: 'Your article today implying it is a 'Mufi' site is incorrect. We like Hannemann, but he has no input or control over the site and as far as I know has not even seen it…' The Hannemann campaign also confirmed yesterday that a campaign volunteer, who works as a special adviser attached to the city Department of Information Technology, was responsible for a parody website that savagely mocked Abercrombie. Tanaka said Rollman, the campaign volunteer and city adviser, created the 'Atomic Monkey' website on his own time and without the campaign's approval. The website, which has been taken down, included a disclaimer stating that it was not operated or financed by Hannemann or any other candidate for public office… A Hannemann campaign volunteer who works as 'a special adviser' at Honolulu Hale allegedly produces Atomic Monkey

which occurred. In sum there was a website/blog that was clearly anti-Abercrombie, with critical statements and cartoons, done in what was essentially a juvenile schoolyard brand of humor. The problem was that no one took responsibility for these unsavory statements. Although the Hannemann campaign leadership were friends of the site, they all denied any involvement or knowledge as to who was running it. It was as though someone was throwing dirt from the other side of the fence, but you couldn't tell who it was. When the perpetrator was identified as a city employee and political operative of the mayor, all hell broke loose.

Politics has always been seen as a dirty business. Many people use the word in the same vein as when they discuss corruption or crime. For many, a disdain for politics is surpassed only by their disdain for paying taxes. Politicians can't be trusted, right? And yet, we are still fascinated by politics. It's like a soap opera (or in Hawai'i, like a Korean drama). We view it as entertainment and get a certain perverse pleasure from watching politicians whacked. That's probably why some politicians do so well—or at least the entertaining ones do. Many liken politics to the Japanese theatrical art form of *kabuki*. Personally, I think of it more as Greek or Roman tragicomedy.

However, the use of pseudonyms in blogs and their surreptitious use by candidates probably says more about our society than about the candidates themselves. Why we find such titillating "news" so fascinating reflects a society in which truth and facts have little influence.

I believe that media has a societal obligation in such matters. Fortunately, we have responsible journalists who do their jobs well. The *Star-Advertiser*'s Dave Shapiro, for example, took great pains in exposing the obfuscations of the Atomic Monkey scandal. I found it refreshing that he noted Hannemann's contradictory statement about the matter:

It's ironic for supporters of a political candidate to make claims of superior godliness with tactics that are anything but. Attempts to evade responsibility for the actions of operatives who have clear ties to the campaign skirt the bounds of honesty; it crosses the line to

---

on his own—but took it down when ordered to do so by the Hannemann campaign. This could be seen by a court as the Hannemann Committee controlling the website. If so, the website would be an illegal false name in-kind contribution to Hannemann's campaign. The campaign would then have showed an 'intent to deceive' by claiming that the site was not a Hannemann site. This is a felony under HRS 11-201 and 11-202. Conviction of a felony or misdemeanor under HRS Chapter 11 automatically renders Hannemann ineligible to serve in office for four years."

surreptitiously erase the name of a campaign committee member after the fact and hope nobody notices.[141]

Shapiro issued even more specific commentary on his blog site:

Keith Rollman has been a shadowy figure in local politics for much of the last 25 years, a behind-the-scenes operator whose job is to draw attention to his candidate, not himself. The Atomic Monkey website was registered under the fictitious name of "Bob Wiesel." By acknowledging that it was Rollman, the Hannemann campaign potentially linked Rollman to further online attacks on Abercrombie and other Hannemann rivals. The concern is that such anonymous character assassinations reduce political campaigns to the intellectual level of the locker room interviews on professional wrestling shows. Partisans of other campaigns are guilty of the same thing, but when the Hannemann camp is seen as giving more than it gets, it runs the risk of enhancing a reputation for bullying.[142] [143]

This view of Mufi Hannemann as a bully has been pervasive. Even today the polling research to which I have been privy, from various sources, reinforces this perception. I've been told this rankles the former mayor. In some cases, it has been attributed to his imposing physical appearance, but others have tied it to his demeanor. In any case I have never experienced that side of Mufi. Maybe it is due to the decades we have known each other, maybe it is because I was less than relevant to his ambitions. In either case I am thankful not to have experienced that side of the man.

Why have I spent so much time setting this table by quoting contemporary media sources? I believe that many people forget about such events over time. History is never the most popular course in school curricula, but an understanding of history is essential to understanding

[141] David Shapiro, "Hannemann's tactics take the hit-and-run route," *Honolulu Star-Advertiser*, September 8, 2010.

[142] David Shapiro, "Mufi's Rock 'n Rollman," Volcanic Ash, July 12, 2010, https://blog.volcanic-ash.net/2010/07/12/mufis-rock-n-rollman/.

[143] Keith Rollman repudiated these news reports and allegations in an article written in the *Hawai'i Reporter*, "The Short Life and Premature Demise of the Hawai'i Political Satire Blog Atomic Monkey—a Word from the Author," dated July 7, 2010.

Why Hawaiians Support Arnold Morgado for Mayor.

Honolulu City Council chairman Arnold Morgado
ran for mayor against Jeremy Harris in 1996.

Jeremy Harris (opposite top, with author) trumpeted his strong track record in his 1996 campaign against Arnold Morgado.

Family Man, Educator, Environmentalist and Can-Do Mayor!

As Mayor of Honolulu and its managing director from 1986 to 1994, Jeremy Harris has proven to be an award winning administrator and an energetic leader.

He's a 1972 graduate of U. H. Manoa and a trained environmental biologist, with a passionate interest in protecting Hawaii's fragile environment.

He taught college-level oceanography and biology on Kauai.

He was elected to the Kauai County Council and immediately became its chair.

He helped write the State's Constitution as an elected delegate to the 1978 Constitutional Convention.

He has lived all his adult life in Hawaii; he lives in Kalihi Valley with his wife, Ramona Sachiko Akui Harris, and his mother, Ann.

PAID FOR BY
Jeremy Harris Campaign Committee
733 Bishop Street, Suite 170-122
Honolulu, Hawaii 96813
Ann Kobayashi, Chair

Harris flyer, front ("Devotion, respect and love...")
Harris flyer, back ("We're proud to be supporting...")

Jeremy Harris. Mayor.

The best man for the job.

"What does it take to make a city truly great? What challenges must we answer to provide our citizens with the highest quality of life possible? How can we, together, make Honolulu one of the world's premier cities of the 21st century?

I am committed to making Honolulu a city that provides economic opportunity for its citizens, and maintains a healthy and pristine environment. A city that offers a wide array of parks, cultural and recreational programs for its families. A city that provides good mobility for its residents through public transportation. A city with safe streets, and communities free from crime.

This is a vision we all share and a reality we all desire. And it is within our grasp.

We can realize this vision because our citizens, and our dedicated city employees, have been willing to join hands and work together to find new and creative solutions to problems. We can realize this vision because we believe in ourselves, and because we believe in our values. We can realize this vision because of our values of caring for one another and sharing our unique spirit of Aloha."

Thank you for your support.

Harris flyer ("Jeremy Harris. Mayor. The best man for the job.") Campaign literature touted Jeremy Harris' vision for Honolulu in his 2000 mayoral campaign.

For Hawaii's Future...
For Our Future.

Iwase and Solomon

Above and opposite bottom: Malama Solomon came out of retirement to join Randy Iwase in his 2006 gubernatorial bid. Opposite top: (left to right) Charlie Toguchi, John Radcliffe, Jim Boersma, newly elected Governor Neil Abercrombie, former governor Ben Cayetano and Iwase celebrate on election night 2010.

Iwase flyer ("Randy Iwase. Governor. You Gotta Believe.")

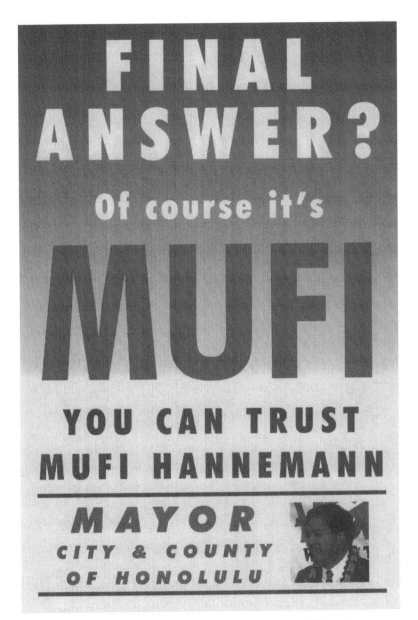

Mufi Hannemann channeled *Who Wants to be a Millionnaire* in his 2000 mayoral campaign against Jeremy Harris.

the principles and lessons of politics. Marcus Tullius Cicero again:

> When a small group of people control a nation because of their
> wealth or birth or some other advantage, they are simply a faction,
> even if they are called an aristocracy. *On the other hand, if the multi-
> tude gains power and runs a country according to its wishes at the mo-
> ment, it is called freedom, though it is in fact chaos.* (Emphasis added.)

The Atomic Monkey scandal was an evolutionary change for the worse.
Hawai'i politics has long endured murmuring campaigns. This may be due
partly to the quiet Asian influence on local culture, but also to the contrary
part of human nature that finds perverse pleasure in seeing something torn
down rather than built up. Atomic Monkey was this in spades—an un-
welcome import, a viral invasion of commentary, which neither helped
society nor elevated the discussion. Rather it denigrated the view that all
viewpoints are welcome in Hawai'i. It created and fanned the flames of
discrimination and character assassination. It made acceptable the personal
attack on a politician based on nothing more than a claim of free speech.

The unanswered question despite numerous denials was why it was
allowed to continue. The Hannemann campaign leadership disavowed
any connection, and yet they must have known what Rollman was up to.
Certainly they should be given the benefit of the doubt, but is it credible
to have a city employee connected to the campaign doing something like
this without the knowledge of either the candidate, the city administration or the campaign? This scandal said much about how a Hannemann
administration might govern—and to what extent dirty tricks would be
part of the tools of a Hannemann administration.

The Atomic Monkey affair also began a line of questioning about how
much of a "Democrat" Mufi really was. Andrew Walden again wrote:

> For someone seeking the Democratic Gubernatorial nomination,
> Mufi Hannemann's campaign sure has a lot of current or former
> Republicans among its leadership. And it starts at the top. Mufi's
> personal GOP connections lead straight to the Bush family and go
> back three decades. More than a few Democrats found it cheeky
> for a guy who spent all those years working to elect Republicans to
> present himself as the voice of old-line Democrats. How will they

feel about voting for a candidate who spent all those years as part of the Bush administration?[144]

Indeed, Mufi's cavorting with Republicans was well known, but now bi-partisan game playing was coming to the top among Democratic voters, who had tired of eight years of GOP control of the state capitol's fifth floor. How would Democratic primary voters react to a Bush confidant and friend? This notion of being able to play both sides of the aisle is intriguing, almost beguiling. However, in Hawaiʻi, one must always understand our roots. The older generation is still deeply tied to "plantation values." People today call this "local values," but their origins are deeper and more cultural. From my perspective as an AJA, I see the influence of the camps and Japanese or Asian ethics as all-pervasive. The plantation camps were like mini collectives, which also fostered a deep social bond in the face of the common "enemy," the *luna* and the plantation managers. Like the coal miners on the continent, people in the camps demanded better pay and better working conditions.

But a desire to get out of the camps drove the personal demand for achievement. For many immigrants, education was the ticket out. Add to this the overlay of Japanese culture and the sense of sacrifice for the next generation, and you had a "movement" among these workers. This became the key to core "local values"—hard work, the ganbatte ideal, a tolerance of others and what they believe (essential to organizing the labor in the various camps), education (that ticket out) equal treatment (an end to economic domination by the elite) and fundamental fairness (equality before the law, both by the police and by the courts).

In this context, Mufi consorted with a modern-day luna and plantation manager class. Mufi appealed to businesses, the centrists, who leaned more GOP. But could he still appeal to the core of traditional Democrats, the old-time AJA and labor constituency? Would core local values determine the outcome of the gubernatorial race?

By August, just a month out, the Atomic Monkey fallout and Hannemann's Republican connections were having an effect. "You don't win campaigns," Bob Oshiro had said to me many years ago, "you lose

---

[144] Andrew Walden, "Mufi's Republican Army: The Bush Family Connection," *Hawaii Free Press*, August 8, 2010.

them." Hannemann made a critical and campaign-turning mistake by mailing out a flyer asking voters to "compare and decide." Among other comparisons, the flyer listed the candidates' wives opposite one another, compared Neil's victory in a beard contest with more serious accolades won by Mufi, and appeared to contrast Hannemann's Harvard degree with Abercrombie's University of Hawai'i credentials. *Advertiser* reporter Dave Koga wrote:

> The compare-and-decide format is classic political advertising, [political observer Neal] Milner said, and many of the elements in the flyer "were precisely along the lines of the campaign: 'have experience running a city. I have solved problems. I have a vision for Hawai'i.'" It was the gratuitous stuff—the wives comparison, the beard contest, the school for dummies—that caused the problems.
>
> To [political observer Tom] Coffman, it was in some ways "a clash of new culture versus old culture." "My definition of old culture in Hawai'i would be that if you don't have something good to say about somebody, don't say anything. That's one of Jack Burns' lines," he says. "There's a strong tendency in Hawai'i not to attack people. It just goes against the grain. We just don't attack people in a way as if we're trying to push them away from the table."[145]

Significantly, Mufi calculated that the haole/local dichotomy, which had always floated under the surface of Hawai'i society, could be used against Neil. If you looked at Mufi's previous contests with Jeremy Harris, this same subtle (or maybe not so subtle) appeal to racism was always present. The difference was that this time it was front and center, with trumpets blaring. Neil's image made this move even easier—the brash Mainlander versus the local boy.

It's fair to say that Neil was known for his combativeness, which some people saw as typically haole. But like Ben Cayetano, you needed to know why. One insider noted, "We saw it in the focus groups—they didn't like Neil, even chose Colleen over him in a mock vote! Why the dislike? There was the old urban legend about the haole hippie who burned down the ROTC building at UH. He hadn't, but it was a story

---

[145] Dave Koga, "Negative political ads a risky tactic," *Honolulu Star-Advertiser*, October 7, 2010.

and an image that many older voters clung to, which was clearly evident in the focus groups. His aggressive personal style—at times a loud critic of 'the establishment' back in his younger days—just fed into the myth of the loudmouthed haole hippie. Yet the voters had sent Neil to Congress, perhaps attracted to his assertive qualities, but more content to appreciate them from a distance. Sort of like your forceful curmudgeon uncle: You wanted him on your side in a fight, but you didn't want him living with you. But Neil was passionate about the causes he believed in. He was fighting for us because his history is our common history. Wouldn't you fight like Neil did? The story of his schoolteacher mom [a victim of gender discrimination] was especially powerful to me."

Neil wasn't just some loudmouth; he was on a mission to free the people from what he felt was an oppressive power structure. He was, in the Robert Oshiro sense, deeply dedicated to this cause, to the point at which he was willing to do anything to accomplish it. As a colleague once said, "Having worked on his two campaigns, I came to really respect Neil. We knew that he was a liberal who fought for and deeply cared for the causes he believed in—peace, equality, respect for the elderly, the education of our *keiki*, creating a better future. But I came to see his deep love for Hawai'i and its people. He was thoughtful, he had a good heart, he wasn't petty, and he had a big picture view of Hawai'i, indeed the world."

One of Neil's favorite phrases is "Our diversity defines us; it does not divide us." Neil lived those words. I believe the Hannemann camp thought they could take them and somehow turn them against him. It was a disastrous mistake. Civil Beat's Chad Blair wrote about the "Compare and Divide" flyer:

> Abercrombie immediately responded to Hannemann's tactics, arguing that Hannemann was, among other things, making veiled racial claims, inappropriately comparing spouses and insulting the state's university. Republican Gov. Linda Lingle—no fan of Hannemann—condemned Hannemann's tactics, and U.S. Sen. Daniel K. Inouye—who officially stayed neutral in the race but appeared to lean toward Hannemann—asked his fellow Democrats to keep the election clean.[146]

---

[146] Chad Blair, "Abercrombie Rolls Over Hannemann," *Honolulu Civil Beat*, September 17, 2010.

The attack on Neil's UH credentials shocked people. Here was a gubernatorial candidate attacking his opponent for going to our only state university, and implying that his attendance at Harvard was significantly better—so much so that you should vote for him. Apparently it was OK to be local and go away for your degree, but not cool to come from outside Hawai'i and earn a degree from the local university. This would come back to haunt Hanneman's campaign, as did his playing of the race card. Here's John Temple in Civil Beat:

> I was taken aback when I read what Honolulu Mayor Mufi Hannemann told union carpenters at their convention this weekend. "I can identify with you. When I look in the audience, I look like you, you look like me," he told the gathering, according to a thorough story by *Honolulu Star-Advertiser* reporter Derrick DePledge, confirmed by Civil Beat's Chad Blair, who was also there... [T]o hear Hannemann make a racial appeal in a political speech is troubling. He's basically saying: I look like you. All of you. The other guy doesn't. He can't relate to you. Vote for me. It's difficult to hear Hannemann's words and not hear the sound of division, even if he didn't intend to send that message. He's telling the crowd that Abercrombie, because he's white and not born in Hawai'i, isn't really one of them. Even though he's represented the state in Congress for two decades, served in both the state House and Senate and on the Honolulu City Council... So, yes, Mr. Mayor, you were wrong to bring up the color of your skin the way you did. Of course it's not wrong to bring up where you come from or your pride of accomplishment. You have a great personal story. But it is wrong to make yourself seem better than somebody else because of the color of your skin or the blood in your veins.

The fact that Mufi used racism to advance his candidacy was a real affront to Democrats. George Ariyoshi, John Waihee, Ben Cayetano, Linda Lingle and now Neil Abercrombie were and should be judged for who they are, not what ethnicity they happen to be. For a modern politician whose political career followed on their legacy to intimate such an argument is truly abhorrent. Whether we were born in the Islands or arrived later in life, being a part of Hawai'i is not a matter of birth, but attitude. To think otherwise and to say otherwise is to repudiate all that came before.

The local angle may have been used more subtly, and more fairly, in John Waihee's gubernatorial campaign. His "Us Guys Together" approach was decidedly local-focused. The crucial difference was that Mufi said, in so many words, "Don't vote for the haole." That was a different thing. The distinction between locals and haoles is not a new phenomenon,[147] but it was usually played in the background, not used up front as an offensive weapon. Mufi had crossed the line, and like the proverbial Rubicon there was no turning back. No amount of explanation would make it go away. The key to winning an election is addition and multiplication, not subtraction and division, and Mufi was quickly subtracting from his support. To paraphrase Lincoln, he was appealing to our lesser angels.[148]

By September 10, 2010, Neil was moving way ahead in the polls, as reported by Civil Beat: "Former Congressman Neil Abercrombie has a wide lead in the Democratic governor's primary, according to a new Civil Beat poll. Abercrombie would get 48 percent of the vote, compared to just 31 percent for former Honolulu Mayor Mufi Hannemann, an automated telephone poll of 1,226 likely primary voters found."[149]

Two days later the Abercrombie campaign challenged a Hannemann newspaper advertisement that gave the impression that Hawai'i's two US senators were supporting Mufi. An Associated Press article noted:

> Democratic gubernatorial candidate Neil Abercrombie is criticizing a newspaper ad bought by the Mufi Hannemann campaign that features laudatory remarks by U.S. Sens. Daniel Akaka and Daniel Inouye. The ad was published Sunday in *The Honolulu Star-Advertiser*. It quotes Hannemann, a Democrat, being praised by Inouye at a 2009 dinner. It also uses a portion of a letter Akaka sent Hannemann in conjunction with a 2008 banquet. Abercrombie said

---

[147] For some local folks, the unfortunate schoolyard tradition of "Kill Haole Day" or "Kill Jap Day" still resonates decades later.

[148] Abraham Lincoln in his first inaugural address said, "We are not enemies, but friends. We must not be enemies. Though passion may have strained, it must not break our bonds of affection. The mystic chords of memory will swell when again touched, as surely they will be, by the better angels of our nature."

[149] John Temple, "Civil Beat Poll: Abercrombie on Top, Hannemann in Trouble," Honolulu Civil Beat, September 10, 2010.

in a statement Sunday the ad creates the "false impression" that the senators are endorsing Hannemann. A subsequent statement from Hannemann spokeswoman Carolyn Tanaka says the quotes are accurate and both senators were aware of the ad. Aides to both senators say they remain neutral in the race.[150]

The ad was truthful, but was it honest? Parsing the language, you'd have to agree the ad implied something that wasn't true. Hannemann's veracity, already in question, was now even more so.

Our campaign couldn't let any of this go unanswered. Letting a lie stand is paramount to acknowledging that it's true. And what role do media publishing these ads bear in such determinations? Surely they cannot be a censor, but, like the Iwase-Solomon ads two years earlier, they should at least have questioned the ad's veracity.

The Abercrombie campaign's decision to take the high road paid off. Instead of slinging mud with Mufi, Neil stayed above it all. Chad Blair wrote in Civil Beat:

Voters ultimately were turned off by the negativity and found Abercrombie's take-the-high-road approach more palatable. Hannemann, in part because of his early financial edge, appeared to be the favorite, with Abercrombie the underdog... Hannemann—who never led in the polls and whose fundraising fell behind Abercrombie's during the last two months—never recovered from his blunders, and a last-minute negative hail Mary pass never materialized, though Abercrombie insiders said they were prepared for it![151]

On primary night the efforts of the previous year's hard work were evident. The site of the old CompUSA store was set up for a huge crowd of Abercrombie supporters. There was a small back room for close friends. Everyone that night was a close friend, or wanted or thought themselves to be. There was a keen anticipation of the results, and the wait for the first printout was oppressive. Chad Blair observed in Civil Beat:

---

[150] "Abercrombie criticizes Hannemann newspaper ad," *Honolulu Star-Advertiser*, September 13, 2010.

[151] Chad Blair, "Abercrombie Rolls Over Hannemann," Honolulu Civil Beat, September 17, 2010.

It was over by the first printout. And it wasn't even close. In the contest for the Democratic nomination for governor, former congressman Neil Abercrombie beat former Honolulu Mayor Mufi Hannemann 59.4 percent to 37.8 percent. Abercrombie had 134,955 votes to Hannemann's 85,891, according to final results from the State Elections Office late Saturday evening… On Saturday, at Abercrombie's campaign celebration in downtown Honolulu, the president's sister was on hand to congratulate "Uncle Neil." "This place hasn't been this wild since my brother's election," Maya Soetoro-Ng told the crowd of enthusiastic Abercrombie supporters. It was not an exaggeration. It was a cathartic experience for many in the room— but especially for Abercrombie.[152]

It was a glorious night.[153] The campaign that had started with just a few people now numbered supporters in the thousands. It was the return of the Democratic presence to the fifth floor of the capitol. It was a euphoric moment!

The Abercrombie gubernatorial campaign was a good example of a "flat" campaign, an organization with very little top-down control. Lloyd Nekoba, Harry Mattson and Marvin Wong mostly held it together with persuasion. Our campaign meetings were group-think events, and everyone's opinion was welcome. Bill Kaneko, who coordinated us all, was very good at that. Amy Asselbaye and Andrew Aoki managed the day-to-day and worked with Neil on policy. No one was excluded. It was a coalition of differing groups, in many cases the first in decades to come together in such a fashion, under the singular flag of Neil Abercrombie. For those of us fortunate to have been around for decades, it was a special campaign, especially as the once-disparate parts came together as a complementary working group. Here I was, a Burns guy, with Art Park, a Gill guy, together under one roof. How could this be? I believe it was all about the candidate, Neil Abercrombie. He was an unlikely hub for this diverse group, but it spoke to the man, that he was able to summon such cohesive support from such diversity. "Our diversity defines us; it does not divide us"—his words were more than a handy slogan or catchphrase.

---

152 Chad Blair, "Abercrombie Rolls Over Hannemann," Honolulu Civil Beat, September 17, 2010.
153 Ibid.

It was true of the whole campaign.

There were no chiefs, as Bob Oshiro had suggested, only Indians. For me, it was the culmination of all of my years of campaigning. In part, it was the fulfillment of many of the theories and experiences that Bob had espoused. It was a flat organization, one built on the four tests of a productive volunteer, built by collaboration, and built around "the cause" of equality and fair treatment. It was an odd moment that my theories would find expression in a campaign in which I contributed but had little involvement tactically. To see the campaign operation function without a hierarchy was revealing, not only about the character of those involved, but also the attitude that each of us had about the goal—Neil's election. While there was much expectation, there were no spoils to divide.

When you come from nowhere as we did in 1980 and 2010, the elation and exuberance you feel is indescribable. As they say, success has many fathers, defeat is an orphan. There were many fathers that night. Everyone contributed to the victory. Everyone had a role in winning. Few understood that the dynamics was less about Neil and more about Mufi. But that analysis and discussion was for another day, not tonight. Tonight was a night to savor the victory. Tonight was a time to remember where we came from, and to reflect on how we had all come together to support Neil.

In my office is a picture of newly elected governor Neil Abercrombie surrounded by his close friends, Governor Cayetano, Randy Iwase, Charlie Toguchi, John Radcliffe, Jim Boersma and me. Not everyone who should have been in that picture is there, which is unfortunate, but Neil inscribed my copy of the photo with the words, "To Rick Tsujimura, a _Real_ Winner." That night, we were all winners.

This campaign created a deep sense of camaraderie. It was heartening to see such a flat and inclusive organization succeed. We were allowed to disagree with even the candidate and there were definitely times that we did.

This election dispelled the notion that disparate parts of the political establishment couldn't come together for the election of a candidate. Burns, Gill, Waihee, Cayetano and Ariyoshi people were all in this mix of supporters. From that perspective, the election not only healed wounds but did so in a way that gave us all a sense of being one.

And I would have a chance to try to replicate this in the very next election.

CHAPTER SEVENTEEN

Kirk Caldwell: Hope Floats

~✤

"Hope is definitely not the same thing as optimism. It is not the
conviction that something will turn out well, but the certainty
that something makes sense, regardless of how it turns out."

—Vaclav Havel

In 2010 there was one other important local election—to fill the
position vacated by Mufi Hannemann. The office of mayor of the City
and County of Honolulu is one of the most significant in the state. But
no one who became mayor of Honolulu has ever become governor of
Hawai'i, although several have tried. The mayoralty has always been
considered a key step towards a local politician's future ambitions. In
2010 Peter Carlisle, then the city prosecutor, and Kirk Caldwell, Mufi's
managing director, both threw their hats into the ring.

Kirk had a handicap. Hannemann decided to wait until the last minute
to announce for governor, which gave Kirk scant time to run for mayor.
Kirk and I had been friends—not close, but more than just acquaintances.
I had known his wife, Donna Tanoue, for many years from her days as
the State financial institutions commish. I got to know Kirk a little better
during his term in the House of Representatives. In 2010 he gave me a
call. I was already working for Neil's campaign. I told Kirk that since he
was Hannemann's MD, I couldn't really help him. He was just too close
to Mufi, and I would appear to be straddling the fence if I signed on. I
told him that if he quit as MD, I might be able to help since he wouldn't
have ties to Mufi. But of course he didn't, and so of course I couldn't.

Kirk came close in 2010, but close wasn't good enough. In the end he
was closing on Carlisle's lead, but there just wasn't enough time—that

enemy of all campaigns that trail behind.

In 2011 Kirk again came to see me. I told him I wasn't much interested in county elections, that when I'd participated in the past it had been under special conditions. But then Donna Tanoue caught me on Bishop Street and asked me to reconsider. I told her that I would.

It took a couple of weeks to ruminate over Kirk's pathway to victory. You always need to think through whether a candidate really can pull off an election. I decided that Kirk actually could, but it would take a new campaign team, money and strong commitment by Kirk and his family.

We sat down and outlined the strategy. The initial order of business was to start building a new team. First on the wish list was Harry Mattson, my old buddy from the Harris and Abercrombie campaigns. I'd known Harry for decades and he was one of the best campaign guys around. He came with a bonus, Norma Wong. I owed Norma for her Harris campaign involvement, and I knew if Harry committed he could persuade Norma to join us. Harry agreed to meet Kirk and me for breakfast at the Asahi Grill on Ward Avenue. Breakfast turned into lunch. Harry and Kirk were deep in discussion. At the end of the day Harry was in. Ray Soon, who had done polling for many other campaigns, had been recruited to do Kirk's polling. The three of us formed the initial nucleus of this new campaign organization. But we needed a finance guy. I recalled that Marie Imanaka, Mitch Imanaka's wife, was Kirk's former campaign treasurer. So I asked Mitch to be Kirk's financial guy. He hesitated, then agreed. With Mitch we were the four musketeers.

This was not going to be easy. We got wind that Ben Cayetano was considering a run as well, but his focus was to kill the rail project. Carlisle and Kirk would be pro-rail. The equation meant that Ben was assured victory since the two campaigns would split the pro-rail vote. Ben knew this, we knew this, Carlisle knew this. So what was the strategy?

It was the "bear" strategy. Remember that old story about the bear chasing two guys in the woods? One says to the other, "We got to outrun the bear!" and the other guy responds, "No, I only have to outrun you!" Our strategy was to cede Ben the lead position, then beat Carlisle. In a head-on race we had an even chance to beat Ben in the general. This meant we needed to get ahead of Peter in the primary and deny Ben more than fifty percent of the vote. If we did this, we'd get to the next level and a chance to beat Ben.

We needed a PR firm. We had engaged the Olomana Loomis firm early on, but for various reasons that relationship didn't work out. They did a great job, but we needed more. Then we found out that Dennis Christianson from Anthology Marketing might be available. Dennis was and is one of the best political marketing guys in town—a latter-day Phil Wood and Jack Seigle. If you got Dennis, you had the best. Harry, Ray and I had a long history with Dennis, and we knew we were headed in the right direction.

Ray, Harry, Mitch and I, along with candidate Kirk, started holding a series of that time-tested event—the breakfast meeting with the Merchant Street business crowd. We needed seed money. The formula for these meetings was simple: We needed to exude confidence that we could win. Ray would get up and analyze poll results that showed we could pull this off. Harry would get up and explain how we would do it. Harry had introduced me to a new tool of persuasion, a book by Quintus Tullius Cicero entitled *How to Win an Election*. I still have my copy at my desk, along with my Drucker and my Napolitan. I don't exactly recall what we said, but citing Cicero seemed to provide assurance to these folks gathered together that we knew what we were doing, and that we were determined to do it. Then Kirk would give his stump speech and we concluded. We hosted several of these breakfast meetings, thanks to Mitch, and gradually started bringing in support, both personal and financial.

It reminded me so much of the Anderson campaign. And because Mitch, Ray, Harry, Norma and I had also been involved in Neil Abercrombie's campaign, we had the ability to ask the governor and his team to stay out of the race. At that point, Neil and Ben were best pals, and Charlie Toguchi was a friend on both sides, as was John Radcliffe. To ask them to stay neutral was difficult for them. After all, Ben was their friend. We knew we were asking a lot, but they were well aware that we had been there for the Abercrombie campaign when it needed us two years earlier.

We also knew that any promise of neutrality was a fragile one. Neil and the campaign did remain relatively neutral. There were the occasions when Neil's chief of staff would appear at a Cayetano function, or when Neil might make a positive comment about Ben. In April 2012, Civil Beat ran a story headed "Cayetano Won't Get Abercrombie's Endorsement," where a blog post by Ian Lind read:

At the same time that the administration is gung ho for development, Gov. Abercrombie told people in a recent informal conversation that he backs both Ben Cayetano's mayoral bid and Cayetano's opposition to rail. Abercrombie said he had favored the original rail plan for a system that would link Kapolei with Waikīkī and the University of Hawaiʻi's Mānoa campus, but that isn't the system that is now being built, according to two people who were present. Neil has sidestepped the public rail debate, but I think he could make a difference if he privately backs Cayetano. [Abercrombie spokeswoman Donalyn] Dela Cruz said her boss has not formally endorsed Cayetano for mayor. Asked about whether he opposes the current Honolulu rail project, she said the governor has "long supported mass transit."[154]

We didn't make a fuss; we knew that they were in a difficult position and if we barked about it, that fragile status might become outright support for Ben, to our detriment.

Ben was the alpha dog in the race, the one to beat. He had good name recognition, and Kirk's was way below Peter's. We needed to get on the radio to build Kirk's name recognition. Once he was known, we could go to the issues, but you can't do both. This was a tough time. Kirk didn't have the incumbency; that was Peter's asset. And Ben had his old guard, and a friend in Neil Abercrombie. We had, well, us. We did have Dennis Christianson, and his ads on the radio were beginning to make progress. Union endorsements and business support were growing. The grassroots were gradually coming around.

Eventually, we began to pull away from Carlisle. First, Peter never really had a campaign organization, at least not in the sense that we knew campaigning. Second, our level of campaign expertise was as good as it gets in Honolulu. Third, we had a great candidate who wasn't afraid to campaign.

Fourth, we had Dennis. You may recall his hilarious radio ads. This was a first for Hawaiʻi—humorous political ads, not the usual soapsuds spots, but entertaining ones. So much so, we had heard that kids were repeating them at school. Here's one example, which addressed the confusion over the rail issue:

---

[154] "Cayetano Won't Get Abercrombie's Endorsement," Civil Beat, April 8, 2012, http://www.civilbeat.com/2012/04/cayetano-wont-get-abercrombies-endorsement/.

VALLEY GIRL TYPE: So, you know, I was, like, listening to the whole rail transit argument thing? And Ben Cayetano was saying, like, "No way!" and Peter Carlisle was saying, "Way!" and so Ben was all "Nu-uh," and Peter was, like, "Yu-huh," and then Ben is all "Bus rapid transit!" and I'm, like, "Where are you going to put all those buses, dude?" and he's all, like, "I have a secret plan!" and I'm, like, "Whatever! But we gotta do something!" and he's all, like, "Nu-uh," and Peter's, like, "Yu-huh," and I'm, like, "I'm outta here!" and Ben says, "No way!" and I'm, like, "Is that all you ever say?" and he says, "No way!" and I'm, like, "Way!" and he's, like, "I'll sue you!" and I'm all, "Whatever!" and then they say... [fades]

ANNOUNCER: Tired of the mindless argument about rail transit? Think we need a little more honesty and openness in the discussion? So does Kirk Caldwell.

Here's another one, aimed exclusively at Ben Cayetano:

                    [Game show theme music. Applause.]
GAME SHOW HOST: It's time for the final round of "Know Your Ben!" Ready?
CONTESTANT: Ready!
GAME SHOW HOST: How will Ben Cayetano improve traffic on O'ahu?
CONTESTANT: Oh! Kill rail transit?
                    [Ding! Applause.]
GAME SHOW HOST: That's right! And how will Ben Cayetano fix the potholes?
CONTESTANT: Kill rail transit!
                    [Ding! Applause.]
GAME SHOW HOST: Right again! And where will Ben put the landfill?
CONTESTANT: Kill rail transit!
                    [Ding! Applause.]
GAME SHOW HOST: And his favorite restaurant is?
CONTESTANT: Kill rail transit!
                    [Ding! Applause.]
GAME SHOW HOST: Finally, what is Ben's favorite color?
CONTESTANT: Red. No, wait! Kill rail transit!
                    [Ding! Ding! Ding! Music. Applause.]
CONTESTANT: Wow! You really know your Ben!

[Applause fades.]

ANNOUNCER: Think our next mayor should be focused on more
                    than just one issue? So does Kirk Caldwell.

Money was in short supply so we had to be extremely judicious in how we used our funds, especially in the primary. Our goal, remember, was to beat Peter, not Ben. We needed to be the strong second, and then coalesce the pro-rail vote under our banner after the primary.

The campaign was not without controversy. The PRP ads, in which Pacific Resource Partnership attacked Ben for alleged improprieties while governor, were a distraction to our campaign. We felt they were beginning to hurt us. No matter what we said, it always appeared as though we were somehow benefiting from these ads. In fact, we may have been, but it wasn't my style, nor Kirk's. They were an independent group, however, and we couldn't stop them.

Did the PRP ads affect the outcome of the election? It's debatable, but I believe they did. Negative campaigning, as much as we publicly abhor it, is not new in Hawai'i. Back in 2004, during the mayoral race between Duke Bainum and Mufi Hannemann, a negative whisper campaign against Duke Bainum's new wife was considered the worst in modern Hawai'i elections. Like the later Atomic Monkey scandal, local politics became embroiled in innuendo and dark accusations.

Duke Bainum had been leading in the polls.[155] But neither candidate received more than fifty percent, which resulted in a runoff between Hannemann and Bainum in the general. Howard Dicus wrote in the September 18, 2004, edition of *Pacific Business News*: "The Honolulu mayoral race wasn't settled Saturday. Duke Bainum outpolled Mufi Hannemann but didn't win 50 percent. Result: a November runoff."[156]

In November, Hannemann beat Duke Bainum, and many attributed the victory to a smear campaign using emails about Bainum's wife, re-

---

[155] Crystal Kua, "Bainum leads in race for mayor," *Honolulu Star-Bulletin*, August 8, 2004. "Duke Bainum is leading opponent Mufi Hannemann in the race to become the next mayor of Honolulu, according to a *Honolulu Star-Bulletin*/KITV-4 News poll… But with a sizable number of undecided voters and many respondents saying they may change their mind, the race is still a toss-up… And the poll indicates that former mayor Frank Fasi could win enough votes to force a runoff at the general election."

[156] Howard Dicus, "Runoff for Honolulu mayor; Kim, Carlisle re-elected; Kawamoto, Aduja out," *Pacific Business News*, September 18, 2004.

garding an alleged caregiving incident years before. Crystal Kua and Rob Perez reported in *The Honolulu Star-Bulletin*'s November 3, 2004 edition:

> Mufi Hannemann came from behind to beat Duke Bainum in the race for Honolulu mayor last night. Hannemann had been trailing in the polls throughout the campaign but eked out a win with a roughly 1,300-vote difference at the third printout… Bainum officials and supporters said that negative attacks against Bainum and his wife in the final days of the campaign might have made the difference in the race… "I think we did everything right. I'm very disappointed," [Bainum supporter] City Councilman Gary Okino said. "It's absolutely due to the smear that contributed to loss." Campaign co-chairman Roy Amemiya said, "If it did, then it's a sorry day for Hawai'i politics…" Hannemann spokeswoman Elisa Yadao said she did not know anything about the organization and said Hannemann had no part in any smear campaign.[157]

In many ways this 2004 whisper campaign about Bainum's wife was much more toxic than the well-publicized allegations by PRP eight years later. At least the PRP ads were out in the open, and not underground like the salacious Bainum slurs. Ken Conklin, PhD, in a November 17, 2004, article, questioned the "morality" of smearing family members in a campaign:

> Is it right for the press to "drag family members" into political campaigns? Is it right to "smear" a political candidate or public figure by pointing out the bad behavior of family members or close associates? Is it right to focus the media spotlight on "innocent" people who just happen to be family members or friends of a controversial public figure? Was it a smear of mayoral candidate Duke Bainum when [*Hawai'i Reporter* writer] Malia Zimmerman published unsavory facts and court documents pertaining to Bainum's wife Jennifer?[158]

---

157 Crystal Kua and Rob Perez, "Hannemann wins," *Honolulu Star-Bulletin*, November 3, 2004.

158 Kenneth R. Conklin, PhD, "Smearing Public Figures By Reporting the Behavior of Family Members," November 17, 2004, http://www.angelfire.com/hi5/bigfiles3/smearingpublicfigures.html.

The outrage in 2012 over PRP's attack ads can be contrasted with the lack of (or less intense) outrage in 2004. No one called for an investigation; few observers even spoke out against such an outrageous act. In fact, one would be forgiven for drawing the conclusion that this was now the new norm. Hawai'i, you'd have thought, was becoming the same as the rest of the country. The Atomic Monkey incident in 2010 likewise got press, but not the levels of outrage expressed in 2012. What was the difference? The 2004 and 2010 smears were, in my opinion, far more heinous than the 2012 allegations, because they were done surreptitiously and without attribution. In 2012 they were out in the open. You knew who was making these allegations. This was tough negative campaigning, but not a smear in the 2004/2010 sense.

Blogger Ian Lind pointed out that these were not the first such political smears in the modern era. That inauspicious award may go to the unsubstantiated sexual misconduct allegations that surfaced in the 1986 John Waihee-Cec Heftel gubernatorial race. As Lind noted:

[T]he Heftel smear as I recall it was largely based on unverifiable rumor and innuendo, the attack on Bainum's wife is based on court documents and innuendo. The documents, at least, can be checked and another side to the story can be verified, as you ably did with very little apparent effort or discomfort. In all these circumstances the attacked candidate might decide not to respond to the allegations as a matter of principal or strategy, but the mainstream media really has no excuse not to look into what was said, attempt to set the record straight and attempt to trace the insidious behavior back to its source (and I don't just mean the writer of the piece).[159]

Of course there were others who reported on and analyzed the Heftel smear, including columnists Bob Jones, who had once been a newscaster and reporter for KGMB. Jones wrote in a February 10, 2010, *MidWeek* column:

The state Narcotics Investigation Unit got a statement from an arrested-convicted-imprisoned druggie…claiming to have observed

---

[159] Ian Lind, iLind.net, October 30, 2004, http://ilind.net/diary/oct_5_04.html.

Heftel at a party where drugs were used. The state gave a copy of that statement to the city prosecutor, the late Charles Marsland, and it got photocopied in his office and was distributed to reporters, who did not use it, and anti-Heftel labor unions, who did. But few ordinary voters saw that document. It could not have been a deciding factor. So what did in Heftel? I say a combination of his often-odd mannerisms, his flip-flop politics and Hawaiʻi not being ready to elect a never-held-local-office fellow from the Mainland... I suspect a lot of people had a change of heart in the voting booth. Then the boom fell on him and he was never again a player in Hawaiʻi politics.[160]

Back in 2002 then Democratic Party chair Lorraine Akiba challenged the GOP to abide by a "clean campaign" pledge. *The Honolulu Advertiser* noted:

The proposal came from Democratic Party Chairwoman Lorraine Akiba, who was obviously trying to get the goat of the local Republican Party... Micah Kane, executive director of the state Republican Party, was not about to take the bait. The GOP, he said, already is committed to running clean and factual campaigns. No new pledge is required. *If the two sides want to do something to elevate the quality of local campaigns (and the turnout that comes with them), they should take a personal vow not to accuse the other side of dirty politics. Run your campaign as you wish, negative or positive, soft sell or hard sell. But knock off the accusations that the other side isn't playing fair. All it does is reinforce the idea in the mind of the voter that all politics is dirty. And we know that isn't the case.*[161] (Emphasis added.)

No pledge necessary? The GOP would rue that statement just nine months later. Many may have forgotten the 2002 smear against LG candidate Duke Aiona. *Honolulu Star-Bulletin* writer Richard Borreca

---

[160] Bob Jones, "Remembering Heftel's Heady Days," *MidWeek*, February 10, 2010, http://archives.midweek.com/content/columns/justthoughts_article/remembering_heftels_heady_days/.

[161] "Clean campaigns are all about being positive," *Honolulu Advertiser*, February 1, 2002, http://the.honoluluadvertiser.com/article/2002/Feb/01/op/op01a.html.

recorded that allegation:

> Yesterday, attorneys across the state and all members of the Legis-lature got an anonymous letter in the mail about James "Duke" Aiona, the former Family Court judge and attorney who is the GOP lieutenant governor candidate. The letter, which made reference to Aiona being Hawaiian, said he was not bright and that he had been rewarded his judgeship by his law partner, Gerard Jervis, in return for settling a lawsuit in Jervis' favor when Aiona was a deputy city corporation counsel. Yesterday, Aiona called the letter "all lies." His campaign chairman, George Lindsey, said the unsigned, one-page letter is "designed to make people feel bad about each other..." Laura Figueira, who was Heftel's assistant and worked on his gubernato-rial campaign, said the anonymous attack was difficult to defend against because it came just days before the primary election and made voters doubt the integrity of the candidate. "The candidate is forced to deny outlandish charges," Figueira said. The Aiona letter says GOP gubernatorial candidate Linda Lingle picked Aiona to be her running mate in meetings with Jervis, but Lingle said she had never met Jervis, an attorney and former Bishop Estate trustee. "It is false and misleading, and it is an out-and-out lie," Lingle said. Pre-viously in the campaign, Lingle said her campaign was targeted by anonymous racist mailings. As for the anonymous newspaper ads, Robert Watada, Campaign Spending Commission executive direc-tor, said the ads appear designed to escape reporting requirements. Political ads that mention a candidate must state who paid for them, but the anonymous ad only attacks the GOP and does not mention a specific candidate.[162]

That wasn't the only smear in 2002. According to *Honolulu Star-Bulletin* reporter Rick Daysog:

> The lawyer for Honolulu Mayor Jeremy Harris charged yesterday that Harris is a victim of a smear campaign to link him to a for-

---

[162] Richard Borreca, "GOP decries anonymous letter taking aim at candidate Aiona," *Honolulu Star-Bulletin*, October 31, 2002.

mer Maui beauty queen who was indicted for theft and arrested for allegedly promoting prostitution. William McCorriston said that Harris and his wife, Ramona, have never met Lisa Katherine Otsuka, nor do they know the 32-year-old former Ewa resident. McCorriston also said the Harris campaign did not employ Otsuka, nor did it make any direct payments to her. "Enough is enough. The mayor is outraged by attempts to link him to Ms. Otsuka," McCorriston said. "This is nothing but a hatchet job."[163]

The naïve suggestion in that February *Advertiser* editorial that accusations about negative campaigning should be discarded seems hilarious in hindsight. The notion that exposing negative campaigning only reinforces the public's perception of dirty politicians reeks of Neville Chamberlain's attitude in dealing with the events unfolding in 1930s Europe. To suggest that we deal with such negative campaigning by not calling it out is at best appeasement and at worst encouragement of more smears.

So is it now the new norm that negative advertising is acceptable? There have been many other instances in local politics, online, in flyers, in television ads and elsewhere. I was taught that if you can't say anything nice about someone, "no say nottin'." But that old-school discipline has faded with the electronic connectivity that provides the cloak of anonymity, one in which disparagement can be accepted as truth. I am sympathetic to Ben Cayetano's reaction; no candidate should be subject to unfair aspersions and innuendo. But the reality is that the "atomic monkeys" cannot be controlled. At least Ben knew who was casting the aspersions; Neil and Duke did not. The challenge for us as a society is to

---

[163] Rick Daysog, "Attorney says Harris is victim of smear campaign. 'This is nothing but a hatchet job,' says William McCorriston," *Honolulu Star-Bulletin*, September 27, 2002. The link was Otsuka receiving an investment from two Harris political allies, Norma Wong and Harry Mattson, through their business. Daysog reported, "McCorriston cited a news release issued by Mattson's attorney that said Otsuka had no connections to Harris and that Mattson thought he was investing his own money with a reputable businesswoman... 'Mr. Mattson is deeply disturbed by a situation where his investment of personal resources in a legitimate business with someone he believed to be a successful entrepreneur has turned out otherwise,' the release said. McCorriston also took issue with Bob Watada, the head of the state Campaign Spending Commission, who questioned the payments. Watada's remarks are based on 'innuendo and rumor' and come from a person who did not want Harris to run for governor or serve as mayor, McCorriston said."

eradicate or control such behavior.

The difficulty is that we can't restrain first amendment right to express opinions, including independent-, Democrat- or Republican-leaning groups that buy print ads and broadcast spots and send out flyers. In many ways, this is a boon for the media, adding to their bottom lines every couple of years during the political season. So how can you defend against this negative campaigning? To this the credibility of the candidate is critical. If a candidate is vulnerable on his or her character, he's obviously more susceptible to this kind of innuendo. Duke Bainum was the "nice guy" who was an exception to that rule. But in his case, the smear wasn't against him but against his wife.

It is extremely unfortunate that such behavior is tolerated and excused. I believe most people find it objectionable, but recent campaign events suggest that there's a sense of voyeurism in watching politicians squirm. It can be a spectator sport. Have we descended to this type of "entertainment?"

But politics isn't entertainment; it is serious business. Choosing our leaders shouldn't be done on a whim or on emotion, but on cold hard facts. In many ways our obsessive reliance on media in all its forms has transformed politics from its noble roots of debating broader policy implications to an institution constantly enduring a "gotcha" mentality. We revel in the twists and squirms of candidates, not whether they have the best programs, or whether they can work well with others. And as citizens, we don't always ask the right questions, because we often don't know what the right questions are. As a result, we must rely on an independent media to do so. But how independent is a media that relies dependent on political ads? Someone selling a service by definition always has an agenda.[164]

To my mind the 2012 general election couldn't have ended soon enough. When all the votes had been counted, Kirk Caldwell had rolled to victory over Ben Cayetano by a margin of fifty-three to forty-five

---

[164] I once represented Gannett Corporation locally and am aware of the so-called Chinese wall between the sales and editorial departments. But should this be left to chance and self-regulation? Shouldn't there be some yardstick upon which to measure this claim? Do ad departments have an influence on the stories and outcomes? And when does opinion qualify as news? Clearly we need to restrict the opportunity for a candidate like Cec Heftel to use his media ownership position as a bully pulpit for political purposes.

percent. As Nathan Eagle and Nick Grube in Civil Beat reported on November 5, 2012, Ben "blamed his loss on the special interest groups that spent millions of dollars on attack ads and other campaign tactics to prevent him from becoming mayor."

> "The election will usher in a new era in Hawai'i politics," Cayetano said. "Basically what it means is if you have money you have influence. You will be able to sway the way people who vote..." "This election was very divisive," Caldwell said. "There was negative campaigning. I know Ben didn't like it and I know I didn't like it. I wish we could've just talked about the issues..."

Kirk's come-from-behind victory engendered the same elation among his campaign staff as Eileen Anderson's had thirty-two years earlier. It was a magical night. As in Abercrombie's upset victory in 2010, it seemed there was a new day dawning. But for every action there is an equal and opposite reaction. Ben Cayetano's loss was a bitter pill for him to swallow, and this would have ramifications in the governor's race two years later. And as we would soon learn, a longtime friendship would be sacrificed on the altar of politics.

The flat structure that we had built for the Abercrombie campaign was efficient here as well. I was in charge, but only nominally, as we replicated the group meeting/group think that we used in Neil's campaign. My theory was that we already enjoyed great mutual trust—Lex, Harry, Ray, Gary Caulfield, Hubert Minn, Mike Freitas, Dan Ide, Dennis Enomoto, John Serikawa, Gary Nakata, Dennis Christianson, Georgette Deemer, Norma Wong, Mitch Imanaka, Glenna Wong, et.al. And since we trusted one another, then we shouldn't need to ask permission in our day-to-day operations, unless we were making big expenditures or a major policy statement. No one needed to see me to schedule a sign holding or a coffee hour. A few people were concerned about giving our people too much freedom, as had happened during the Anderson campaign. But we found that once they were free to do their jobs, they rose to the occasion.

While conceptually easy to understand, the reality of running an organization in this manner is quite different. It requires a watchful eye, especially in matters of timing. Our group dynamic was such that we all got along, which is one of the keys to successful campaigning. This demands respect, thoughtful consideration an openness to other ideas, and doing what's best for the campaign, not for your own position. Many times this means just listening rather than talking. That's sometimes difficult for people who are leaders, but it's essential for maintaining a strong organization. A good leader, Peter Drucker wrote, "considers only what is right and never who is right." This is true whether you're running a corporation or a campaign. Bob Oshiro taught me that. Anyone attempting to run a political campaign should first become a student of management.

The flat organization definitely works, but it depends mightily on the people involved. It is built on trust. If you want to work this way, you need to trust one another. If that trust isn't there, you'll have a hierarchy. Ask yourself how you want to run your organization. On trust or distrust?

In our Caldwell campaign, we also depended a great deal on the unions, and we received most of the major union endorsements. Of course, you still had to persuade the rank and file. Kirk did that at many pau hana and lunch meetings, attended by both active members and retirees. For those who believe that an endorsement by union leadership guarantees rank and file support, I can tell you it's not always true. The rank and file need as much attention as any other group, maybe even more so given the fluid internal politics of each union. Again a campaign and the candidate must respect all the people, both leaders and membership. None can be taken for granted. Keep in mind that all politics is retail. That is to say, all politics is personal. It is one on one, whether the one is the candidate or the campaigner who represents him.

Another cardinal rule is to start with the low-hanging fruit—that is, tap the supporter base first, not those who need a lot of convincing. If you touch the individuals who are naturally affiliated with you, they will eventually reach out to the others. In school, there was a science experiment where you'd put a leaf in a jar of colored water, and the color would gradually spread into the leaf's large veins and then the smaller. Politics is the same. The best approach is to tap the big organizations and then work your way to their grassroots.

The critical element in any campaign is the grassroots. A committed force of volunteers is like gold; treasure them. In many ways, a campaign without volunteers cannot sustain itself. And while it takes time to build, the structure once built is the sinew upon which the organization moves. Be they union members or business people, housekeepers or shop clerks, these unsung heroes are usually less indulged than they really deserve. Remember that volunteers don't have to do anything. After all, they're volunteers! The campaign needs to embrace them as family and make them feel an essential part of the election effort. Valuing people means respecting them and honoring their contributions, and volunteers, of course, can tell whether they're truly valued. A sweaty volunteer who's just been out holding signs on Nimitz Highway in the hot afternoon sun is as valuable, if not more so, than the company president stopping by campaign headquarters in his air-conditioned car. A genuine recognition of a volunteer's service and sacrifice is critical to building a relationship.

Speaking of sign holding, or sign waving, this may be the most visible feature of campaigning, Hawaiian style. Most campaigns do it, just because it's expected. For this, they can blame Charles Campbell, who is generally acknowledged as the first local politician to stake out a spot on the roadside in this manner, back in the early '70s. Charlie was an African-American teacher at Farrington, a gracious, well-known politico and civil rights activist who served as a state legislator and city councilman. He's the one who presented Martin Luther King Jr. with the *lei* Dr. King wore on his famous 1965 march across the Edmund Pettus Bridge in Selma, Alabama.

Curbside campaigning is really a Hawai'i thing. One of the reasons candidates like to do it, of course, is to be able to interact with the public. Kirk Caldwell, for instance, receives very good responses when he's out holding signs. It's a good way to gauge public opinion, although obviously not scientific. It's reinforcing to get those positive shakas and waves and honks from the drivers, or even being able to walk up to cars stopped at intersections. Of course, the reverse is also true. It's no fun when people give you the finger or yell obscenities. So whether or not a candidate actually likes sign waving, or finds it useful, depends in large part on the response he or she gets.

We often spread our sign holders about five to six feet apart, although ten feet is really preferable, because of the angle of sight as people drive by, so ten sign holders might take up anywhere from sixty to 100 feet. That's a lot of roadside real estate. But crowding them together only compresses things and makes the scene appear frenetic. Then again, if that's the effect you want, then that's what you do.

Getting people out to sign wave can be tough, and that's why you might be seeing less of it these days. Organized groups such as labor unions seem to be more adept at this than the individual campaigns. Many unions do so at or near their headquarters. For example, in Honolulu ILWU members typically hold signs in front of their Atkinson Drive HQ, the Carpenters rank and file on Waiakamilo/Houghtailing in front of their headquarters, the laborers on Palama Street, the UPW on School Street. Some, like the Ironworkers, tend to be on the west side rather than in town. And then there are the movable crews—the Fasi campaign was very good at busing their people around from location to location.

In 2010 Neil Abercrombie's women's group boasted a line of supporters stretching along King Street from downtown to Ward Avenue. It was an amazing sight. But this kind of mobilization is unique and in many ways serendipitous. It grows organically and is based more on relationships than campaign mobilization. Although it started as a women's event, Abercrombie's King Street turnout quickly became a campaign event with a much broader reach.

Perhaps the ultimate Hawai'i sign practitioner was State Senator Steve Cobb, who took sign waving to new levels of technology. When Steve was running for the legislature from east Honolulu in the 1970s, he had a regular spot near the intersection of Ainakoa Avenue and the H-1 Kāhala viaduct during morning drive time. In the beginning he was like all the other sign wavers, but he soon equipped his signs with flashing lights and even added a coffee cup holder. Then he made himself a seat at the end of a painter's extension pole, which made it look as though he were standing even when he sat down. Steve was really good at this. (Sadly, his political career went into the tank after he was arrested for propositioning an undercover police officer posing as a Chinatown transvestite. That didn't play well in conservative east Honolulu. He later moved to Russia.)

In addition to sign waving, simple walkthroughs of workplaces, shopping centers or just down the street—downtown, 'Aiea or Kaimukī, for instance—can be very worthwhile. Just being out there among the people is the best campaigning. Jeremy Harris, Mufi Hannemann and Kirk Caldwell are and were great at this. A solid campaigner from dawn to dusk and beyond, Ariyoshi was like the Energizer bunny, working long hours and never complaining. Eileen Anderson, on the other hand, complained a lot. Sign waving, canvassing and working the crowds are all retail politics. Some are good at it, others less so. ⳬ

CHAPTER EIGHTEEN

Neil Abercrombie: I'm Not Your Pal

~&

"In every field of endeavor, there are people who could easily be successful
but who spend their entire lives making one political mistake after another.
They become so absorbed in themselves that they ignore the very
people they would most like to influence. Rather than recruit allies,
they limit their horizons to missions they can accomplish alone.
Instead of confronting or seducing their adversaries, they avoid them.
In making important deals, they become obsessed with intangibles
and give away the store. They become crippled by handicaps
when they could be exploiting them."

—Chris Matthews, *Hardball*

Two thousand fourteen was a year much anticipated. This was to be
Neil Abercrombie's year. His general election opponent was considered a political lightweight, if not an unknown; he had more money
than any other candidate; and he had a well-oiled campaign composed
of many diverse Democratic elements. But in the end, no matter how
much money was in the war chest, no matter how many human assets
there were, the critical element—the candidate—was damaged, and damaged substantially. His loss was due not to campaign shortcomings but to
Abercrombie's decisions on governance during his first term. I apologize
to Neil and others in his administration if this seems harsh. But in the
cold light of day, had certain actions and issues been handled differently,
the outcome might have been different.

Here are three adages to remember:

"Good government is good politics." —Joe Napolitan

"Politics is about addition and multiplication, not subtraction and division." —Bob Oshiro

"You don't win elections, you lose them." —Bob Oshiro

I was involved in the Abercrombie-Ige contest, but not nearly as much as in Neil's 2010 gubernatorial campaign. This time I was more of a pinch hitter, a consultant. Because of my role in the Caldwell election two years earlier, in which I was deeply involved, I was cautious about appearing at Abercrombie functions and decisions—I knew it would give the impression that the two campaigns were linked, which they weren't. Some of the same people worked on both Abercrombie campaigns, but the leadership was definitely different this time around.

In many ways, it's more fitting to start at the end of this campaign rather than the beginning, as the lessons learned will become clearer that way. So let me start with the failings of the Abercrombie administration as listed by journalists Loren Moreno and Robbie Dingeman in *Honolulu* magazine:

9. Proposed taxing pensions
8. "I'm not your pal"
7. Angered Hawai'i teachers
6. Nurses contract
5. Same-sex marriage special session
4. Dying wish
3. Pro Bowl
2. Canceled debates
1. Big wind[165]

Each of these items in and of itself was not entirely devastating; but cumulatively they were. To address each of these one by one:

Taxing pensions riled the pensioners. And as most politicos are aware, people in that sixty-five-and-over group are consistent and habitual vot-

---

[165] Loren Moreno and Robbie Dingeman, "9 Reasons Neil Abercrombie Lost the Hawai'i Governor's Race—Neil Abercrombie is the first elected Democratic governor in the state of Hawai'i to lose his bid for re-election," *Honolulu* magazine, August 11, 2014.

ers. Threaten their economic security and you'll feel the backlash. Neil lost a chunk of primary voters with that proposal. Was the proposal necessary? Could some other solution have been found? The measure was DOA at the legislature. And it stirred the AARP to action, as it did the state pensioners, who were also HGEA retirees. Many were deeply angered. And for what? The lesson here was not to put forward a proposal that would fail at the legislature and cost you votes with no positive return. It may be a good idea, but a good idea isn't always good politics. This is one example of counter-productive result. Someone didn't do the basic political math here, and Abercrombie lost the seniors.

When Neil said, "I'm not your pal, I'm not your counselor, I am your governor," this was supposed to be shorthand for, "I can make the hard decisions even when it's painful." But it came across as, "I don't empathize with you; I don't care about you." I know Neil and I know that's not what he meant, but those looking for a reason to vote against him were given a match to light the tinderbox. Again, someone had failed to choose the words carefully. And instead of apologizing, he doubled down. He was right intellectually, but he was wrong politically. He lost the union rank and file.

In the 2010 election, the teachers' union went all out for Neil. While there was no agreement to reciprocate, the Hawai'i State Teachers Association (HSTA) still didn't expect a proposal by Neil to cut pay and benefits. But that's exactly what he did. To be sure, the state was in dire financial straits. Neil hadn't realized just how dire until he took office. In an effort to stem the tide he had to take drastic action, even with his supporters such as pensioners and teachers. This was hardly a position that would engender support from these same groups when he ran for re-election. Again, who was doing the political calculations? Often a first-term politician approaches such problems gingerly—as they are, or soon will be, seeking re-election. Most second-term incumbents can afford to be bolder, but not a newly elected politico. He lost the teachers, irrevocably.

Neil also vented at nurses on Maui, which was caught on video with a cell phone and went viral. Neil was consistent, at least, and essentially asked the nurses to help bear the pain and the budget cuts. But Maui had been one of Neil's early strongholds. He lost the nurses.

Many evangelicals and other conservatives took umbrage at the speed at which the same-sex legislation sped through the legislature, called into special session by Neil. While the public had its say and the legislature made its determination and all was done according to the law, the bill's opponents felt that the process was managed to their disadvantage, that the cards were stacked against them in an unfair fight. They held a number of individuals responsible, but no one more than Neil.

In 2014 his statements about the National Football League's Pro Bowl—whether the money spent by the state was worth the cost—rubbed local sports fans the wrong way. Football is a big thing in Hawaiʻi. Neil didn't calculate that reaction. We know now that the NFL abandoned Aloha Stadium for Orlando after the 2016 Pro Bowl, but in 2014 the idea was incomprehensible to many in the sports and tourism community. He lost the local sports enthusiasts.

The canceled debates may have added fuel to the fire, but I didn't really consider them a big factor in Neil's fall from grace. More apparent were the effects of polling conducted by the newspaper and other news organizations. Once the *Star-Advertiser* surveys showed Ige in the lead, Neil's numbers began to slip, reported Harry Mattson, who conducted the campaign's in-house, get-out-the-vote phone bank. According to Harry, while Neil was trailing only slightly in the phone bank polls behind Ige, he suffered a precipitous drop right after the newspaper released its own poll.

As the election approached, many people in the community accused Neil of taking advantage of Hurricanes Iselle and Julio, in using his emergency television appearances for free publicity. But the reality was that by now, the die had already been cast, and those who disliked Neil were already migrating toward his relatively unknown opponent, State Senator David Ige.

But the big issue, and the one I believe contributed most substantially to Neil's ultimate defeat, was his appointment of Lieutenant Governor Brian Schatz to fill the vacancy left by the passing of Hawaiʻi's senior senator, Dan Inouye, the grand old man and *de facto* head of the state's Democratic Party. Inouye's storied career, his legacy and his reach among the rich and powerful, made his wishes law. Neil's decision to disregard Inouye's "dying wish" that Colleen Hanabusa replace him was to sever many of the ties he would have with the AJAs, and bind them instead to David Ige.

Bob Oshiro's words from long-ago campaigns—you don't win elections, you lose them—rang loud and true. Despite his good intentions,

Neil found himself and his administration on the subtraction and division side of the political ledger. Even understanding his logic for many of his proposals and positions, it seems he lost sight of the fundamental fact that he was a representative of the people, and what he did and what he said slowly separated him from those same groups that had always supported him. In many respects Neil was like that Athenian leader, Themistocles, who had the support of the people and fought the entrenched aristocracy. He had saved Greece against the onslaught of Persia at the Battle of Salamis. He earned the accolades of victory and enjoyed the admiration of all Athens. But eventually the adulation turned to spite because of his arrogance and the jealousy of his opponents and those who did not share in his aura of greatness. In the end he was ostracized which, as Plutarch wrote, "was not a penalty, but a way of pacifying and alleviating that jealousy which delights to humble the eminent, breathing out its malice into this disfranchisement."[166]

Neil was to suffer the same fate but for different reasons. When he had first moved into the governor's office after eight years of Republican Linda Lingle, local Dems breathed an air of anticipation and relief that they held the fifth floor once again. Neil and the team chose some really impressive cabinet members, including Kalbert Young as budget chief and David Louie as AG. They brought much to the team. Neil also had a strong relationship with Shan Tsutsui, his LG, and they worked well together on projects, just like in the good old days.[167] Neil had veterans like Bruce Coppa, Blake Oshiro and Mike Kido to handle the day-to-day ops in the governor's office.[168]

But in the end, the Abercrombie administration's faux pas on the issues were fatal shortcomings, from which the 2014 campaign could not recover. Neil had lost the groups upon which his 2010 election had been based: AJAs, teachers; nurses; unions and local voters in general. But

---

[166] Plutarch, "Themistocles," *Lives of the Noble Greeks and Romans.*

[167] A governor can make or break his LG's future. Governor Waihee's ceding of the A-Plus program to Ben Cayetano was a classic boost. Governor Ariyoshi's empowerment of John Waihee to help resolve a month-long United Airlines strike was another.

[168] He also got an unsung but vital assist from Amy Luke, Bruce's assistant and right hand, who formerly had worked in the legislature for Representative Sylvia Luke. She was the other bookend in the office to Kathleen Chapman, who was Neil's right hand. Add the scheduling expertise of Vicky Borges (who was also Jeremy Harris' chief assistant when he was mayor), plus the services of Kate Stanley, and you had an A-team.

maybe just as important, he didn't have a Mufi Hannemann running against him. The yardstick this time wasn't an opponent who had high negatives, but someone who people didn't know. In some ways the old saying, "The enemy of my enemy is my friend,"[169] entered the equation. It wasn't so much that people loved David Ige but rather saw him as a friend against the "enemy" Abercrombie.

Bob Oshiro's admonition about losing elections rings true for another reason. David Ige didn't win this election; Neil lost it, in the same way that Hannemann had lost it four years earlier. But there were similar outcomes in several races in 2014. Senate president Donna Kim, for example, was running against state house member Mark Takai. All of the early polls said she was the leader. Yet Takai won. And when Mufi ran for the congressional seat vacated when Colleen Hanabusa ran for the US Senate against Brian Schatz, it was accepted that he would win. He didn't. A relatively unknown local politician and Iraq War veteran, Tulsi Gabbard, beat him. Was there a thread running through all of this?

One might conclude these races were won because people were voting against and not for someone. Much like our Eileen Anderson campaign more than thirty years earlier, the anti-vote was critical to winning. These days, voter anger is precipitating results one hardly could have imagined in years past. This trend of voting is disturbing, because the public is often making choices not on the job performance of the candidates but on their likeability. If they don't like you, you won't win. So are we now in the age of beauty contests at the polls? An age of popularity contests? Is this now all about Miss or Mister Congeniality? How does a politician deal with voter anger or displeasure? The Greek story about Themistocles is instructive. The popular leader was notably responsible for victories against the Persians at Salamis. But his arrogance cost him that popularity more than once and he was ostracized by the *polis*, the people, of Athens. And so, a great leader was dismissed as a way to satisfy the crowd. Themistocles' fate deserves the attention of any leader, especially political leaders. His story reminds that even then, the polis preferred a leader who didn't boast about his accomplishments in public. Today, Themistocles and Alcibiades provide insight into how we look at politicians and

---

[169] Kautilya, *Arthashastra*.

how they look at themselves. In Alcibiades we see a person who had physical attributes that captured the hearts of the people; he was an accomplished and successful general. But like Themistocles, he too had an inflated ego. His desire for approval led him to defect from his native Athens to Sparta, its archrival. His only concern for loyalty was how it met his goals. Contrast this with the life of Cincinnatus, who was known for his selfless service to the community, and the abrogation of accolades and power that would descend from success.

But back to the twenty-first century. Of course, there were good reasons to vote for David Ige, not just against Neil. David is a longtime friend, whom I knew throughout his many years in the state senate. He is a truly nice guy—honest, trustworthy, fiscally prudent, intelligent—all the attributes one wants in a leader. The one thing he didn't have was a base. Abercrombie created that base for him. So in many respects, David owes his win to Neil. You can be sure that Hannemann was second-guessing the math as well. Had he run against Neil a second time, would he have won?

At the same time, all was not well between Neil and his longtime friend Ben Cayetano. In a surprising move, Ben turned on him during the election, as recorded by *Star-Advertiser* political reporter Richard Borreca:

> Former Gov. Ben Cayetano, one of Gov. Neil Abercrombie's closest political allies, says he will not support the veteran Democrat's re-election… Cayetano said he feels Abercrombie has changed his positions on key issues, and therefore, will back Abercrombie's primary opponent, state Sen. David Ige, chairman of the Ways and Means Committee. "I'm going to help David Ige; I'm going to help him. He is an underdog and Neil has a lot of money," Cayetano said. "I think David shows the contrast with Neil. He listens, he gives people respect and he is not afraid to make decisions and he is smart… [Neil] has changed completely—the things he criticized and the principles he was for, he seems like he has abandoned… If he wins, I hope he reflects on why people who used to support him don't support him now," Cayetano said.[170]

---

[170] Richard Borreca, "Abercrombie loses support of former ally Cayetano," *Honolulu Star-Advertiser*, November 17, 2013.

This action by Ben deeply hurt Neil. The two had endured many political crises together, each coming to the other's defense when necessary. Ben might have been more the net beneficiary of this relationship, and thus Ben's criticism of had a profound impact on Neil. After all those years of supporting Ben through thick and thin—in difficult negotiations with unions, in the early days in the legislature, fighting together in the trenches to change Hawai'i politics and power structure—now Cayetano was walking away, not quietly or privately but outwardly and openly.

Consider that during Ben's term as governor, Neil Abercrombie and John Radcliffe had helped settle a major strike at UH. Jerry Burris wrote in the *Advertiser*:

> There were…positive personal relationships that, in the end, brought the strike to a close. This was the close friendship between Cayetano, U.S. Rep. Neil Abercrombie and veteran lobbyist John Radcliffe, associate director of the UH Professional Assembly. These three go back a long way… Abercrombie, Cayetano and Radcliffe share certain personality traits as well, including a tough-talking, in-your-face combativeness. The years have made them comfortable with each other to a point that even when they disagree, they disagree as comrades rather than as enemies… A level of trust built through years of political wars made room for a degree of brutal frankness that would otherwise be impossible.[171]

Neil also assisted Ben in union negotiations with the HSTA in April 2001, along with former DOE chief Charlie Toguchi. Ben, Neil, Charlie and Clayton Hee were a big part of the old senate dissident group. But thirteen years later, Ben would disavow Neil, as recorded in the *Hawai'i Herald*:

> Cayetano has been upfront about his decision to part company with Abercrombie, his longtime friend and political ally, and instead support Ige. He said he had supported Abercrombie with campaign contributions and his personal vote in each and every one of his election bids. But he could not this time around. He said Abercrombie has

---

[171] Jerry Burris, "Personality had big role in UH deal," *Honolulu Advertiser*, April 22, 2001.

changed, from being a vanguard for the middle class and the disen-franchised to serving big money interests. He said his efforts to point out that change to his friend, Neil Abercrombie, were unsuccessful.[172]

Having worked up close and personal with both men, although admittedly not as an intimate, I will share some observations here. In politics, loyalty is first and foremost. In politics your word is your bond; all you have is your integrity. Money, wealth and power are transitory. My experience in politics leads me to conclude that the breakup of an alliance and friendship of decades wouldn't happen only on the basis of what was made public. I don't know the "real" reason, and maybe it is best that we don't. But the lesson here is that in politics friendships are to be cherished. In the end Neil, like Themistocles, suffered the attacks of those who knew him and what he had done. Whether his actions justified Ben's reaction is ultimately up to those two men to decide.

In the end 2014 was really about anger, and it was directed primarily at Neil Abercrombie. It became personal to Neil, especially considering that Brian Schatz beat back a determined effort by Colleen Hanabusa, in effect confirming Schatz' appointment two years earlier. If his 2014 election was a proxy fight between Neil and Dan Inouye, then Neil won. But in his own race, Neil suffered the consequences. This suggests it wasn't just his disregard of the late senator's wishes, but the many issues—the same-sex marriage legislation, the union confrontations, taxing the pensions—that combined to defeat Neil. And not David Ige.

It also demonstrates the power of social media and cell phone cameras. The recording of Neil lambasting a teacher went viral. Like other candidates, Neil had to learn a lesson of careful discipline in the techno era, when new tools can make every statement, every incident into a news item backed up by indisputable evidence. The power of such visuals creates a new campaign front, and another yardstick against which politicians and candidates are measured.

No longer is it good enough just to accomplish goals, or to simply get things done. Now the "who" of the candidate, the character of the candidate, can be revealed with great transparency. A candidate has to be

---

172 Michael Markrich and Karleen Chinen, "The Great 2014 David Vs. Goliath Match-Up," *Hawai‘i Herald*, June 2014.

on his or her toes, from a simple walk down the street to the most intense confrontations.

In Neil's case, voters ultimately gauged not the accomplishments of the man, but whether he was likeable or not.[173] The lesson for all politicians is that an election is a temporal glory. The last lines from the movie *Patton*, in the words of the general himself, have always resonated with me.

> For over a thousand years, Roman conquerors returning from the wars enjoyed the honor of a triumph—a tumultuous parade. In the procession came trumpeters and musicians and strange animals from the conquered territories, together with carts laden with treasure and captured armaments. The conquerors rode in a triumphal chariot, the dazed prisoners walking in chains before him. Sometimes his children, robed in white, stood with him in the chariot or rode the trace horses. A slave stood behind the conqueror, holding a golden crown, and whispering in his ear a warning: that all glory is fleeting.

While an election seems to set a course for an elected politician, it is but the beginning of the journey. As Joe Napolitan wrote, "Good government is good politics." I think the converse is also true: Bad governing is bad politics. I would add that governing doesn't mean doing what people want. Sometimes you have to do what they need, as prescribed in the old Rolling Stones song:

> *No, you can't always get what you want*
> *You can't always get what you want*
> *You can't always get what you want*
> *But if you try sometimes you just might find*
> *You get what you need.*[174]

The unfortunate nature of politics is that sometimes the politician believes he or she needs to win every argument. This isn't always true. What

---

[173] Neil's gubernatorial defeat also led to the loss of Kalbert Young as budget director and David Louie as AG, as well as the other cabinet members who had rebuilt state government after eight years of Republican budget cuts that had resulted in the likes of teacher and state worker furloughs.

[174] The Rolling Stones, "You Can't Always Get What You Want."

they need to do is make good decisions. Arguing with someone does nothing but heighten emotions. If you do the right thing for the right reasons, then voters who lean your way will support you just because you did so—even if they disagree with the decision. Politics is about listening and being humble, not timid, and not being a bully either. All people want is someone to whom they can relate.

But that's the world of politics these days. It can be cruel and merciless, unforgiving and treacherous. The rules have changed, and there are more diverse interests and philosophies than you can count.[175] The next election will represent a new measuring stick. By what gauge will the public measure the next governor? ~

---

[175] In 1998, Mike Tokunaga reflected on the state of Hawai'i's Democratic Party in the book *Japanese Eyes, American Heart*: "[I]n the old days, if you take the Nadao Yoshinagas, and the John Ushijimas, and the Kazuhisa Abes and Nelson Dois throughout the state—these people in the 1950s and '60s had a common purpose, because they were of plantation stock, and they wanted equality. And they worked for equality; they improved the educational system. Now I kind of sense that the Democratic Party is splintered, and it looks like everybody is out for himself."

CHAPTER NINETEEN

A Sparrow's Story

✒

"Life isn't about waiting for the storms to pass.
It's about learning to dance in the rain."

—Anonymous

Life is generational. One person can make a difference; it takes many people to change the world. It is important for each generation to impart its knowledge and experience to the next. But education can only be truly effective if the student wants to learn. Most of us have endured the experience of sitting in a class we didn't really care to take, but were required to. We found the subject uninteresting and the professor less than engaging. Life lessons are much the same. Unless you really want to know; you won't.

I had the great fortune to meet one particular young man on my political journey. At first glance, he didn't appear to be exceptional. You'd be forgiven for thinking he was plain and ordinary, but you'd be making a grave and unfortunate mistake. It would be like walking through a diamond field, finding an unusual stone, but tossing it aside because it wasn't exactly what you were looking for. Exceptional people are sometimes just under your nose, and while you may notice them, you don't really see them. Gary Nakata is such a person. When we met during the Harris campaign, he was just another campaign worker. Just another sparrow. But I learned differently. Here, in his own words, is Gary's story.

Someone asked me to write my own personal story of political and election campaigning in Hawai'i and I thought, *No sweat, easy!* Then I realized how many years it's been since my first time at a coffee hour. Twenty years went by really quickly, including several campaigns for governor, Congress and mayor, plus one house rep primary election just to see what it was like at that level.

It took some time and festering to get into political campaigning. I grew up wanting to be the governor of Hawai'i because I thought John Waihee was the coolest cat I ever saw on TV. Never mind all the squid water jokes—this guy could make you feel like climbing the Pali barehanded, like it was a walk in the park, and that was just watching him on TV. I remember the union talks and him doing the midnight talk with union leaders on the railing, and I could feel the power right through the television. Naïvely, I thought I could do that too. After all, I had been president of the freshman honor society at UH!

I went to work at Bank of Hawai'i after college and was introduced to the world of haves and have-nots. A kid from Kāne'ohe who went to Castle High School had no chance against all the private school pedigrees. At least that's what some of the pedigrees led me to believe. Others were not that sure. Robert Piper went to Damien High School but never forgot he came from 'Ewa Beach. He made sure that I didn't forget my roots either, and that it didn't matter where we came from, as much as where we were headed. In our minds it would just be a few short years before we became COB and CEO of the bank, then served out the rest of our lives in Congress representing Hawai'i.

During our short tenure at the bank, there were two senior managers whose nicknames were the Admiral and the Emperor. Our nicknames were the Senator and the Congressman. We had so many talks about how we'd change the world, the nation and Hawai'i for the better. To make sure successive generations inherited a better place. To get rid of politicians that thought only of themselves, and their cronies that did the same, and replace them all with good solid people like us, who thought only of making life better for others. Politics was a bad word to a lot of our peers. It was fun to be young, arrogant, motivated, idealistic and, to great extent, naïve.

I loved the idea of being in office and having influence, and changing the lives of others. But this head-butted strongly with the sick feeling I got every time I thought of election campaigning. I couldn't reconcile the two. Campaigning, I reasoned, was for others—people who liked to pander to the masses, sometimes with lies or half-truths, candidate T-shirts and cute jingles on radio and TV. I, on the other hand, would just wait until I was anointed into public office or befriended by someone who was. Like I said—idealistic and naïve.

Enter Bert Kobayashi Jr., who represented the biggest reality check of my life up till then. After a few years with the bank, having received the best business and financial analysis training possible, I trotted off to law school in Sacramento, after which I went to work at Bert's law firm. He was the Kobayashi in the Kobayashi, Sugita and Goda law firm, as well as its predecessor firm, Kobayashi, Watanabe, Sugita, Kawashima and Goda.

After I'd been working there for a year or so, Bert pulled me aside one day and asked what I was doing to become a successful lawyer. I said I was working hard, learning all I could about the law and gaining as much practical experience as I could. He asked me where I wanted to be in the future. I said I'd like to be on the letterhead. (Apart from being naïve, I was also arrogant!) I was lucky he didn't slap me upside the head. He asked how I expected to be a rainmaker and bring business into the firm. I said my work would speak for itself, plus I'd network around town and join the right organizations to get to know people who could throw business the firm's way.

He stared at me for what seemed like a long time. I think he was trying to figure out what to do—walk away, tell me off or offer some practical advice. "Forget all that," he said. "You need to get into politics." I don't think I made a sound. What he was telling me was I'd have to be one of those people waving at cars, handing out brochures and basically pandering to the masses. I thought, *But I'm a lawyer now. Can't I just wait till one my friends becomes governor or mayor, then appoints me attorney general or something?*

I asked Bert why, and he proceeded to give me a rundown on the practical realities of being a rainmaker in Honolulu. He then asked me who I liked in the 1996 elections. I don't remember what I said. "I'll set you up" was the last thing I heard him say as he walked away.

I wasn't sure what he meant by that. So I was waiting for some politician to call me to be a policy advisor when I got a memo to show up at a campaign meeting. I thought this was my big chance. Instead, I arrived at an elementary school cafeteria to find myself at a coffee hour. Nearly the entire firm was there. Bert had gotten about thirty of us there to attend a function for Arnold Morgado.

I met Gary Nakata for the first time at that function. If I didn't impress him at first, the lack of feeling was mutual. But we have since become fast friends and he has become my mentee, one way for me to repay my debt to generations past. Our activities mirrored each other. I understood his ambition and his drive; I had shared much of the same in my youth. But Gary had an advantage: He had a close cadre of friends, while I had very few. Growing up an only child can be both a curse and a blessing. You're comfortable by yourself and don't need the presence of others, but you also might not develop socially quite as well. My friends are close in that we share the same values and the same causes. In this regard, Bob Oshiro forever changed my life. Thanks in large part to him, my life purpose has focused on such issues as equality, justice, honesty and integrity, but executed with people through personal relationships.

I was fortunate to be part of a group of young people involved in community affairs. We called ourselves, quite unimaginatively, the Pau Hana group, which included Ben and Frank Kudo, Gary Caulfield, Randy Iwase, John Hara, Donna Tanoue, Meredith Ching, Neil Hannahs, Robin Campaniano, Judge Darryl Choy, Kaiulani De Silva, Mike Flores, Guy Fujimura, Clifford Higa, Rex Johnson, Pat Liu, Bob Miyasato, Mario Ramil, Ray Soon, Jim Stone, Robert Wo Jr., Delmond Won, Norma Wong, Al Yamada and Gregg Yamanaka. It was a diverse group. Our goal was to form a networking group, and this was before networking was an organized business practice. It allowed us to fellowship in a structured way. But we were always respectful of our jobs and would avoid anything that would compromise that role. This was especially true with Darryl and Mario, given their judicial careers. While we have all gone our separate ways, the Pau Hana group is still a fond memory of our youth.

Gary was part of a similar group. It came, like so many things in politics, from small beginnings. It started with the Harris campaign, as Gary tells it...

Generation X had big plans, and so did Roy Amemiya. I knew Roy from a past life, and our common bond was the Jaycees. In my life, it seems anytime I need someone to champion me, Roy shows up. A few years earlier, his opinion of me was critical in my hire at my firm, even though I totally botched the job interview.

In 2000, I got a call to have lunch with him. Roy was in charge of the Harris campaign grassroots effort and wanted a co-chair. Roy was again giving me a chance to take on greater challenges, and to sit at the main committee table. I wasn't sure how my Gen X acquaintances would take this. Some weren't too happy, but others were elated, knowing that they had someone at the table. So went the political posturing, but then life got really busy and I didn't have time to think about it anymore.

With Gen X's support, I set out to organize the grassroots. But I needed more help, so I called another Jaycee—Rick Taniguchi. Roy was clearly the boss, but I was given free rein to do whatever was necessary to make the grassroots work. Coffee hours needed the biggest fix and organization, and I set out with gusto. Roy needed my help, and I was going to give it to him, and Gen X was right there to help. Rick Taniguchi, Jim Lyon, Brian Uy, Brian Sen and I were constantly running around making sure Jeremy Harris was staffed up at his events.

Soon after the election, we learned that Roy had not been asked back by the Harris administration. This was a real setback, since we had hitched our wagon to Roy's star. I felt bad for him. I felt bad for us. Gen X was on its own. We didn't get the positions we wanted, but I was learning that there was more to be gained from a campaigns than just jobs. Jobs come and go, but relationships last a lifetime. After all, it's in the wee hours of a campaign, maybe not having slept for two days, that you come to understand who you can count on:

- Rick Taniguchi and I became inseparable during campaign seasons. He became my brother and always will be.
- To this day, I'd drop anything I'm doing to help Jim Lyon or Brian Uy. Gen Y, Gen Z, Gen whatever, and the millennials have all come and gone. But in my mind, it was a Gen X band of volunteers who kicked ass all over Honolulu during that one shining season.
- Nor was it a bad thing to be on a first-name basis with the mayor, the managing director and the deputy managing director. The mayor's secretary knew us by name and by face. This was heady stuff for a young associate attorney from Castle High School.

Then there was Mike Amii. From working with people like him, I also found that the real lessons of politics are learned at the front line, and not up in the stratosphere. If you hung around the campaign HQ long enough, you'd come across Mike eventually. He had a drill sergeant way about him that I took to quickly. What Mike wanted, you gave him.

Mike was the premier, go-to, large event organizer. I got the call one day when he was planning a large fundraiser. He'd usually start his phone calls with, "Hey, champ!" On this occasion he said he needed someone to watch over the site, and so I was anointed site chair. It was a fairly easy job since Mike was providing all the sub chairs and had done this many times over. Besides, he would be on-site himself. He did let me pretend to be in charge, and even pretending, I learned what it took to put it all together.

My real job was to man the front door on event night. Supporters were being bused in from all over. It was one of those events designed to show attendance, as opposed to money raised. By 4 p.m., the lines snaked around the block and into the parking lot at Blaisdell Center. At 4:45, people were pressed up against the glass doors at the front of the Exhibition Hall. The place was all set up. The food was hot. The bars were stocked. The entertainment was good to go. I called Mike and told him we were ready—could we let 'em in? Mike said no.

Five minutes later, it looked like a mob scene. One big, angry local guy yelled that if I didn't open the door that second, the first thing he would do when he got in was kick my ass. Little old ladies were being jostled around. It didn't look good. I called Mike back and said we had to let them in. I told him about the death threat I'd just gotten. He said I could either deal with the guy myself or deal with Mike later. I took my chances dealing with the guy. Mike wanted to create buzz, a frenzy about the event, knowing that the media was outside taking all of this in. Later news reports would prove Mike right, but at the time I didn't think I would live to see any reports.

At 4:55 Mike called me with what I hoped would be the OK to open up. But all he said was "Hold that door, champ!" in his best drill sergeant manner. I held it until he said go, and then it was like Walmart on Black Friday. People came swarming in. The big local guy? I never saw him again. But the dramatic buildup paid off—the message was that our supporters couldn't wait to rush in and support the candidate.

Another time, we were planning a 200-person coffee hour of young business professionals for Jeremy Harris. We just needed a free venue, the people and the logistics to get the mayor there. We also had to feed all those people; coffee hours don't happen if you charge folks to attend.

We were sure we could get the bodies, but what about the venue and the food? I went to see Mike Amii. "What you got yourself into now, champ?' he asked, then laughed out loud in that Mike Amii way. Then he said, "I'll call you back tomorrow." The next day, we had a venue and a commitment for food and drink, donated by an anonymous sponsor. I asked Mike what I owed, and he just replied, "This is for the mayor, right?" Mike was one of those guys who was always there to back you up—as long as it's for the mayor.

Attendance at the coffee hour topped out at 210, not counting us volunteers, and they filled the entire ballroom. We ordered dark blue polo shirts for ourselves with "Young Leaders for Harris" embroidered on the sleeves. It all looked pretty slick, and it made us look like Jeremy's young corps of shock troops.

I suspect the mayor knew that Mike was behind this, but he never let on. And Mike never appeared out of the shadows that evening. He stayed out of sight near the kitchen—cigar in hand, Nokia earpiece in his ear, wearing his trademark windbreaker—always just a holler away in case something went wrong. After the event, he finally emerged to say, "Good job, champ! I'm sure the mayor appreciated it." I thanked him profusely, but he only replied, "Thank you." Then I asked Mike what I owed him, and he said he'd call one day. To this day, he has never called in the favor. I don't think he ever will, but I'm sure he'd want me to pass on what help he gave me to other young people coming up in the ranks.

Soon after that, I was called to a campaign meeting, When I arrived at HQ, Mayor Harris' cabinet was there. I took a seat at the end of the long conference table, where the mayor was already talking strategy. When I sat down next to Mike, the mayor pointed our way and said, "Now *that* is how a coffee hour is done!" We got a standing ovation from the cabinet, and Jeremy led the applause. Mike was beaming. At that point, I would've taken a bullet for the mayor—and for Mike.

Gary was experiencing and learning much. He's felt the pains of losing, and the elation of winning. You can't learn about campaigns from reading books, or by watching them on TV or online. Politics is all about being up close and personal. You can't feel it if you haven't experienced it. Gary went through many other political races, including working on Ed Case's congressional campaigns. In many respects my obligation to him is similar to Bob's gift to me; being a friend and mentor, a confidant who can respect his confidences while providing counsel, not advocacy for my positions but objective advice for his life and career. Politics will never be out of his life.

I've included these words from Gary to show that sparrows are still being born and nurtured in our political community. It's a reminder that life transcends politics in many ways, and that we can write our history. I am proud and humbled to be Gary's friend, and as with my other mentees I'll provide such counsel as long as I'm around to give it. Gary's story also energizes me, as do other younger folk come up through the ranks. Passing the torch fulfills my obligation to Bob and all the other people who helped me. ❧

CHAPTER TWENTY

Reflections

~❧

"Never give up on the principles that define your culture."
—Jim Collins, *How the Mighty Fall*

I began by describing my early years in politics, and I close after forty-six years in the political arena. Many of my colleagues have their own stories, of course, and I encourage you to ask and listen. So much about politics isn't written down, but passed along by word of mouth.

I was fortunate to be a fly on the wall in many campaigns. Hawai'i politics have been described many times, in many ways, but mostly through the recollections of people that journalist Denby Fawcett calls "the high *makamaka*." I can't claim to be a *garut* today, but I once was. I was there in the trenches with the everyday folk who work on elections. I felt the pain of defeat and the elation of victory. I was fortunate to make a lot of friends, and I made some enemies too. But the relationships I formed greatly inspired me and the writing of this book.

In many respects, this book is an acknowledgement to all who preceded me, who accepted me, worked with me and supported me. While this is primarily my story, in truth it is their story as well. The old song "No Man Is an Island" rings true here. It was my high school class graduation song, but the lyrics speak to me as clearly today as they did some fifty years ago:

I saw the people gather
I heard the music start
The song that they were singing
Is ringing in my heart

No man is an island, no man stands alone
Each man's joy is joy to me
Each man's grief is my own
We need one another, so I will defend
Each man as my brother
Each man as my friend[176]

I am but a sparrow. Sparrows flock together because they seek the relationship of the group. They experience the same depredations and joys together. This book is about the sparrows—their sacrifice and their joy and pain. I hope in some small way it stands as a tribute to them, and to the efforts of my mentor, Bob Oshiro—to inspire others to get involved, and to remember that politics is indeed a noble profession, something that we as members of a free society should seek out and embrace.

People too often forget the contributions of the less glamorous, the unremarkable, the quiet but effective, the noble but humble, the ardent but unheralded. The squeaky wheel gets attention; the well-oiled one does not. I salute those who made campaigning seem so easy, but worked so hard to make it so.

To the next generation of politicos, both candidates and campaigners, I hope these recollections both embolden and temper you. In a broader sense, I hope that the lessons of history will provide a new beginning for politics, in terms of both issues and character. And I hope that they will focus more on the latter, because you can learn about the issues, but you can't learn character. The recollections contained in this book should give the reader some clear takeaways:

Candidate and Campaigns

There's a clear distinction between the candidate and the campaign organization. Successful campaigns need both. A good candidate with a bad (or no) campaign organization cannot be successful. Neither can a bad candidate with a great organization. A good candidate with a great organization will win every time.

---

[176] John Donne, "No Man Is an Island," adapted from *Devotions upon Emergent Occasions*, 1624.

Politics is About People and Relationships

Campaigns are all about people. It's politics, after all, and politics is built on relationships. Friendships are the underpinnings of politics. If you sit with some old politicos, you will often find them reminiscing about these old campaigns. They do this because, as in the war stories told by military veterans, these experiences are the stuff that binds them together, in the same way that a battlefield encounter does. Most of these stories are and will be lost as this generation fades away. That's unfortunate, because there's much to be learned from the old warhorses. After many decades in politics, I'm still learning. Even apparently innocuous stories can be consequential, as they fill in the gaps about what actually happened, and lend a human perspective to the hard facts you read in the history books.

Money and Campaigns and People

A campaign with strong financing but no, few or bad human assets cannot win. Money can't buy you love; neither can it buy you an election. But fundraising is not for the timid or the weak of heart. It is hard and unrelenting and truly valued by only a few. No one really likes a fundraiser. People will cross the street to avoid them. And it's in fundraising where there is the most risk of legal exposure, because of all the rules. I tip my hat to those who raise money for candidates. Theirs is a lonely job. Yet without them a campaign can't run. They provide the fuel for everything else. Even here the utmost of ethics is required. A little slip here and there can lead to bigger sins down the road. A fundraiser must never surrender to the temptation of expediency and money over integrity and honesty. As that Bible says, "Ill-gotten gains have no lasting value."[177]

Depending on the quality of the human assets, a campaign's chances of success increase exponentially. Recall the Oshiro adage: Campaigns are about addition and multiplication, not subtraction and division. The campaign that acquires the most capable human assets will be the most successful. People get it done, not candidates or leaders. Someone once said you can't be a leader if no one follows. For a candidate and campaign, it's critical to remember and honor the commitment of the volunteers. That recognition is rewarded with loyalty. Loyalty allows the organization to mobilize and perform miracles like a rally at Aloha Stadium. Again,

---

[177] Proverbs 10:2.

politics is people. And while quantity matters, so does quality. Seek out the best people. Ask those people to do the job. Train them to learn the job well. Take a chance on people. Never believe there's a finite number of leaders; there's always a good leader out there who hasn't been discovered. Find them. Test them. Give them a chance.

To young people seeking to get involved: Learn to start small; take the most menial job and do it well. Good leaders will recognize and promote you. Be wary of promising to do more than you can. Humility is not only a good policy; it is an insurance policy against failure. Do things as a team. Always solicit friends to help. Never embark on your own with the idea that you'll enjoy all the glory. Sharing success is more important than bearing failure by yourself. When many hands are participating, failure is less likely because many eyes and ears are keeping tabs on things.

Leadership and Identifying Talent

Campaign leadership must acknowledge the various skills of all volunteers. There is a position for everyone, albeit maybe not to the liking of that particular volunteer. As Bob did, current leaders must keep an eye out for future leaders in their ranks. You'd be amazed at the talent hidden right under your nose. The key is to hone your skills in identifying it— and to acquire the ability to assess character and potential. Leadership is less about telling and more about suggesting. Trust people to do the job. Watch that they do. Be prepared to assist if they fall, but never let them fail. A good leader doesn't have failures; good leaders build character from failures. Each of us will fail at some point, but the real lessons lie in why and the how. Falling off a bike the first time might be inevitable, but once you learn how to fall, success is guaranteed. You learn that falling isn't fatal, but just an obstacle, and obstacles can be overcome.

Finally, leaders must trust. A failure or inability to trust others is the bane of leadership. Without trust an organization, a campaign or otherwise, cannot grow. This doesn't mean that trust ensures harmony. The latter requires a trust of the motives of other people. If you know innately that the motives of all parties involved are fundamentally the same, then forward progress is inevitable. But if your motives aren't synchronized, then your progress will be either blocked or reversed. I cannot stress the concept of trust more. It is a belief that I hold dear. Where there is no trust, conflicts abound. Steven Covey's words resonate with me: *"Trust is the glue of life*. It's the most essential ingredient in effective communication. It's the foundational principle that holds all relationships."[178] (Emphasis added.)

Campaigns need leadership. This leadership must be built on character. I encourage anyone interested in becoming a good candidate or campaign organizer to study and take to heart the millennia of treatises on leadership, character and integrity. Peter Drucker's admonitions about character should be in every leader's handbook. Character, character, character. You can't teach it; it is within you. But you can detect it. Seek out people with character. Character doesn't require perfection. We are all imperfect beings. But an imperfect person can exhibit strong character—demonstrated in integrity and honesty, accepting responsibility, acting in a forthright manner, and agreeing to disagree with grace. Character is a human trait that we can sense and yet find hard to define. I've found it in the person of Cincinnatus; in Jimmy Stewart's title role in *Mr. Smith Goes to Washington*, and in the person of Father Francis Chisholm in A.J. Cronin's book, *Keys of the Kingdom*. Father Chisholm provides my favorite example of character. Orphaned as a child and raised as a Catholic priest who later struggles to open a mission in China, he is first portrayed in the book as a failure. But in retrospect his Monsignor discovers that Father Chisholm's life was an incredible success. Father Chisholm never looked at a person in judgment. Rather, he looked upon people as fellow humans and loved them for who they were—not for their influence or wealth, but as human beings. Those who sought his indulgence because of their wealth or their place in society were dismayed by his reaction, or rather his lack of one. Perhaps the book's most poignant scene is when his good friend Willie is dying. He tells Father Chisholm that even in death he will love the priest, because he didn't preach to him about salvation, but just loved Willie for who he was—an atheist. Father Chisholm could have used this opportunity to make a convert, but he leaves that between his dying friend and God. In the end our relationships with our friends can be no less and no more. I believe that leaders just need to "love" people, not change people. Leadership is conducted by example, not by force. Leaders with character will necessarily draw others to their life work, but a leader shouldn't use the opportunity to

---

[178] http://www.brainyquote.com/quotes/quotes/s/stephencov450798.html?src=t_trust.

advance his or her own agenda.

Campaigns Need a Moral Compass

A campaign's moral compass is set by the candidate and campaign organization leadership. A candidate and campaign leadership that cuts corners or skirts the law will have followers who do likewise. Birds of a feather do indeed flock together. An exacting adherence to principles is necessary for leadership to run a campaign—and for a candidate to lead a community. As Drucker suggests, good leaders demand adherence to high principles. So it is with campaigns. Politics often devolves to the lowest common denominator of human desire. As Spencer Tracy's character points out in *State of the Union*, it's easy to offer all kinds of promises to people, but is that the higher moral compass to which we want leaders to aspire? Maybe I'm naïve, but I believe leaders need to be much more. Theodore Roosevelt was one such leader. He was a person of great character, Lincolnesque in many ways—not perfect, but someone worth emulating. He took down big business for the working people; he created the national park system and saved great swaths of the outdoors for generations to come; he fought corruption in New York as police commissioner. We tend to remember the swashbuckling Roosevelt, but his legacy was so much more. In a 1912 speech entitled "The Progressive Covenant with the People," he said:

> Political parties exist to secure responsible government and to execute the will of the people. From these great tasks both of the old parties have turned aside. Instead of instruments to promote the general welfare they have become the tools of corrupt interests, which use them impartially to serve their selfish purposes. Behind the ostensible government sits enthroned an invisible government owing no allegiance and acknowledging no responsibility to the people. *To destroy this invisible government, to dissolve the unholy alliance between corrupt business and corrupt politics, is the first task of the statesmanship of the day.* (Emphasis added.)

Roosevelt got it right. Campaigns and politics should be, as Lincoln said, dedicated to ensuring "that government of the people, by the people, for the people, shall not perish from the earth." We must and should demand that our moral compass be redirected for the benefit of the people. Much of the anger today is because the rich are getting richer and the poor, poorer. Business is by law and fiduciary duty bound to increase stock prices and dividends rather than to consider the interests of society, their employees or the public. Surely we must change the rules or, to paraphrase Einstein, we'd be crazy to expect a different result from the rules as they are.

Just as we should expect character and morality from candidates and campaigns, so must we expect it of volunteers. Is a potential campaign volunteer available, reliable, loyal and committed? If any of these attributes are missing, so will be the volunteer. Individuals will deliver what is expected of them; if you demand more they should deliver more. Of course this is a balancing act, but as a campaign leader, do you want large numbers of uncommitted volunteers or a smaller group of quality volunteers? I'd pick the latter every time.

Flat Campaigns Are the Epitome of the Politics of Equality

A campaign leader should keep in mind that ideally there are no chiefs, only Indians in his or her organization. A campaign doesn't really need a hierarchy if everyone knows what to do and agrees to do whatever needs to get done. Don't complain about the trash; take care of it. Don't complain about a lack of sign holders; go out and do it. Leaders serve; they aren't served. "Rank," Peter Drucker wrote, "does not confer privilege or give power. It imposes responsibility."[179]

The moment you feel privileged as a leader is the time to stop being a leader. The designer and marketer Michael Janda wrote:

I believe you are a better person if you've ever had a job that required you to clean a public restroom. This humbling task teaches so many lessons, among which is the willingness to do whatever the job requires. I have seen over and over again in my career that the people who are willing to go the extra mile and do whatever task is required of them by their boss or client are among the most valued in the company. Ultimately, cleaning public toilets early in life is not the only way to learn gratitude and humble service to others. Many people are fortunate

---

[179] http://www.brainyquote.com/quotes/quotes/p/peterdruck134727.html.

to learn these lessons in their homes. Others are born with service built deep inside of them. Regardless of how you learn to serve, learn it and learn it well.[180] (Emphasis added.)

So maybe the best leadership test is cleaning toilets? Mahatma Gandhi practiced this same philosophy. Here's a story told by his great-grandson Tushar Gandhi:

> In Bapu's ashrams, the first task entrusted to new entrants was the cleaning of latrines. In those days there were no flushing toilets. Latrine duty meant emptying and washing chamber pots and toilets. Since toilets were buckets in those days they had to be carried and emptied into cesspits and cleaned frequently. Bapu's reasoning for this kind of initiation was that this would strip the person of any residual ego and make them humble enough to be able to recognise truth and be prepared to serve the weakest and the poorest. Every Satyagrahi went through this initiation, which is the reason why even today when one meets a freedom fighter or a true Gandhian the first thing one notices is their dignity and humility. There is a story from Sevagram Ashram. One of Bapu's close associates, a rich industrialist one day brought his son to meet Bapu. The young scion had just returned from abroad after completing his studies and was brimming with ideas. He expressed his desire to do something for his country before he joined the family business. His father felt that Bapu would be able to utilise his son's services, so he took him to meet Bapu. The young man told Bapu he had many ideas and wished to solve the problems facing India and asked that Bapu assign him a task. Bapu accepted him into his ashram and told him that he must clean the latrines from the next day. Being obedient the young man performed the task assigned to him. A week later he went to Bapu and said, "I have cleaned latrines for a week now can I move on to bigger more important tasks?" Bapu shook his head and asked him to continue cleaning latrines. Thus a month passed, the youth felt his talent was being wasted, but he could not disobey Bapu so he obediently continued to clean the toilets. Finally he asked Bapu,

---

[180] Michael Janda, *Burn Your Portfolio: Stuff they don't teach you in design school, but should.*

"I have become used to cleaning the latrines, initially I felt it was demeaning but now I have got used to it. But Bapu I think I am capable of doing better work, I want to know when you will allow me to address the problems faced by India?" Bapu told the young man, "*I know that you have been educated abroad and so you feel that you must address the bigger issues plaguing India, like reducing poverty, speeding up development and eradicating illiteracy, but as long as you don't have the humility to do the humblest of jobs you will not be able to recognize the real problems that beset our mother-land. If you really want to make a difference you will have to first get rid of your ego, only then will you be able to understand that it is essential to recognize the importance of the seemingly insignificant, menial tasks and have the humility to perform them, if you learn to do them with dignity and honour, the bigger tasks will become easy.*"[181] (Emphasis added.)

It is much the same way in campaigns. The insignificant is significant, not for the work that is performed, but for the attitude by which you perform. Likewise, the approach of paying your dues has much in common with Gandhi's actions. You cannot walk in someone's shoes if you have not lived their life. It is an admonition for all of us in politics and campaigns—that we must walk in the shoes of both the volunteers and the voters. Remember Peter Drucker's words: "Effective leadership is not about making speeches or being liked; leadership is defined by results, not attributes."[182] Candidates and campaign managers: Seek character first, not likeability. Yours is a tough job. You can be nice or you can be effective; you can't always be both.

There Are No Real Secrets

There are very few real secrets in political campaigns. As soon as more than one person knows a "secret," it's no longer a secret. Campaigns don't operate in secrecy. There is confidential information, but you need to anticipate that a secret will not be a secret for long. Secrecy is a question of timing, not of loyalty or trustworthiness. Seldom can a television show

---

[181] Tushar Gandhi, "Lessons From Bapu," http://www.mkgandhi.org/articles/lessons_bapu.htm.

[182] In some respects, this contradicts Drucker's call for character, but I don't think so. Leadership is defined by results, but a good leader has character—a bad one does not.

claim an enduring quotation, but here's one, from the police program *Dexter*: "There are no secrets in life, just hidden truths that lie beneath the surface." So true. In politics, people can usually uncover secrets with just a modicum of information. So when you think you have a political secret, think again. Many times in this town, someone already knows it.

Expect No Rewards

A campaign volunteer should expect no reward. As Bob Oshiro told me decades ago, the expectation of a reward will often times be met with disappointment. If that's your rationale for involvement in politics, find some other activity that gives you pleasure. Volunteering in politics is a sacrificial act. It is akin to the Greek concept of *agape*, which is defined as a high form of charity; "agápē embraces a universal, unconditional love that transcends that and serves regardless of circumstances."[183]

Thus a volunteer must bear a certain discipline in his or her expectations. In fact, he or she should personally disavow any such expectations, in part to guard against future charges of cronyism. Such high standards should be the goal of all campaigns.[184] I know several individuals who expected a reward of some sort, either for themselves or others. Most often this expectation was not met, and the volunteer left the campaign discouraged and angry. These expectations need to be addressed early on, and must be shared by the entire campaign.

But while volunteers should expect no such "rewards," constant communication is in many ways its own reward. A volunteer is a friend. Friends don't forget friends. That doesn't mean constant contact, but certainly more than *no* contact. One of the fatal omissions of post-campaign activities, and along the way until the next campaign, is not communicating with the volunteers, both in writing and face-to-face. Maintaining this

---

[183] https://en.wikipedia.org/wiki/Agape.

[184] In the forty-six years I've been involved in politics, I have never sought appointment to a governmental position. I did request one appointment, asking Governor Abercrombie for a place on the Board of Governors of the East-West Center, which is a charitable organization, not a government agency. The appointment brought no compensation. I served on the boards of the Hawaiʻi Community Development Authority at the appointment of Governor Waihee; and I was appointed to the Zoning Board of Appeals by Mayor Harris. Neither appointment was sought. I currently am a member of the 2016 Charter Commission, City and County of Honolulu, upon which I hesitatingly agreed to serve as a mayoral appointee. I also served on George Ariyoshi's Governor's Committee on Hawaiʻi's Economic Future in 1984.

relationship is harder once a candidate is elected, due to the nature of the relationship. After an election, of course, the candidate focuses on the new job and not on campaigning, but this can cause problems down the road. It is therefore recommended that campaign meetings continue after the actual campaign, not for electioneering but for relationship building.

Recognize and Respect Loyalty and the People Who Give for the Cause

It also means that the loyalty of the volunteer must be recognized by the candidate. Ignoring a volunteer to maintain an appearance of impartiality usually means the end of the relationship. If a person who did not volunteer, or supported the opposition, has better access or a better relationship with the candidate, because of this desire for impartiality, then the volunteer will feel that the relationship is meaningless, or even a detriment. Thus it is imperative that all successful candidates include a grassroots member on the administrative team. It is likewise imperative that this grassroots member honors the position by honoring the other volunteers, and not succumb to the position and the sycophantic nature that it might engender. Acknowledging volunteers is an art that should always be top-of-mind for the candidate and the staff.

I cannot emphasize more that at the core of any campaign is relationships, in all directions. Consider the following words to the wise by Freek Vermeulen in the *Harvard Business Review*, in his article "Stop Comparing Management to Sports." Vermeulen abhors the analogy of management to sports, as the title states, but he does not merely criticize, he offers an alternative:

> At the end of the day, organizations are collections of people; this means that superior organizations need more effective ways for them to cooperate and work toward a common goal. As the famous management professor Henry Mintzberg noted: "Think of the organizations you most admire. I'll bet that front and center is a powerful sense of community." Research backs this up. Several studies have examined the characteristics of resources that, over time, lead to superior performance. The conclusion of this stream of research is that these resources are usually intangible and community based, such as relationships, trust, culture, identity, or knowledge sharing. That is

because, *ultimately, competitive advantage comes from people,* rather than products or patents.[185] (Emphasis added.)

I couldn't agree more. In business or campaigns, the competitive advantage is people. And it is the relationships of people that builds community—and a campaign.

Humility is Ingrained in Public Service and Politics

In all things, a candidate and campaign organization must exercise and demonstrate humility. Expertise doesn't mean a person has all the answers for all situations. Campaigns are organic in nature and substance, and organic organizations must evolve to meet challenges. The key is for the campaign to honor all opinions that address those challenges. And addressing challenges doesn't mean complaining, but rather providing solutions. Too often in campaigns we spend much more time on complaining than on problem solving. Time spent arguing about solutions is much more productive than arguing about why the candidate is right and the opponent wrong. Always ask people what they think. Never tell people what you want to do, except in the context of soliciting a response to your idea. No matter what the response, be respectful, even if you don't like it.

Remember to Find the Cause

Most important, as Bob Oshiro always said, a campaign must have a "cause." Why are you campaigning? What is this greater good that a campaign is all about? It isn't enough just to want someone elected; it's much more critical to know why. It is often times difficult to think about the cause. It may seem less important in a local versus a statewide race, but articulating a cause will always elevate a campaign from "personality" to real movement.

I hope that my recollections of a life in politics have contributed in some small way to what we're learning about human interaction on the campaign trail. How we interact is complex, and the more we do it, the more complex the process becomes. You might think that in the final analysis politics is nothing more than educated guessing and hunches

---

[185] Freek Vermeulen, "Stop Comparing Management to Sports," *Harvard Business Review,* June 2, 2016, https://hbr.org/2016/06/stop-comparing-management-to-sports.

played. That's partially true, but let me remind you that politics is both an art and a science. And political players who can combine the two will be amazed at the result.

A Candidate is Just a Symbol for the Hopes and Aspirations of the People

In the end candidates should acknowledge that they can't win an election, but they sure can lose one. Such a loss, as my friend Randy Iwase observed, is much more substantial for the volunteer, who feels his sacrifice has been for naught. The candidate should fully appreciate the possibility of losing; the volunteer sometimes doesn't have the same expectation. Thus the candidate and the campaign must provide the solace and compassion to overcome that grief. The ability to empathize is not just good to have; it is a must-have.

Campaigns depend on these "little guys and gals" to win. They sometimes go unnoticed and many times go unrecognized. I encourage candidates and campaign leaders to always be mindful of these unsung heroes, for they are the real champions of a campaign.[186] They are the backbone and the sinew by which campaigns move. Remember them. This kind of recognition alone goes a long way toward making a good leader into a great one.

Continue to Learn

I believe that our generation owes a debt of gratitude to the previous generation, as I do to Bob Oshiro. So how do I repay that debt? One way is to do right by the lessons he instilled in me, but maybe more important is to pass on the values I've learned and am still learning. It is human nature to forget the past, or even to rewrite it to fit the demands of the present. Avoid those traps. Get the facts, question them, then draw your own conclusions. Know history until it is second nature. You cannot predict the future if you don't understand the past.

Leadership is Not Doing It Your Way

To the aspiring campaign manager: Gather as many human assets

---

[186] It's like that great Mary Poppins song "Feed the Birds," written by Richard and Robert Sherman. ("Show them you care, You'll be glad if you do.") Candidates and campaigns must care for their volunteers, not with condescension but with compassion and appreciation for their sacrifices.

as you can. Build the finest team possible, then let them loose to do their best. To manage doesn't mean to control. It means directing, not dictating. Trust the team, but don't be afraid to question and push your team and your candidate. As a leader, never sequester your opinions or the opinions of others to avoid conflict. Vibrant discussions always provide better solutions. But once a decision is made, close ranks. Without a united front, a campaign is doomed.

Create a "Winning" Mentality

Trust your instincts about questionable acts or activities; if something feels wrong, it probably is. Remember that at the end of the day all you have is your integrity and credibility. If you lose either or both, your campaign will be the loser. A "winning" mentality must permeate from the candidate down through the organization. Create such an environment and people will gravitate towards you. Obviously, volunteers will be more committed to a winner than to a perceived loser. Winning is more a mental game than a physical (or even fiscal) one. If you don't think you can win, or are in an election you really don't want to be in, you won't win.

A Parting Word

Keep in mind the oft-quoted maxim by the philosopher George Santayana: "Those who cannot remember the past are condemned to repeat it." Hawai'i has experienced so many volatile political campaigns over the years, yet we still tend to forget what came before. There is much to be learned from the campaigns of the past, both in terms of what to do and what not to do.

Heed these words from Andrew Oliver, a politician who lived back in the nineteenth century:

> Danger is the inseparable companion of honor… With all the temptations and degradations that beset it, politics is still the noblest career any man [or woman] can choose. ~

INDEX

About the Author

~&~

Rick Tsujimura earned a Bachelor of Arts in political science from the University of Hawai'i and a Juris Doctor from the Loyola Law School. He is of counsel to the law firm Ashford & Wriston and serves on the boards of the Queen's Health Systems, East-West Center and Global Hope Network International in Geneva, Switzerland. Tsujimura lives in Honolulu with his wife, Ruth. Together they have three sons: William (married to Gloria with son, Andrew), Jonathan and Matthew.